FINDING GREATER
ACCESS TO THE
SAVIOR'S GRACE
IN TROUBLED TIMES

WHAT OTHERS ARE SAYING ABOUT THIS BOOK

"*Press Forward in Christ* is a collection of remarkable, heaven-sent spiritual guideposts that provide us direction and protection as we attempt to figure out mortality. It contains powerful gospel basics that point us to Jesus Christ. In fact, this book provides a constant reminder of a personal, accessible Savior, His love for us, and His desire that we understand His sacrifice and advocacy in our behalf. Thank you, Chris and Mark, for your fresh focus on eternal truths."

—BRUCE NEWBOLD, CEO of Hearthsong Entertainment
and author of The Baseball Box Prophecy series

"I absolutely loved this book. When I read *Press Forward in Christ,* I was struggling with real life and death challenges. My faith was being tried and tested in a multitude of ways. This book reminded me of the importance of allowing God to prevail in my life, to trust in the Lord and acknowledge Him in all that I do, and to endure to the end so that I may find joy in this life and in the life to come. I wholeheartedly endorse this book to everyone."

—JODI L. SMITH, PhD, MD, FAANS, pediatric neurosurgeon

"This book is exceptional at making exaltation and spiritual ordinances into mortal reality."

—DR. GERALD L. SPETH, PhD, director of Graduate
Business Programs, University of Indianapolis (RET)

CHRISTOPHER R. GREENWOOD
& MARK D. MASON

PRESS FORWARD IN CHRIST

FINDING GREATER ACCESS TO THE SAVIOR'S GRACE IN TROUBLED TIMES

CFI
AN IMPRINT OF CEDAR FORT, INC.
SPRINGVILLE, UTAH

ISBN 13: 978-1-4621-4468-6

Published by CFI, an imprint of Cedar Fort, Inc.
2373 W. 700 S., Suite 100, Springville, UT 84663
Distributed by Cedar Fort, Inc., www.cedarfort.com

Library of Congress Control Number: 2022949057

Cover design by Courtney Proby
Cover design © 2023 Cedar Fort, Inc.
Edited and typeset by Liz Kazandzhy

Printed in the United States of America

10 9 8 7 6 5 4 3 2 1

Printed on acid-free paper

From Christopher R. Greenwood

To anyone who has felt broken beyond repair, this is for you. If you've ever felt excluded, detached, or walked a path strewn with thorns and marked by struggle while being told you were not enough, this book is for you. The sunrise will come and the darkness will dissipate. You never walk alone.

From Mark D. Mason

This book is dedicated to Tricia, who has always encouraged me to press forward.

Other Books by Christopher R. Greenwood

A Mighty Change:
The Process of Going from Good to Better

Spiritual Atrophy

CONTENTS

NOTE TO READERS

By Christopher R. Greenwood

When Mark and I began this book in December of 2013, little did we realize some of the difficulty attached to such a robust, collaborative project. The difficulty became obvious because of the extensive subject matter related to covenants, covenant keeping, and how each of us, as children of a loving Father in Heaven, can raise the bar of spirituality, conversion, and faithfulness in our lives. Although I had written two books before this one (*A Mighty Change: The Process of Going from Good to Better*, 2011; and *Spiritual Atrophy*, 2013), I had never collaborated on a writing assignment, nor had Mark. It was new and uncharted waters for both of us.

As is the case with most of us, life happened. Church callings came that preoccupied much of our time, deaths occurred in families, there were job losses and job changes, a worldwide pandemic happened, there were moves to other states, and so on. Nevertheless, Mark and I kept at it, communicating from time to time and sharing notes and ideas. The changes that happened to both of us widened our understanding and perspective, making us a little wiser for the wear.

As the book progressed, naturally we became more comfortable with the topics and subject matter. However, some concerns materialized that neither of us anticipated. For example, there was a significant contrast in writing styles between us! Because of his experience, Mark tends to emphasize doctrine and theology related to the subjects he writes about. I, on the other hand, tend to illustrate doctrinal points with a myriad of personal experiences and stories. Both methods are good for learning and can help the reader, but combining the two styles presented a challenge when trying to marry them within the same book.

Our original idea was to assign certain topics to each author, and that person would become the lead writer for a given chapter. But as we continued to review each other's work and help each other improve clarity and grammar, another problem emerged. We realized we couldn't successfully add personal experiences into the narrative without confusing the reader as to which writer had the experiences. Therefore, we decided to place our initials under the title of each chapter we were responsible for (CRG for Christopher R. Greenwood and MDM for Mark D. Mason), and the experiences within the chapters are those of the one designated. The entire book has been a collaborative effort, and we have both significantly influenced each other's thinking as we discussed what topics the book would cover and how best to cover them. In the end, writing a collaborative book has profoundly changed Mark and me. Our desire has been to create the combined voice we would share with you.

The last concern we faced was feeling like we were setting ourselves up as a light for others to follow. Mark and I are not trying to indicate, through the message of this book, that we have both somehow been able to achieve spiritual success to the point that we think we are examples of what someone should pattern their life after. Like each person in mortality, we have our strengths and weaknesses, but we hope we share a common bond with each of you—the desire to become converted and to be spiritually self-reliant as we live our covenants. Spiritual rebirth takes time and patience. By writing this book, we hope to provide help to anyone who reads it by identifying some of the key elements and changes we all must go through to benefit from the fruits of spiritual rebirth.

It's been an interesting process to write about finding and staying on the covenant path, and at times it's been difficult for both of us. For example, on November 28, 2021, we spoke over Zoom to discuss the progress we were making with the book. We wanted to make sure we were adequately expressing in writing what we felt in our hearts and the lessons we had learned about spiritual conversion. After we decided to "tighten up" some of the subjects we had already written on and add some more insights, Mark asked me, "Could you have written this book back in 2014?" After a bit of a pause, I responded truthfully, albeit painfully. "No, I could not have. I have learned more since we began this process."

Interestingly, Mark felt the same and bore testimony to me of the process of incremental change we go through as we dedicate and commit ourselves to the covenant path. This resonated with me. It gave me assurance that even though our spiritual growth is incremental, when we look back on where we came from, we can see our spiritual progress when we consider the experiences we've had that make us better people with greater insights—as in the writing of this book. These kinds of experiences enable us to become closer to a loving Father in Heaven and our Savior Jesus Christ. It was a "tender mercy" moment for me that I will always remember.

I am so grateful for the experience of writing this book, as I know Mark is as well. Such insight does not come without effort. After much preparation, after much study and work, and after seeking for the truth in the right places, we can receive needed insights. We begin to "see" where we had not "seen" before, we begin to "hear" what we may have not "heard" before, and this motivates us to live a higher, more Christlike life.

ACKNOWLEDGMENTS

Having an idea, then turning that idea into a publication requires the efforts of many people. The experience is both challenging and rewarding and takes an incredible amount of time. However, the world is a better place because of people who share the gift of their time with others, like the people who have assisted in the publication of this book. Our spouses, Tami K. Greenwood and Tricia Mason, who read draft after draft and corrected us on our spelling and grammar. Jesica L. Rodriguez, Dr. Gerald Speth, PhD, Larry Waldron, Ryan Jenkins, and Jaron Packer offered incredible and timely suggestions and improvements. We are grateful for Liz Kazandzhy, Shawnda T. Craig, Heather Holm, and the entire CFI team for taking a chance on us. Thank you from the bottom of our hearts to each of you mentioned and those not mentioned for helping us to press forward in Christ.

INTRODUCTION

CRG

"It's time for each of us to step up; to live lives more worthy of . . . divine power and privilege."

—Elder Kevin W. Pearson[1]

The Savior taught that there are two gates: a strait gate and a wide gate. "Enter ye in at the strait gate: for wide is the gate, and broad is the way, that leadeth to destruction, and many there be which go in thereat: Because strait is the gate, and narrow is the way, which leadeth unto life, and few there be that find it" (Matthew 7:13–14).

If something is strait, it can refer to a situation or a condition that is strict, unbending, inflexible, or of a high degree of difficulty. Our Father in Heaven requires everyone who enters the gate leading to eternal life to begin a journey along a path that is narrow and more difficult to travel. This is simply because there are covenants we need

---

1. Kevin W. Pearson, "Priesthood Power in the Home—Brethren, It's Time to Step Up," Pacific Area Presidency Message, Mar. 2013, pacific.ChurchofJesusChrist.org.

to make and commandments we need to obey, and we need to change into something better than what we are now (a human *becoming* as opposed to a human *being*). Conversely, the path that leads away from eternal life—the way the world is traveling—is a broad path, attractive in its appeal, and has several distractions.

We know that many will choose the broad path. In our limited, mortal understanding, we may even think that the broad road is easier to travel, but it isn't. Yes, it's easier to get *on* that path because the gate to sin is wide and open to all, and sin is so easy to fall into. However, our Savior has said, "Take my yoke upon you, and learn of me; for I am meek and lowly in heart: and ye shall find rest unto your souls. For my yoke is easy, and my burden is light" (Matthew 11:29–30). I believe that the burden of traveling the world's path is much heavier and not as easily traveled as one may think. Though it's easy to get onto that path, it's far more difficult to travel along it because of the consequences of sin. Whether in this life or the next, each of us will face those consequences, and they always result in spiritual pain.

The first gate is for those who have found the truth and are determined at all costs to be faithful and obedient to what our Savior taught, and "few there be that find it" (Matthew 7:14). Conversely, because the world of sin at times seems very appealing to our weak, human (carnal) nature, there will be many who will be drawn to this second gate.

It seems impossible to imagine that any honest thinking member of The Church of Jesus Christ of Latter-day Saints would believe they could go through the wide gate, follow the broad path, and believe they will end up in the celestial kingdom by following the trends, fashions, and wickedness of the world. It is a scary thought that a member of the Church could walk the path of life, only to find that he or she had followed the broad and wide path. The Savior said such people would cry out, recognizing they were on the wrong path the entire time. As He taught in Matthew 7:21–23: "Not every one that saith unto me, Lord, Lord, shall enter into the kingdom of heaven; but he that doeth the will of my Father which is in heaven. Many will say to me in that day, Lord, Lord, have we not prophesied in thy name?

and in thy name have cast out devils? and in thy name done many wonderful works. And then will I profess unto them, I never knew you: depart from me, ye that work iniquity."

President J. Reuben Clark, First Counselor in a former First Presidency, observed how Satan uses certain tactics to try to get us to walk on this broad path. He explained, "As I read the scriptures, Satan's plan [or path] required one of two things: Either the compulsion of . . . man, or else saving men in sin. I question whether the intelligence of man can be compelled. Certainly men cannot be saved in sin."[2] Obviously, none of these possibilities would have worked, but we do see elements of these tactics used today. For example, we see civic leaders and political activists seeking to limit religious freedom while compelling and coercing society to accept sinful behavior.

Sometime ago, this concept of dual gates rested upon my mind. I recall one Sunday morning speaking in sacrament meeting and reading aloud Alma 37:44: "For behold, it is as *easy* to give heed to the word of Christ, which will point to you a straight course to eternal bliss, as it was for our fathers to give heed to this compass, which would point unto them a straight course to the promised land" (emphasis added). In my address, I shared how I found it very interesting that Alma, while instructing his son Helaman, would use the word *easy* to describe obeying the commandments of our Father in Heaven. Then the revelation hit me like a ton of bricks—Alma was correct! It *is* easy to "give heed to the word of Christ" because when we *deviate* from that, all the difficulties begin in our life. We do it to ourselves! We create our own difficulties. Deviation from the covenant path results in broad and miserable consequences. We can expect compounding difficulties in rejecting the Lord's gate to eternal life.

"O then, my beloved brethren, come unto the Lord, the Holy One. Remember that his paths are righteous. Behold, the way for man is narrow, but it lieth in a straight course before him, and the keeper of the gate is the Holy One of Israel; and he employeth no servant there;

---

2. J. Reuben Clark, in Conference Report, Oct. 1949, 193.

and there is none other way save it be by the gate; for he cannot be deceived, for the Lord God is his name" (2 Nephi 9:41).

Jesus Christ is the keeper of the gate. He employs no servant there. He is the way. Jesus Christ is helping us individually and collectively back into the presence of our Father in Heaven. This is the way to consider: "Thus saith the Lord of hosts; *Consider your ways*" (Haggai 1:7; emphasis added).

Thank goodness for our Savior Jesus Christ who made it possible through His Atonement for us to return and live with our Father in Heaven. It's never too late to experience the joy, confidence, and peace that comes from living the gospel. We can still unlock the secrets to happiness. Our Savior Jesus Christ has the answers to all of our problems and offers the lasting joy we each seek in our lives. All the wonderful concepts and principles of the gospel can't save us—but Jesus Christ can. President Russell M. Nelson has taught:

> Under the Father's great eternal plan, it is the Savior who suffered. It is the Savior who broke the bands of death. It is the Savior who paid the price for our sins and transgressions and blots them out on condition of our repentance. It is the Savior who delivers us from physical and spiritual death.
>
> There is no amorphous entity called "the Atonement" upon which we may call for succor, healing, forgiveness, or power. Jesus Christ is the source. Sacred terms such as Atonement and Resurrection describe what the Savior did, according to the Father's plan, so that we may live with hope in this life and gain eternal life in the world to come. The Savior's atoning sacrifice—the central act of all human history—is best understood and appreciated when we expressly and clearly connect it to Him."[3]

There is much hope for us, but we have to do our part. However, because we are mortal, there are times we feel discouraged, frustrated, or unmotivated, and it's easy to think that being a member of the Church is not easy. There are things we must do to show our Father in Heaven that we are able and willing to do all that He asks of us. The

---

3. Russell M. Nelson, "Drawing the Power of Jesus Christ into our Lives," *Ensign* or *Liahona*, May 2017, 40.

sacrament prayer we hear each week clearly says that "they are *willing* to take upon them the name of thy Son, and always remember him and keep his commandments which he has given them" (Doctrine and Covenants 20:77; emphasis added). The word *willing* is a powerful motivator. We must be willing to submit to all that He wants of us if we are to become true disciples and truly converted.

But like any journey, this path toward enduring discipleship starts with a conscious decision to take that first step. Consider the following two statements. When Elder Dieter F. Uchtdorf was serving as the Second Counselor in the First Presidency, he said, "The first step on the path of discipleship begins, luckily enough, in the exact place where we stand! We do not have to prequalify to take that first step. It doesn't matter if we are rich or poor. There is no requirement to be educated, eloquent, or intellectual. We do not have to be perfect or well-spoken or even well-mannered."[4] And Elder Robert D. Hales of the Quorum of the Twelve Apostles offered us this timely council: "Unless you are fully engaged in living the gospel—living it with all of your 'heart, might, mind, and strength' (Doctrine and Covenants 4:2)—you cannot generate enough spiritual light to push back the darkness."[5] The bottom line is that all of us need to find sufficient strength and power to successfully defend against the adversary's attacks and the difficulty of the journey if we are going to successfully make our way back into our Heavenly Father's presence.

Back in July 2012, I was corresponding with my son Collin on this very subject matter. At the time, he was serving as a Mandarin Chinese–speaking missionary in New York City. He replied to me about the extent of the love our Savior has for each one of us individually, and it deeply resonated with me. He said, "If you were the only person in this world, would the Savior still have sacrificed Himself for you? Yes, he would have. Your soul is of great worth to Him, and no

---

4. Dieter F. Uchtdorf, "The Way of the Disciple," *Ensign* or *Liahona*, May 2009, 77.
5. Robert D. Hales, "Out of Darkness into His Marvelous Light," *Ensign*, May 2002, 71.

price is too great to have you back in the kingdom of God."[6] We, in turn, can reciprocate that love from our Savior and Heavenly Father by allowing ourselves to achieve a higher level of spirituality and obedience indicative of true conversion. President Howard W. Hunter taught that "developing spirituality . . . will not happen by chance, but is accomplished only through deliberate effort and by calling upon God and keeping his commandments."[7]

Let us not be so focused on the destination that we lose focus on the process of getting there, which is often more important. We are very results-oriented people who focus on the endgame, but the *process* is the key to success. Think of Oliver Cowdery. He saw Joseph Smith translating the Book of Mormon with relative ease and thought he could do the same thing. He didn't see the struggles and the process of learning that perhaps Martin Harris had seen in Joseph Smith while they were translating the first 116 pages of the manuscript. Maybe Oliver had come into the picture having missed all of the growth that came from those first weeks of translating, including the processes that Joseph Smith had learned in order to reach the end result of translation. Oliver took no thought in studying, pondering, or preparing for translating "save it was to ask [the Lord]" (Doctrine and Covenants 9:7) to help with the translation—a very interesting principle when you think about it.

If we truly desire to return home to our Father in Heaven, who genuinely wants us to succeed, we need to let these words of President Hunter, Elder Uchtdorf, and Elder Hales resonate within us and apply them in our lives. We must live the gospel of Jesus Christ with all of our heart, might, mind, and strength if we want to return and live with Him. There is no room for second place, nor is there a "do-over" button like there is on a video game. Each day presents new challenges and opportunities, but with the help of our Savior Jesus Christ, we can do it!

---

6. Email dated July 16, 2012. My son, Elder Collin Greenwood, attributes this quote from a teacher he knew named Luo Laoshi.
7. Howard W. Hunter, "Developing Spirituality," *Ensign*, May 1979, 25.

You may have struggled in years past to follow the Savior perfectly. Maybe it's time for you to realize that enduring to the end as a covenant disciple isn't about you following the commandments perfectly. It's about you continuing in the struggle—continuing on the narrow path regardless of mortal failings. It's about pressing forward in Christ and accessing the Savior's grace in troubled times that we all have occasionally. So, today is the day for you to decide again. Don't put it off. Say to yourself, "I'm going to pick up the burden one more time and try another day."

The objective of this book is to assist each of us as members of the Church to become *truly* converted. It is our intention to set forth what is expected of us as sons and daughters of a loving Father in Heaven if we truly are to "come unto Christ and be perfected in him" (Moroni 10:32). Our hope is that as you read this book, your testimony may be strengthened, your spiritual resolve might be kindled, your heart may be softened, and you may experience true conversion. As President Thomas S. Monson implored, "The spiritual nature within us should not be dominated by the physical. It behooves each of us to remember who he or she is and what God expects him or her to become."[8]

Additionally, each of us knows someone who fits the following description: Mary grew up in The Church of Jesus Christ of Latter-day Saints. She planned in her young life to find the man of her dreams, get married in the temple, have a family, and find the joy promised to her in all the many Young Women lessons she listened to. Now, in her forties, she finds life is not what she thought it would be. Maybe her son is inactive, her husband has a pornography addiction, or she discovered she really doesn't enjoy working in the Primary, which is the only place she's ever had callings.

Or you may know someone who had the same dreams as Mary, but he found that going to work each week, paying the bills, and fixing the house up wasn't the exciting dream he thought it would be. His relationships with his children are strained, he feels dissatisfied with his work, and he questions whether he has fulfilled his purpose

8. Thomas S. Monson, "The Will Within," *Ensign*, May 1987, 67.

in life. Even though he has married in the temple and found many things satisfying, he continues to have moments of crisis in his heart about the purpose of his life.

These two people could be someone you know, or maybe elements of their lives could represent what you feel personally. Yet these moments of trial and challenge are but a few that faithful members of the Church of Jesus Christ experience: children with anxiety and depression, marriages that feel like they are not progressing, various addictions, and disappointments and struggles that begin to overshadow the joy each of us hoped we would experience as members of Christ's true church.

We as the authors have experienced our fair share of challenges, setbacks, and downright unfair moments in life as disciples of Jesus Christ. But this book is not an opportunity to vent our frustrations and soak our souls in the hot tub of self-pity. Together, we have been searching for answers to help us joyfully endure to the end of life's journey with our testimonies intact, thriving in the gospel, and finding deep and meaningful purpose. We feel we have found answers that have strengthened us—answers that we believe will lift you as well so that you can joyfully endure to the end.

These answers have come as we have studied and pondered the scriptures and writings of modern-day prophets and apostles. We also will include our personal perspectives on what we think can help someone maintain their faith and continue along the covenant path.

The answers and our perspectives have been broken down into chapters about pressing forward in Christ, considering your ways, becoming a disciple, baptism, the Holy Ghost, the oath and covenant of the priesthood, the sacrament, studying the scriptures, attending the temple, increasing your access to the Atonement of Jesus Christ, and ultimately increasing your own happiness that can come to you from the Savior.

Additionally, there are writings of prophets and apostles that we have utilized that can help us endure and motivate us to press forward in Christ. These have been broken down into chapters about the need to consider your ways, becoming a disciple, baptism, the

Holy Ghost, the sacrament, the oath and covenant of the priesthood, studying the scriptures, attending the temple, increasing your access to the Atonement of Jesus Christ, and ultimately increasing your own happiness that can come to you from the Savior. These resources are gifts of grace from our loving Heavenly Father to help us along the covenant path.

We will present stories, scriptural analysis, and prophetic and scholarly commentary to help make it clear in all of our minds how to access the Savior's power through these resources. We have not sought to create a comprehensive list of resources our Father in Heaven has given us; instead, we hope the list is sufficient to help anyone see how gospel resources can provide the strength necessary to make it successfully through this life, facing the challenges each of us will face, and remain on the covenant path.

Lastly, in Appendix A, there is a diagram we've called "Consider Your Ways," and we suggest you take a few minutes to read, study, and ponder this. This diagram may help you understand the process of choosing to take the covenant path, and how we can become better than we are once we make the conscious decision to press forward in Christ. It demonstrates in a cyclic motion what can happen to us as we each "consider our ways" and journey on the covenant path that our Father in Heaven has designated for us.

We believe with all our hearts the statement from the Prophet Joseph Smith that "happiness is the object and design of our existence and will be the end thereof if we pursue the course that leads to it."[9] Our hope is that each person who reads this book will see more clearly the glory of the gospel of Jesus Christ and what the Savior offers us so that they can endure life's challenges faithfully and find lasting joy.

We know personally the satisfaction of enduring difficult challenges with faith in the Savior. We know that the resources presented in this book can strengthen anyone, and the power they offer each of us is real. We know this both through our personal experiences and through the experiences of others we have seen who have faced

---

9. See chapter 3 of this book.

challenges and come through them with their faith intact. We invite you to join with us as you read this book to find the courage, strength, and faith to continue along the covenant path to the very end of your life.

1

PRESS FORWARD IN CHRIST

MDM

"Ye must press forward with a steadfastness in Christ."

—2 Nephi 31:20

As a child, I learned from my mother the stories of the Restoration and the First Vision. Listening to mom read the Book of Mormon instilled in my heart a faith that seemed unshakable to a young, faithful, yet somewhat naive member of the Church with a fairly black-and-white perspective about the gospel. At least that was the case until I reached my teenage years. Then life became increasingly difficult. My relationships with some of my family members were rocky, and I began to question what I was taught and what I thought I knew so well. Some of my choices no longer reflected my faith, and before long I became inactive in the Church.

By the time I graduated from high school, I left Utah Valley where I was living and headed to the Bay Area in California. I went there hoping for a fresh start, trying to enroll in a prestigious university I thought would lead me to my goal of law school and earning an impressive salary.

With my personality, I made friends easily and excelled in school. After two years of living in San Francisco, I was experiencing what the world said would make me happy: a good job for my age with an amazing boss who was my friend as much as my employer. I developed friendships with people who provided connections in the art community. These people provided access to what I thought were even more important people. I attended gallery openings where I ate exquisite food and saw world-class art. I associated with intelligent, entertaining, and often pretentious people, and I loved all of it. I felt an overriding sense of adventure in my life.

One of my friends worked for the San Francisco Ballet, and he gave me tickets to attend the opening night of *Swan Lake*, a premier event for the social elite. Along with all this excitement, I was in love with my girlfriend, and we were talking about marriage. My friends helped me get elected as president of the honor society at my college, and I attended socials with the student body president of the school. I felt like I had everything the world could offer, living in one of the most beautiful cities in the world—but also one of the most worldly.

Despite all my success and a life of worldly fulfillment, over time I felt increasingly dissatisfied with my life. Then, one Sunday in November 1988, my life took an abrupt turn. While doing my laundry at the laundromat with my girlfriend and her mother, an unexpected spiritual impression penetrated my heart: "Everyone you associate with wants nothing to do with God. Is that really who you want to become?" The thought shocked me. In fact, it frightened me.

Secretly, I always knew God was real, but at the time I felt incapable of fully following Him. While my lifestyle said otherwise, I still believed God was real and often felt the Church was true. However, because of past pain inflicted by some people who should have loved me and also some poor personal choices, the pain I felt caused me to seek relief. Instead of turning to Christ and His gospel, I was turning to the world for that relief and personal satisfaction. This misguided placement of my values was seriously halting my spiritual progress. I had fallen way off the covenant path.

After feeling that penetrating thought in the laundromat, I said nothing to my girlfriend about the impression. I quickly took my clothes to my apartment while she went home with her mother. I threw my clothes into my bedroom and raced to find the phone number of the local Latter-day Saint church. When I called, a counselor in the bishopric told me sacrament meeting started at 12:30. I had only thirty minutes to travel across town. It seemed impossible to arrive on time, but I felt compelled to try despite my concerns.

I pulled my hair into a ponytail, grabbed my nicest shirt and pair of jeans, got dressed, and ran to the bus stop. The bus took me to the corner of Van Ness and Market, but because it was Sunday, the bus schedule was limited. I eventually realized I would miss church if I waited for the next bus, so I flagged down a taxi, begging the driver to get me to Pacific Avenue and Gough Street in five minutes. I told him I would make it worth his while.

He drove like an insane race car driver. I thought I was going to die before we made it to the church. After paying the driver and giving him a big tip for his courageous and successful driving, I hesitantly but anxiously approached the front doors of the church. As I opened them, the Spirit greeted me with a completely unexpected loving, spiritual embrace that completely enveloped me. I felt this strong, shockingly powerful greeting. The Spirit gave me the courage to slip quietly onto the back pew. That day, I began a journey toward letting God prevail in my life and returning to the Savior's covenant path.

Nothing about the subsequent changes came easily for me. I faced the challenge of letting go of the world. I fought temptation to return to sin, my old friends who didn't want me to change, and the incessant call of the natural man who enjoyed my previous lifestyle.

Yet I began to rely on the powerful feelings inside me, and they drove me forward. These feelings were centered in the love I felt that day I returned to church. I felt that love as members of my ward surrounded me. They encouraged and lifted me. My bishop, George Matthews, loved me, met with me regularly, and encouraged me to read the Book of Mormon and come to know my Savior Jesus Christ.

Over time, more frequent thoughts and feelings penetrated my mind and heart, inviting me to continue casting off the world and subsequently changing my perspective when I felt tempted to return to sin. Desires I had not felt for years began flowing back into my heart like a well of water quenching a thirst I forgot I once had.

Each of these experiences were evidence of a power in my life helping me to change. Since that time, I learned I was experiencing the grace of Jesus Christ, which He willingly gives to those who exercise their faith in Him and repent. When I began this journey, I didn't know how hard changing would be, but I was equally oblivious to the unforeseen tremendous blessings God would bring into my life, both in the moment and also throughout my 35-year journey of seeking to follow Christ. Now, the depth and intensity of the Savior's love and power to change my life stuns me. I feel like I have become a living witness to the tremendous power the Savior Jesus Christ has. I feel He has purchased me from the consequences of my choices, thus redeeming me and filling me with His precious love. His blessings truly are "most sweet, above all that I ever before tasted" (1 Nephi 8:11).

The End Goal

Each of us needs to come unto Christ, regardless of our past or present condition. He is "mighty to save" (2 Nephi 31:19) anyone who chooses to come unto Him. So, what changes do you want to make in your life? What joy do you wish was present that you have not yet received? What forgiveness do you need to extend to people who have harmed or offended you? What repentance do you need to seek in order to draw closer to God? What greater love could you bestow on those around you? If our ultimate goal is becoming like Jesus Christ and returning to live with our Father in Heaven, each of us might identify a gap between where we are and where we need to be. Yet the goal of Christlike development is lofty and requires us to break it down into smaller, daily changes we need to make. When goals are too great to visualize, the best way to travel the path of change is by creating daily habits.

President Henry B. Eyring has said, "Most of us have had some experience with self-improvement efforts. My experience has taught me this about how people and organizations improve: the best place to look is for small changes we could make in things we do often. There is power in steadiness and repetition. And if we can be led by inspiration to choose the right small things to change, consistent obedience will bring great improvement."[10] When we implement small alterations to our behavior, we can consistently repeat our new actions. Doing so also breaks down large, lofty goals into more manageable efforts. With this strategy, we begin our efforts to obtain eternal life.

This book is intended to help you examine yourself, comparing your current situation with where you want to be, which ideally is closer to the Savior and His gospel. As Stephen R. Covey taught in his landmark book *The Seven Habits of Highly Effective People*, intelligent, thoughtful, effective people "begin with the end in mind."[11] Knowing in advance that living the gospel has an intended purpose helps each of us to remain focused as we seek to live for that purpose. The goal is to become like and return to live with our Father in Heaven; to inherit all that He has, including His character and attributes; and to receive His abiding joy. We call this attainment eternal life or God's life.[12]

Jesus Christ is the way we reach this goal. He taught, "I am the way, the truth, and the life: no man cometh unto the Father, but by me" (John 14:6). In the Savior's famous Bread of Life sermon, He said, "I came down from heaven, not to do mine own will, but the will of him that sent me" (John 6:38). Jesus continued, explaining that He was the Bread of Life or manna from heaven; that is, He sustains us and fills us with the understanding and strength we need to continue along the path to everlasting life. His life and teachings literally are our spiritual food.

---

10. Henry B. Eyring, "The Lord Will Multiply the Harvest" (an evening with Elder Henry B. Eyring, Feb. 6, 1998), 3.
11. Stephen R. Covey, *The 7 Habits of Highly Effective People* (New York: Simon and Schuster, 1989), 172.
12. Guide to the Scriptures, "Eternal Life," scriptures.ChurchofJesusChrist.org.

I see one aspect of Christ's role as this: Jesus, the perfect example of the Father, who became as much like God in the pre-earth life as was possible, came to earth to show us the way. In effect, by coming to earth and living a godlike life, Jehovah brought heaven to a mortal, fallen earth. Through His acts of righteousness, He revealed how heavenly people live, think, and feel. Thus, we learn from Him how to respond to situations of temptation as well as opportunities for obedience, sacrifice, and faith. We see how to treat others and what things we should make our highest priorities. And in addition to His example, He continued through His teachings to clarify the process of becoming like Him.

The recent implementation of the Children and Youth program has helped us all better understand the Savior's role in our daily development. We learn from Luke 2:52 that Jesus developed a well-rounded character by emphasizing His standing with God and man as well as his growth in wisdom and stature. With these four descriptions of His development, we see in us the need to improve spiritually, socially, intellectually, and physically. To continue our progression, we might consider each category and then ask, "Which aspect of my life falls short of hitting the target of being a holy disciple of Jesus Christ?"[13]

Knowing the Savior's role in our progression and the goal of becoming like Him gives meaning and purpose to life. Accepting Him as our God charts the course we travel. Thus, the Savior provides us with the means and motivation to begin right now to create as much heaven on earth as possible within our circle of influence. Through the many affordances of His gospel, He can empower us to fulfill the plan of salvation, hence changing our nature to become more divine and influencing our surroundings. By performing His glorious Atonement, He enabled us to receive forgiveness and sanctification. In so doing, He offers to us continued strength to press forward along the journey President Russell M. Nelson so often refers to as the covenant path.[14]

---

13. See Wendy Nelson, "One Question That Can Change Your Life" (worldwide young adult devotional, May 15, 2022), ChurchofJesusChrist.org.
14. See Russell M. Nelson, "As We Go Forward Together," *Ensign*, Apr. 2018.

Setting Our Feet More Firmly on the Path

Whether we are a lifelong, active member or the most recent convert to Christ and His Church, each of us will face challenging times when our resolve to remain on the covenant path is tested. In such anxious moments, what will we do to press forward? Where will we turn for greater strength to continue enduring along the path of Christ?

Chris and I have written this book with the intent of reaching anyone who wants to progress. Both of us have faced many challenges to our faith throughout our journey, yet we have always come back to the primary decision, "Will I continue following the Savior?" His grace has helped us continue in faith. Our purpose in writing this book is to share what we have learned with the hope that you too will increase in strength and understanding and continue pressing forward to overcome your challenges. Specifically, we know that no matter how far we have come along the strait and narrow path, we "have not come thus far save it were by the word of Christ with unshaken faith in him, relying wholly upon the merits of him who is mighty to save" (2 Nephi 31:19).

The overarching message of this book comes from a verse in the Book of Mormon. Seeking to inspire those who had taken the name of Christ upon them through baptism, and wanting to help them continue in their faith, Nephi wrote, "Wherefore, ye must press forward with a steadfastness in Christ, having a perfect brightness of hope, and a love of God and of all men. Wherefore, if ye shall press forward, feasting upon the word of Christ, and endure to the end, behold, thus saith the Father: Ye shall have eternal life" (2 Nephi 31:20).

This scripture describes a life devoted to the Son of God. It is a life of growth, development, and progression. It requires energy, intensity, and strength. This devotion develops with steady, applied effort in the right direction. That direction is faith in Jesus Christ, His life, His teachings, and the restored gospel.

We cannot press forward unless we have decided where we want to go, or else we will simply wander aimlessly. Our relationship with

Jesus sets our aim and goal. This relationship defines the means and method of obtaining the end we seek. Our connection to Him strengthens our motivation and understanding so we keep striving to press forward and become more like Him. As we develop His attributes and character, we taste the fruit of His all-encompassing love and experience His joy. In all, our relationship with Christ is everything if we are to endure to the end with our faith intact and ultimately obtain eternal life.

The Change We Need to Experience

A parable shared in general conference by President Dallin H. Oaks characterized the expectation and influence of enduring faithfully. In the parable, President Oaks described a son and a wealthy father talking about the father's wishes for his son's future. The father explained to his son that he wanted to give his son everything he possessed and more. He said, "All that I have I desire to give you—not only my wealth, but also my position and standing among men."

As I read these words, I pondered the difference between the man's wealth and his position and standing. The father could easily bequeath his wealth on his son through a legal document, but if his son were to inherit not just his physical possessions but all that the father *was*, he would need his character and attributes as well. Without this kind of personal development, the inheritance of wealth would likely be wasted.

I felt a keen personal appreciation for the story because of my interactions with a friend from my college days. This friend's father possessed tremendous wealth. Despite his father's encouragement, my friend would not attend school, and he failed to hold down even basic employment. His father had spoiled him with luxuries I never dreamed of having. His jewelry was lavish and his car excessive, especially for someone his age. Yet his boredom was continuous. He got into trouble with the law and showed disregard for other people's feelings and well-being. During a serious moment together, I asked about his future. He casually replied, "Oh, I'm going to inherit my father's company. I don't need school or jobs. I'll be rich."

In my mind, I thought, "More likely you'll destroy your father's company with your lack of understanding and selfish behavior. Or you'll be unable to maintain the discipline and direction needed to lead a company like your father has." I liked my friend and hoped for his future, but I could see he didn't know the first thing about managing a multi-billion-dollar business, let alone disciplining his personal life. Of course, my friend could hire competent people to manage his business affairs, but he personally had no skills or character traits to maintain or grow in his relationships or business. He at that time was devoid of his father's character and standing among men.

While I don't know what ultimately happened to my friend, I have often thought of the value of becoming the right kind of person as opposed to having great possessions. President Oaks went on to explain the purpose of the wealthy father's conversation with his son. He said, "That which I *have* I can easily give you, but that which I *am* you must obtain for yourself. You will qualify for your inheritance by learning what I have learned and by living as I have lived. . . . Follow my example, mastering as I have mastered, and you will become as I am, and all that I have will be yours.'"[15]

If we imagine the wealthy father as our Heavenly Father, and ourselves as the potential heirs, we grasp the meaning of the parable. I believe sometimes we erroneously think that if we're good, God will give us a ticket to the celestial kingdom. We might believe this false idea when we say things like, "I hope God lets me go to heaven." But, in accordance with President Oaks' parable, admittance into God's kingdom seems less about permission and more about development—what we think, how we talk, what we do, and ultimately who we become.

While heaven certainly is a geographical place, prerequisite to entering into it is becoming the kind of person who is capable of being "equal in power, and in might, and in dominion" (Doctrine and

15. Dallin H. Oaks, "The Challenge to Become," *Ensign*, Nov. 2000, 32.

Covenants 76:95) with Jesus Christ. This thought evokes awe and worship. To become like Christ—what an inspiring and daunting challenge!

We Need Christ Now

We all know we are living in the last days before the Savior's return. How long do we have? When will He come again? President Oaks taught that whether "through our premature death or through His unexpected coming," the Second Coming of Christ will happen in our lifetime.[16] This is a sobering thought. Either way, whether we are "taken home to that God who gave [us] life" (Alma 40:11) or Jesus stands before us on the earth, we need to prepare now. "This life is the time for men to prepare to meet God" (Alma 34:32), and we "should be anxiously engaged in a good cause" (Doctrine and Covenants 58:27) to fulfill our preparation. What better cause is there than seeking to follow Christ along His covenant path and to become more like Him so we can return and live with God?

Despite the imperative nature of our situation and our earnest desires to follow Jesus, for many reasons we often feel anxiety, doubt, despair, and fear. For me, the fear is less about God's ability to set the right course and more about my ability to follow. Maybe you feel the same way. One way we might approach our anxiety is to categorize the types of challenges we face. While the kinds of challenges vary as much as the people who face them, there are common ways to respond to challenges with faith. First, let's examine the categories of challenges we might face.

Some experience physical and mental trials. An elderly person might ask, "How will I get out of bed today with all the pain in my body?" A student might think, "I can't pass this class! My teacher thinks it's the only class I'm taking, and with work, church, and a social life, I feel stretched thin. I'm failing at life!" A father or mother

---

16. Dallin H. Oaks, "Preparation for the Second Coming," *Ensign* or *Liahona*, May 2004, 9.

may feel, "The expectations at work are constant. My pay stays the same, but the demands keep increasing. I'm going to work my whole life and then die. That's my purpose." Another person might feel buried by their stress and anxiety, thinking, "How can I know God is real? I can't feel anything. I pray and nothing happens. I can't sleep. I feel panicked at school and work. I am falling further and further behind. My medication makes me feel sick. When will I get relief? Where is God when I need Him?" The physical challenges of being bound to mortal existence are common to humanity.

Others face trials of their faith, possibly related to certain doctrines or policies of the Church. A woman might ask, "I'm confused about my role in the gospel. I believe the Brethren are called of God, but what can I contribute since I can't hold the priesthood? Is it a doctrine or just policy that only men hold the priesthood, and will it ever change? Will I ever feel satisfied with my life in the Church?" Another person might question, "Does God love me, even though I have feelings of same-sex attraction? What is my future in God's kingdom? Can I receive celestial glory despite my feelings? Do I have to spend my entire life without love to please God? What is my role in the plan of salvation if I am not married to someone of the opposite sex?" Someone else might feel, "What is my place in the Church when my spouse has lost their testimony? The gospel is so family-oriented—how can I remain connected to the plan when I'm not living the ideal?"

Many experience challenges with sin. One might think, "Since I'm already so far gone, maybe it's hopeless to ever change. Should I just forget about the Church? I wonder if I'd feel happier if I did." Another might think, "Everyone else drinks or smokes or does drugs. Why is it so bad? Is the Church against having fun?" Someone else might feel, "I'm never going to be able to stop looking at pornography. How many times will I have to go see my bishop? Sometimes I just want to hide and not deal with this anymore. I just want this to come to an end." The challenge of sin is ever-present in a fallen world, and the guilt that can come with it might feel interminable. Maybe you are experiencing this right now.

Finally, there are people who might feel, "There's no serious trial, temptation, or sin in my life right now. I just want to strive to become more like Christ. I'm trying to keep His commandments, but the journey is long, and the trail is often steep and rocky. It's difficult to develop all His attributes." Someone striving for perfection might feel discouraged with the protracted effort needed to be so refined and might ask, "When will I learn patience?" Another may think, "For years, I've fought the urge to lash out at people who frustrate me. When will I be able to control my tongue?" Another still might feel, "I'm too unkind, selfish, and prideful." Finally, someone else might think, "The world is so full of sinful things. I can't watch a movie without hearing profanity. Everyone seems so impatient, and I'm feeling the same pull. I struggle to participate in ministering even on a basic level. Do I have to be that good and pure if I'm going to make it to the celestial kingdom? I mean, no unclean thing can dwell with God, right? Being like Jesus—exactly obedient in all things—feels unattainable. Am I doomed to terrestrial glory?"

For this last category, we would do well to remember Paul's words, that we all "come short of the glory of God" (Romans 3:23). Repentance is not just for people committing serious sins but also for those who are seeking to become better and more Christlike in every way. We all at some point face the challenge of continued refinement. Maybe that's where you are right now.

Each of these categories of challenges represents an opportunity for growth. They are all simply ways to recognize our need for the Prince of Peace. To find your need right now, you might ponder the following questions: "What brings me anxiety about my spiritual well-being? What diminishes my hope that I will be equal to the challenges of life and ultimately make it to the celestial kingdom? What creates distance between me and the Savior and His commandments?"

The need for Jesus Christ is all-encompassing. There is no one, whether currently in His kingdom or out of it, who has arrived at perfection. The key is remembering Him. We are told by the Savior, "Look unto me in every thought; doubt not, fear not. Behold the wounds which pierced my side, and also the prints of the nails in my hands and feet; be faithful, keep my commandments, and ye shall inherit the kingdom of heaven" (Doctrine and Covenants 6:36–37). With the Redeemer, there is hope. With the expectation to accomplish so much in our lifetime, we need faith in the Good Shepherd if we are going to make it. We cannot accomplish this life without pressing forward with faith in Him. He will help us to fulfill our purpose despite our feelings of inadequacy, regardless of their sources—whether they are challenges to our faith, the trials of mortality, the seriousness of sin, or the need to continually progress toward perfection.

President Russell M. Nelson has stated, "Faith [in Jesus Christ] is the power that enables the unlikely to accomplish the impossible."[17] I know at times with our challenges we may feel that eternal life is unlikely. Sometimes our concerns are closer at hand. Sometimes they feel as if they will never end. Other times, they are on the distant horizon and approach us at unexpected moments. But knowing the right source to look to for strength is half the battle.

Despite the modern nature of many of our challenges, the ancientness of Christ's scripture does not make His words obsolete, and the power of Christ's gospel has not lost its efficacy with all that is happening in our current day. With the swirling, billowing winds of opposition roaring around us, now more than ever we need the Rock of Christ, His sure foundation, His rod of iron, and His strait and narrow path; we need Him to become the anchor to our souls.[18] We all need greater faith in Jesus Christ, His gospel, and His atoning grace. His grace is always the answer to our need for perfection.

Grace comes to us through the enabling power of our Lord Jesus Christ's Atonement.[19] The Lord's grace manifests itself in many ways. It can come as a priesthood blessing that strengthens us despite our not being healed immediately or perhaps ever. His grace comes to anxious hearts who find peace as they read words to comfort their

---

17. Russell M. Nelson, "Christ Is Risen; Faith in Him Will Move Mountains," *Liahona*, May 2021, 104.
18. See Helaman 5:12; Matthew 7:24–27; 1 Nephi 8:20, 24, 30; Ether 12:4; Doctrine and Covenants 6:34, 36–37.
19. Gospel Topics, "Grace," topics.ChurchofJesusChrist.org.

troubled souls. His commandments can be an expression of grace as they remove the confusion of "What should I do?" when faced with sin or temptation. Or the grace of the Lamb of God can come when we enter His holy house and participate in saving ordinances, there to feel His strength to try again. His grace is all-encompassing, ready to strengthen the weary and lift up the hands that hang down.

Press Forward with a Steadfastness in Christ

Each of us needs to conclude at some point, "I am not the source of strength in my life, even though I often think I am. Jesus is my strength. He is my rock and my sure foundation." Accepting this truth allows us to press forward through life's difficulties with spiritual vitality and greater, eternal success.

As an example of this, my wife and I have felt over the past years that we should put our names in for a work transfer. We believed doing so would allow us to follow the direction President M. Russell Ballard gave in the April 2020 general conference. During his talk, he recounted the sacrifices of Hyrum and Joseph Smith for God and His kingdom. He then invited his listeners to act by saying, "Consider what offering you will present to the Lord in righteousness in the coming days. Be courageous—share it with someone you trust, and most important, please take the time to do it!"[20]

This challenge resounded in my heart. Leaving our home of sixteen years to uproot our family and move somewhere outside of Utah felt daunting, but the more we talked, the more the change made sense. Originally, we were told the positions would post in October 2021 and that we would know if we were going somewhere. October came and went with no change coming. We applied to a few positions but were not selected. When May 2022 came, a surprise opportunity arose to apply for an assignment in Tampa, Florida. We applied, and to our tremendous surprise, we were offered the position there. What

---

20. M. Russell Ballard, "Shall We Not Go On in So Great a Cause?," *Ensign* or *Liahona*, May 2020, 11.

a blessing and what an opportunity to serve in God's kingdom outside of Utah. Yet this move meant we now had only a few months to prepare, whereas we originally thought we'd have another year!

We feverishly began a hurried campaign to complete all the projects we knew were necessary to list our home on the real estate market. Quickly we realized we could not complete the work ourselves. Almost immediately we depleted our savings on the work we had finished and found ourselves in desperate need of assistance from our ward members so we could complete some sweat equity.

My wife and I struggled with asking for help. We're independent people who make lists and work hard to accomplish our tasks. Nevertheless, the predicament we were in required help from others. I posted a message in a group chat we share with the elders quorum and asked if anyone could spare thirty minutes to an hour helping on a list of projects we needed to complete. To my elation, many friends quickly volunteered to come help.

I sat in my office that day, seeing the responses come, and began to weep. I felt so humbled by the love of my brethren. At that moment, I did not realize I was pressing forward with faith in Christ. I simply did what I felt I should do after offering prayers for guidance. After posting my request, one brother "liked" what I said, then about twenty minutes later he posted, "I can come tonight and help with the electrical stuff." I smiled and thought what an awesome man for caring so much.

Later that day, when he arrived at the house, he went to work on the electrical while I continued painting. When he completed his tasks, we met on our front porch to talk about life for a minute. There he told me of his difficult week and how stressed he felt. He said, "When I saw your post at first, I thought I couldn't come. I felt it was too much for what was going on in my life right then. Then the thought came to my mind, 'When ye are in the service of your fellow beings ye are only in the service of your God' (Mosiah 2:17). That's when I posted I would I come help." Then my friend looked at me and said, "I really needed this. I feel so much better right now about my situation." By serving me, my friend was healed of the troubles he carried.

The Savior's power to strengthen us comes when we engage in His gospel. All of us are broken in some way, and we need the Master Healer's strengthening touch in our lives.[21] As I pondered this experience, I realized that my friend expressed his faith in Christ and pressed forward, not knowing beforehand the strength the Spirit would provide as the Lord would heal him. As my friend did what Christ would have him do, the Savior then could lift his burden and comfort his soul. He experienced the grace of Christ.

Furthermore, my friend represented Jesus to me at that moment. The Savior "came to my home," figuratively speaking, because of my pleading for help in prayer. He did so by sending His Spirit to speak to my friend, touch his heart, and inspire him to help me. As a result, my friend's actions helped dispel my doubt and despair. Together we both pressed forward in Christ, putting our trust in Him that He would heal us.

The Purpose of This Book

As members of Christ's Church, we each have covenanted to put our faith and trust in Him and live His gospel. As we face challenges in our lives, we experience trials that test our faith. By acting in faith, we each can press forward, trusting the Savior's message by living His teachings. Acting in faith increases the influence the Good Shepherd can have on our lives as He comes to our aid to bind up our wounded souls. His grace is the power to assist us in facing our trials, lifting our souls, and strengthening our faith.

This book is a collection of ideas of how each of us can more fully press forward with steadfast faith in Christ. We present here not a comprehensive list of ways to do so, but rather a selection of resources God has provided to help us respond in faith to our challenges. As

---

21. See Amy A. Wright, "Christ Heals That Which is Broken," *Liahona*, May 2022.

you read the coming chapters, we hope the Holy Spirit inspires you to see ways you can exercise greater faith in Christ. Some of our words may touch your mind and heart, but more importantly, we hope the Holy Ghost speaks to you so you have ideas and impressions of your own that reveal what you might do to face your difficulties with faith in the Son of God.

Certainly, there were other topics we could have chosen to write about. Yet we feel the ones we chose are important and inspiring. That said, the approach we will take in the coming chapters to implement the gospel in our lives can be applied to any of the teachings of Jesus Christ. For instance, we do not address the topics of prayer or tithing, yet by acting on our faith in Christ, implementing any gospel principle will lead to some degree of the healing power of the Savior's love coming into our lives.

2

CONSIDER YOUR WAYS

MDM

"Thus saith the Lord of hosts; Consider your ways."

—Haggai 1:7

At 1:15 a.m. the sound of horns pulled me from my sleep, slowly bringing me to consciousness. I thought, "Oh, Utah fans! Who cares? We know you won!" In my drowsy stupor, I was conflating Utah's victory over BYU earlier that evening with my experience of the San Francisco Giants winning the National League Championship in 1989. Everyone went crazy in San Francisco, staying out until 5 a.m. honking horns and screaming in celebration. Somehow, my exhausted mind thought my neighbors in Utah were now doing the same thing.

Trying to go back to sleep, I forced the sounds from my mind until I heard the throaty blast of a fire engine horn. "The whole city wouldn't celebrate the Utes' win," I thought, now more alert. As I opened my eyes, I saw our large bay window was lit with red and orange hues, an acrid smoky smell filled our house, and my mouth was so dry I could hardly swallow. I hurried to open the blinds and saw thirty-foot flames about seventy-five yards from our house. The hillside was on fire.

We quickly evacuated to our ward building parking lot, where many gathered to observe the path of the flames. We spent the night praying and checking on everyone to make sure all were safe, as winds going forty miles an hour whipped the towering flames toward our neighborhood. At some point that early morning, I met with Dan, our ward emergency preparedness specialist. He had a clipboard resting on his steering wheel and was checking off the names of our ward members. "Everyone is accounted for," he told me. We both exhaled with relief.

"What about your home?" I asked. Dan and Cherilyn lived on the edge of the neighborhood bordering the wilderness where the fire raged.

"Sheila left the house not long ago. She saw flames inside through the front windows." Dan and Cherilyn's house, as well as another neighbor's home, were engulfed in flames, burning everything to their foundations.

Luckily no lives were lost. Yet that night changed everything for us. We recognized how temporary life is. We all appreciated so much more the Lord's blessings of protection, recognizing that our situation in life is so tenuous in the face of adversity. Situations like the wildfire we faced can invite us in meaningful ways to examine our lives, especially our focus and our priorities. This examination is what the scriptures call repentance.

The Call to Consider Our Ways

The Book of Mormon begins in 1 Nephi during the reign of Zedekiah, king of Judah. The message of prophets to the people was "that they must repent, or the great city Jerusalem must be destroyed" (1 Nephi 1:4). As we know, the majority did not listen. Lehi and Ishmael and their families heard the voice of God, left the city, and were spared. They overcame the most pressing danger of their day. But even though they were saved from Nebuchadnezzar and Babylonian captivity, they were not spared from the challenges of following God into the wilderness. Leaving behind their possessions was difficult, some were reasonably concerned, and others murmured and became bitter (see 1 Nephi 2:3–4; 5:1–3; 17:21). We see a pattern in their family conflicts of how we too might respond to our challenges and trials.

Laman and Lemuel murmured when asked to get the brass plates, saying "it is a hard thing" (1 Nephi 3:5). Nephi (and presumably Sam) responded, "I will go and do" (1 Nephi 3:7). I imagine I would have complained along with Laman and Lemuel at some point. The challenges Lehi's family faced were very difficult. It would be natural to complain and maybe even doubt the sanity of leaving everything behind and going out into the wilderness. "Dad, what are you thinking?" I likely would have asked. Yet through Nephi's actions and attitude, we can see a type of Christ, the ever-obedient Son who always did his Father's will.

A thoughtful student of these events might trace this theme of Christlike acceptance to its conclusion, as the family arrived safely in the promised land—or what we might symbolically consider the celestial kingdom. There the obedient were saved, not just from Babylonian captivity or starvation in the desert but from the Satanic captivity of sin and the eventualities of death (see 1 Nephi 18:22–25)—something we ourselves can be freed from by following in their spiritual footsteps. The story of Lehi's family chronicles the lives of people who rose above their mortal challenges and sufferings, and it shows how God directed them throughout their lives. They are for us a pattern of how we might "consider our ways."

Yet what about those who were taken captive in Jerusalem and eventually languished in Babylon? While many perished in horrific ways during the siege that befell them, God did not leave the survivors to suffer interminably (see 1 Nephi 18:22–25). One of the prophets who foresaw the Babylonian captivity was Jeremiah. While he prophesied that Jerusalem would be destroyed, and many Jews killed or taken captive, he also prophesied that their captivity would end after seventy years.[22]

One of the devastating results of the war with Babylon was the utter destruction of Solomon's glorious temple in 587 BC. As the seventy-year period drew to its conclusion, the people needed to fulfill the prophecy of Jeremiah. Yet they seemed unwilling to act and said, "The time is not come . . . [when] the Lord's house should be built" (Haggai 1:2). In other words, "We don't want to leave Babylon and go back to Jerusalem. We're content to stay here." With confidence, the prophet Haggai challenged the captive Jews to "consider your ways" (Haggai 1:7).

According to Haggai, the people had become complacent in their captivity. While they lived in "ceiled houses," the House of the Lord "lie [in] waste" (Haggai 1:4). Their priorities were misplaced. They had put their own comfort above fulfilling the Lord's commandment to return to Jerusalem and rebuild the temple. As a result, God began to stir them up by sending prophets again to rally them to action. He allowed their crops to produce little, their cups to be dry, and their wages to be so meager that Haggai exclaimed, "He that earneth wages . . . [puts] it into a bag with holes" (Haggai 1:6). It's amazing how, over time, we can allow ourselves to throw up our hands in despair and think, "Well, this seems to be my fate! I'm stuck and can't go forward," despite the fact God has made sacred promises to us through covenants, and that we will be blessed tremendously if we follow Him. The emptiness the Jews felt is something we too may face if we choose to place our hearts, minds, and actions on being content rather than "considering our ways."

God may also call on us to repent and "consider our ways" by using events like fires, earthquakes, financial challenges, health problems, lost jobs, divorce, family troubles, doctrinal questions, faith crises, and even a worldwide pandemic. While I am not suggesting God *caused* the pandemic—a prophet would have to be the one to declare

---

22. See John P. Pratt, "When was Judah's 70-year Babylonian captivity?," *Ensign*, Oct. 1998.

that—we certainly can see all challenges as opportunities to consider our ways. We can faithfully examine ourselves and decide what personal messages God might be sending to us through the difficulties we face. Specifically, we can determine how we will respond in faith when our challenges come.

The word *consider* is a call to action. It's a choice. We need not wait for suffering to begin considering. The Latin word *considerare*, which is where our English word *consider* comes from, means to examine. As I have studied the etymology of this word, I interpret it to mean "consult with heaven" about the condition of my heart, what I love, what I want, and who I serve.[23] In addition to our English word, the Hebrew word for *consider* also means to "set your heart on your ways."[24] Regardless of which word we examine, we end up realizing God wants us to think about this question: "What is the object of your desires?" or "What have you set your heart on?" The Lord is calling each of us throughout life's experience, whether in good times or bad, to examine our lives—but He leaves the choice up to us to do so.

Our hope for this book is to journey together through the many resources the gospel provides. This will help us contemplate our life situation, the direction we are heading, and whether we are fully utilizing all the blessings God has given us to safely pass through our journey to the promised land and arrive with our testimonies intact. As we look to heaven to find direction for where we are going, we especially testify that God can lead us through our deserts of adversity or trial.

---

23. This is my interpretation after examining the word *consider*, based on the etymology from *Oxford Languages*. You can further subdivide *considerare* into *con*, meaning "with," and *sider*, meaning stars. Thus, to consider might mean "to consult the stars." Maybe this reference is to astrology or maritime navigation. Regardless, the root of our English word *consider* seems to mean consulting heaven in one way or another.
24. In Haggai 1:7, the Hebrew word *soom* is used, meaning to place, ordain, or establish your ways—one interpretation is to "set your heart on your ways." This Hebrew definition was found, like many others in this book, using the e-Sword mobile application (see H7760).

How to Consider Our Ways

Nephi was an expert at examining himself and his intentions. For instance, when Nephi broke his bow and the family needed food, he didn't murmur. Instead, he made a new bow and found a straight stick and made an arrow. It was time for action, not complaining. If we are constantly dwelling on the frustration and anger of our lives and never do what Nephi did—develop a plan of action—we're going to remain stuck.[25]

Nephi also didn't face his challenge alone. He turned to his father the prophet and to God for direction (see 1 Nephi 16:18–23). He successfully found food and saved his family's life. This wasn't a one-time thing for him. He followed this pattern throughout his life—when crossing the wilderness, building a ship, and ultimately when sailing to the promised land. Nephi was consistently considering his standing in relationship to God. This kind of repentance allowed him to progress from problem to problem, finding solutions and growing in faith.

During one of the great moments at the end of Nephi's life, he summarized a powerful insight about the effects of following this pattern of repentance. In 2 Nephi 31, Nephi taught his reader the doctrine of Christ. He wrote that despite being holy, Jesus willingly submitted to His Father's commandments to be baptized. In doing so, Nephi said Jesus "humbleth himself before the Father, and witnesseth unto the Father that he would be obedient in keeping his commandments" (2 Nephi 31:7). Nephi taught that Jesus was setting the perfect example for us through His behavior, His character, and His attributes. In all things, the Savior was perfectly humble and obedient.

Nephi further explained that Jesus, "having set the example," was now inviting us, "Follow thou me" (2 Nephi 31:9–10). Thus, as we compare our ways to the example of Jesus Christ, we can consider

25. That said, I think it's okay to feel frustration or even anger about our situation. And sometimes venting about our difficulties can help get bottled-up emotions out so we can think straight. At one point, I held a priesthood calling where people would talk to me regularly about their problems, and after a while, I concluded that solving human problems is always messy. Emotions make things very difficult to sort out, and it helps to have someone to talk to.

God's expectations for us by looking at the Savior's divine attributes and character. In this light, our challenges become opportunities as we consider how to become more like Jesus while overcoming the challenges of life.

In addition, Nephi invited us to not only consider our ways as we *begin* our journey of discipleship but also as we faithfully *endure* to the end of our lives. One definition of enduring to the end is "to remain firm in a commitment to be true to the commandments of God despite temptation, opposition, and adversity."[26] If we combine enduring to the end with following Christ, we develop a powerful combination. Thinking of Christlike attributes that relate to enduring, we might develop such a list as being committed, disciplined, diligent, consistent, resolved, determined, and strong. These words describe a relationship of action to stay on course for the long haul, doing the right things throughout our lives.

However, it's not enough for us to get ourselves going along the path. There are also attributes we should seek to develop as we help others, such as being encouraging, brave, patient, and loving. We could help them endure *their* paths so they are not alone as we journey alongside them. With this addition, we might add more attributes, such as being compassionate and accepting. While these attributes could relate to feelings for other people, we can also apply them to ourselves since we're often our worst critics. "So, you broke your bow," Nephi might say. "It's seems really bad right now, but after you make your new one and solve this problem, you'll see you are a lot stronger than you thought you were."

As we develop Christlike attributes while enduring our challenges, we are repenting in new ways. This kind of change is not the repentance of "I've done something terribly wrong and need to see the bishop." This is the repentance of growing closer to Christ by emulating Him in our times of distress and challenge. Here, our choices to follow Jesus's example become the forge that fires our faith into hardened steel.

---

26. Guide to the Scriptures, "Endure," scriptures.ChurchofJesusChrist.org.

Finally, there are attributes like being persistent, steadfast, faithful, trusting, obedient, serving, and humble. These could apply to our relationship with Heavenly Father and Jesus Christ. Each attribute we develop can deepen our devotion to God. We literally become more like Him as we repent and follow His Son. By connecting ourselves with Christ and His attributes, we connect with heaven along the path of life. We develop a character like the Savior's, thus deepening our sense of self and purpose.

Throughout this discussion, I have described various attributes as they apply to specific relationships: ourselves, others, and God. Yet we ought not to be too strict with connecting specific attributes with a specific relationship. Each attribute could relate to many or all of our relationships. The point isn't to see a one-to-one comparison with a specific relationship but to begin thinking of how Christ's attributes can influence all our actions and relationships in many ways. We may see how an attribute of Christ helps with any of the following: (1) with tasks we seek to accomplish as we develop ourselves, (2) with other people who are enduring, and (3) with our Father in Heaven and Jesus Christ.

The Goal of Considering Our Ways

Our goal as we consider our ways is to become lifelong disciples of Jesus Christ. When the Father appeared in the Sacred Grove to the Prophet Joseph Smith, He introduced Jesus by saying, "This is My Beloved Son. Hear Him!" (Joseph Smith—History 1:17). Joseph Smith followed the Savior and Heavenly Father through tremendous adversity and trial until his devotion led to His death (see Doctrine and Covenants 135). When Jesus called the Twelve Apostles in His day, He said, "Follow me" (Matthew 4:19), and these men put down their nets and followed Him to the very end.[27] Jesus Himself set the perfect example of being a true follower of God, committed to do the

27. See also "The 12 Apostles of Jesus Christ: Then and Now," ph.ChurchofJesusChrist.org.

Father's will regardless of persecution or affliction, again even unto death (see Hebrews 4:15; 5:8; Luke 23:46). Finally, we are instructed in our baptismal covenant to serve God and keep His commandments "at all times, and in all places . . . even until death" (Mosiah 18:9).

This kind of devotion—even unto death—can feel unsettling. Is God expecting us to die for His cause? It could be, but this kind of sacrifice is rare. There are relatively few followers who die as martyrs for the cause of Christ compared to how many have lived long, full lives as disciples for Him. Instead, for most of us, the call "even until death" means a lifelong commitment. Will we give our whole lives to the cause, focusing on the big picture every day? In this way, we can look at the level of our devotion to God, deciding if we will commit to becoming lifelong disciples.

I saw this level of devotion in my friend Art Neilson, who taught me many lessons of faith and devotion while he battled an illness in his old age.[28] Art had been a faithful member of the Church his entire life. Raised by active parents, he knew the gospel and loved it. He and his wife Winnie served faithfully in the Church all their married lives. At the age of seventy-eight, Art contracted a viral infection, and the medication doctors gave him to fight it destroyed the tiny hair-like structures in his inner ear, causing Art to suffer from vertigo. For him, the sense of whirling and dizziness was permanent: "I have to constantly fight to keep from falling down," he said. Art endured this trial for over eight years with little relief. He told me the only relief he got was when he was lying down, and he said he faced a daily decision: "Will I get out of bed or not? If I do get up, I know the spinning will resume."

As the years of suffering lingered, Art fell into a deep depression. He began to doubt the gospel was true. He told me, "I felt like right when I needed the gospel most, it didn't work! I have personally given blessings to people in the hospital who were dying, and within the week, they were home and completely well. But me, I would get on my knees and pray—I would just sob and beg and plead with Heavenly

28. Story used with Art's permission.

Father to help me get rid of this. I had six priesthood blessings. I had no help. No help at all!" Hearing my friend share such poignant feelings was deeply troubling. My heart ached for him.

In response to his intense suffering, Art began to plan his own death, believing the end of his life would be the end of his misery. One night while pondering his situation, he realized, "I have always known the gospel is true. Since I was a little boy, I had a testimony. Now I am failing the test! In the last minutes of my life, I'm about to fail." Through this realization and many others, Art began to choose to give his will to God and completely depend on Him for strength. One way Art turned his will to God was to reach out to other people with suicidal thoughts and share his story with them. He told me of many people who would listen to him because of what he went through, and they would begin to find the same kind of hope he had found in Christ.

As Art more fully surrendered to Heavenly Father, I watched him become more sensitive to the Spirit. He was easily moved to tears. Art was not a crying man before this. He was tough. As a martial arts expert, wrestler, and football player, he had developed a strong body. He told me of many grueling experiences he had fought through with physical stamina that few people possess. Now, through this refining process of coming unto Christ through his adversity, Art was given the gift of love through the things he suffered. He became a more Christlike man through his faithful response to endure to the end. God transformed him into a new person. He was a refined son of God.

Speaking of the afflictions we may face, the Savior said, "I, the Lord, have suffered the affliction to come upon them . . . Yet I will own them, and they shall be mine in that day when I shall come to make up my jewels" (Doctrine and Covenants 101:2–3). I am convinced that as we faithfully endure, believing in Him when all seems lost, we can become the Lord's treasure—His precious witnesses who know of His transformative power. We can become beautiful gems of faith. My bishop once wrote a letter to me on my mission where he described this transformation like a caterpillar changing into a beautiful butterfly. We each begin so small and plain and incapable of flight. Yet through the Savior's grace and our willingness to endure, He can transform us into someone greater than we ever could imagine becoming through our own efforts. His power changes our very nature and lifts us to new heights.

In the book of Revelation, the Apostle John wrote of seven churches whose members were suffering intense persecution. Throughout chapters two and three, there is a call to the Saints to overcome their afflictions through Christ, and then John lists the many blessings God would give the faithful. My personal favorite moment in these chapters is the last blessing listed, where the Savior said, "To him that overcometh will I grant to sit with me in my throne, even as I also overcame, and am set down with my Father in his throne" (Revelation 3:21). This promise is stunning and has motivated me as I face my challenges and need continued strength. Thus, to consider our ways means to overcome our adversity, become more like the Savior, and ultimately receive eternal life in the celestial kingdom.

Considering Our Ways through Repentance

Satan, our enemy, desires to thwart our efforts to become lifelong disciples of Jesus and receive eternal life. He attacks us in a variety of ways, from blatant rebellion to lax complacency, from self-loathing to discouragement. The way to overcome Satan's attacks is to put on the whole armor of Jesus Christ so we are prepared to do battle with him. As mentioned before, our plan in this book is to examine the many resources God has given us, thus helping us to arm ourselves against the adversary when we are under attack. With Christ on our side, Lucifer cannot win.

In the Doctrine and Covenants, we read, "Wherefore, lift up your hearts and rejoice, and gird up your loins, and take upon you *my whole armor*, that ye may be able to withstand the evil day" (Doctrine and Covenants 27:15; emphasis added). Note in this verse that the Savior referred to the armor of God as *His* armor. What a thought! In another scripture, we learn that Jesus "suffered temptations but gave no heed unto them" (Doctrine and Covenants 20:22). This means He had power over all temptation, trial, and sin. Clearly, the implication is that His armor is the most effective deterrent against sin that ever was or will be. So, how can we more fully take upon us the armor of Jesus Christ?

In an address to seminary and institute teachers, Elder Kim B. Clark described an experience when he felt a need to arm himself more fully against spiritual attacks. He said, "When I read the words 'put on the whole armour of God,' I felt a powerful witness of the Spirit that this was the answer to my prayers. I needed to put on the whole armour of God—every bit of it."[29]

Elder Clark described the process he went through while seeking to arm himself more fully. Primarily, he found that asking two questions helped in this process: (1) "What am I doing that I should stop doing?" and (2) "What am I not doing that I should start doing?" Elder Clark explained the many changes that came into his life, and the life of his wife, as a result of asking and answering these two questions. Then he concluded, "I know that had we not listened and not acted on what we received, I would not have been called to serve at BYU–Idaho [as university president] and I would not be standing here before you today [as a General Authority]. It was a turning point in our lives."[30] Following Elder Clark's example, if we want to become true followers of Jesus Christ and fulfill our full potential, we need to consider what is holding us back, the negative things we need to stop doing, and the positive things we need to start doing.

We might begin the process by asking, "What is something I have felt lately I need to stop?" As we consider our ways, like Nephi we might formulate a plan to change, turn to the words of the prophets, pray to God, and seek to emulate the Savior's life more fully. Through the Savior's power, we can forsake sin. Furthermore, as we consider the things we know we should be doing, God will help us improve our

29. Kim B. Clark, "Encircled About with Fire" (Seminaries and Institutes of Religion Satellite Broadcast, Aug. 4, 2015), broadcasts.ChurchofJesusChrist.org.

30. Kim B. Clark, "Encircled About with Fire."

discipleship. Through these two questions, we can more fully repent daily.

Brother Stephen W. Owen said, "We often associate repentance with grievous sins that require 'a mighty change.' But repentance is for everyone—those who are wandering in 'forbidden paths and [are] lost' as well as those who 'have gotten into [the] strait and narrow path' and now need to 'press forward.' Repentance both puts us on the right path and keeps us on the right path."[31] In addition, Elder David A. Bednar taught, "Most of us clearly understand that the Atonement is for sinners. I am not so sure, however, that we know and understand that the Atonement is also for saints—for good men and women who are obedient, worthy, and conscientious and who are striving to become better and serve more faithfully."[32]

Our message in this book is that each of us needs the Atonement of Jesus Christ to put off "the natural man" and become "a saint" (Mosiah 3:19). In his famous sermon, King Benjamin described how the Savior's Atonement is the means of this transformation. The change can come as we become more childlike, "submissive, meek, humble, patient, full of love, [and] willing to submit to all things which the Lord seeth fit to inflict upon [us]" (Mosiah 3:19). Notice that each of these attributes is one the Savior exemplifies. Thus, as we fully accept the Savior's Atonement, He arms us against evil and our fallen nature, and He puts His strength upon us. This strength comes from repenting of our sins and seeking to follow Him more fully so that we might develop more of Christ's divine attributes, His perfect character, and the gifts God has given us.

Accept Greater Responsibility to Change

In President Henry B. Eyring's book *Choose Higher Ground*, he presented a powerful idea in the final chapter titled "Raise the Bar."

31. Stephen W. Owen, "Repentance Is Always Positive," *Ensign* or *Liahona*, Nov. 2017, 49.
32. David A. Bednar, "The Atonement and the Journey of Mortality," *Ensign* or *Liahona*, May 2012, 42.

His message was about finding continued motivation to change throughout our lives. President Eyring recalled how, as a high school and college student, he enjoyed high jumping. Later, while attending high jump competitions, probably for family members, he observed how "junior high school students, some of them girls, [were] jumping higher than my best." He realized that the limitation of his improvement was not related as much to a *physical* inability to get over the bar as it was to a *mental* limitation he was setting on himself. He didn't believe he could do more, so he didn't push himself to try. After telling this story, President Eyring issued a challenge to his readers: "Set the bar a little higher for yourself. And then set it a little higher."[33] The idea of continually raising the bar on ourselves is essential to considering our ways.

President Eyring also explained that for missionaries, the Church set the standards for them to be prepared to enter the mission field and serve—they hadn't set the standards for themselves. As I considered this insight, I realized from my experience that I had cut my hair to go on a mission because someone asked me to do it. I was proud back then that I did it, but I never considered that the choice didn't originate with me. Not only had I cut my hair, but I also changed some of my language and taste in music, even though that was a challenge for me. I read the scriptures more than I ever had before. I devoted more of my time to serving God and His children than ever before. But even as I took all these actions, it wasn't me setting the high standards I was reaching for.

President Eyring's words led me to a new insight as he gave the following advice: "You returned missionaries can set your goal not to *maintain* the spirituality you felt in the mission field, but to *rise higher.* That will take work and determination, but you can do it."[34]

When I shared this thought with my oldest daughter, also a returned missionary, at first she said, "Right, we need to be better."

---

33. Henry B. Eyring, *Choose Higher Ground* (Salt Lake City: Deseret Book, 2013), 245.
34. Henry B. Eyring, *Choose Higher Ground*, 243; emphasis added.

Sensing that she didn't catch the full weight of President Eyring's message, I replied, "Sweetheart, he's saying, 'We told you guys what to wear, how to cut your hair, and what to watch and not watch.' So, he's asking, 'Are you not just *as good* as you were when you left, but are you *better* than we asked you to be?'"

A frown spread over her face. "Oh, so we can't have any fun, can we?"

My daughter's comment doesn't reflect her lack of love for the gospel—she's totally committed. But I do think it reflects a lack of understanding each of us may have. Sometimes we might believe "raising the bar" limits our opportunities, when in reality it can expand our potential if we exercise faith in Jesus Christ.

God has tasked us with constantly raising the bar if we want to reach the goal of becoming like Jesus Christ. Paul said, "For all have sinned, and come short of the glory of God" (Romans 3:23). Yet we're not being asked to wear missionary clothes, or avoid all TV, or never listen to worldly music. The point is that we can't just seek to maintain our past spirituality—we need to exceed it. And that effort rests solely upon us.

More so, returned missionaries can't simply come home and rush back to the open arms of the world. Those who set the standards for us previously are not here to challenge us now. Instead, it is up to us to prayerfully seek the Lord's will to know what changes we need to make to overcome the world and become Christlike people. Of course, this challenge is for everyone and not just returned missionaries. Anyone who has covenanted to follow Jesus Christ through baptism needs to find ways to raise the bar on herself or himself. This is considering our ways. And as we do so, we can become more fully enduring disciples, ones who are seeking to rise to "the measure of the stature of the fulness of Christ" (Ephesians 4:13).

Considering Our Daily Walk

This leads us to our final thought. What might "considering our ways" look like throughout our day-to-day life?

First, we can pose three questions: "What am I doing?" "Why am I doing it?" and "How am I doing it?" Asking these questions can help us examine patterns in our goals, intentions, and behaviors. For instance, if we want to get into better physical shape (*what* we are doing), we might consider *why* we want to exercise.

I noticed the influence of asking these questions for myself when I had gained considerable weight. One day, while looking in the mirror, I noticed, "Oh, my goodness! You are fat!" It just sort of crept up on me. I didn't like the way I looked, so I started dieting and exercising. My intentions weren't completely bad and neither was the goal. I worked hard, and over the course of six months, I lost sixty-three pounds and felt better than ever. Yet my motivation was mostly to look better. I found that I compared myself to others and, sadly, thought I looked better than heavier people (including the heavier version of myself). However, over time, my motivation to maintain my weight dwindled. Eventually, I regained the pounds I'd lost and then felt even worse about myself for losing my focus. In the end, not only was my motivation to change insufficient, but I lacked the skills needed to sustain a lifelong habit of eating well.

Several years later, as I served in a priesthood calling, I interacted with a stake president who consistently taught the need to care for our bodies so we could serve the Lord in our later years. His teachings encouraged me to "consider my ways" once more. So, I started exercising again, but this time for a better reason—to serve the Lord. Again, I lost weight, but this time when things got difficult, I reminded myself why I was doing it. I also found I was not comparing myself to others like before. Still, the goal has not been easy. As I continue along the path of discipleship, I find greater motivation to maintain my health because I have a purer reason: I want to be able to serve God.[35] And yet even with this higher purpose, I've often returned to overeating,

---

35. Note that I'm not criticizing someone who might exercise to keep up their physical appearance. That's a personal decision, and each of us needs to consider our own ways. I'm simply illustrating the fact that there are better motivations, and the best ones focus us on serving God.

regained the weight, and found myself back to feeling sorry about my condition.

Now, I find the battle is daily. I have lost and regained the weight I lost four times. In fact, I've lost a total of about 200 pounds in all. That's a whole person—a large person. It's so frustrating. I've found that if I focus on the outcome of looking good or losing weight, I get discouraged. Instead, I'm learning that what is wrong is not the extra weight I'm carrying—it's that there is something in my nature, something in my character, that is not yet Christlike. I lack self-control. I seek to find comfort from food when I feel anxiety. I lack diligence and focus. Through all of these ups and downs, I am learning to be patient with myself.

Recently, my oldest daughter, Michaela, shared with me a quote from President Nelson. It reads, "If you really want to *be* like the Lord—more than any *thing* or *anyone* else—you will remember that your adoration of Jesus is best shown by your emulation of Him. Then you will not allow any other love to become more important than love for your companion, your family, and your Creator. You will govern yourself not by someone else's set of rules but by revealed principles of truth."[36]

When she shared this with me, I was feeling really down about my eating habits. I just couldn't say no to unhealthy food. Later that day, after I read the quote, I saw some cookies I wanted and thought, "Do you love those more than Jesus?" The thought stunned me. "NO! I love Him more." I kept asking this question as I faced each temptation, and slowly I began to conquer my feelings that day.

In my mind, I know that loving Christ is the answer to overcoming temptations and trials. But it's taken more than just the single act of asking myself the question that day. I've faced the same challenges repeatedly since then, failing on some days and succeeding on others. The goal seems less about losing weight and more about changing my character. I know I'm likely going to battle this problem my whole life, and I doubt there will be a single day I don't have this burden. It's a

36. Russell M. Nelson, "Endure and Be Lifted Up," *Ensign*, May 1997, 72.

cross I'm going to have to bear. But in the end, whether in this life or the next, I'll be transformed. And all the striving—all the struggle to learn to resist my bodily desires—will refine me. I'll be more like the One who has perfect self-control, perfect self-love, who wants only to do His Father's will, including taking care of the gift of His precious body.

Now, someone might be thinking, "Is eating cookies really all that bad?" On a scale of serious sin, it's low, I know. But lacking self-control *is* bad—it's not Christlike. And shortening my life expectancy because I fail to care for myself is bad because then I can't serve as faithfully. And certainly I'm not saying that someone who overeats doesn't love Jesus. What I *am* saying is that whatever you feel you need to do to follow Christ more closely, the answer will come in the form of loving Him more, and then He will change your heart to become more like Him because of your faith in Him and His love for you.

We could apply these same principles to any of our goals—going to college, getting a job, improving relationships, becoming more social, and of course, developing spiritually. For example, we could go to college to become rich, or to improve our God-given talents and serve our fellow human beings. We could get a job to seek promotions, or we could think of supporting our eternal family with the money we make. We could improve our relationships to make us happier and have more fun, or we could do so in order to lift those around us. We could seek to make friends so we aren't bored, or we could think of how lonely someone else might by. And we could develop our spirituality to be seen as righteous in someone's eyes, or as a way to create a meaningful relationship with God.

While I am not seeking to oversimplify things or make someone feel guilty for their motivations, I am trying show how every aspect of our lives can become Christ-centered. And when we are Christ-centered, we can find deeper motivations to sustain our good works through faith in Him. We can improve our relationship with God, ourselves, and others. We can more fully fulfill the words of the prophets: to love God with all our heart, soul, and mind, and to love our neighbor as ourselves (see Matthew 22:36–40).

As we consider our ways, we can become more like our Savior Jesus Christ by developing His attributes and character. And as we begin developing the attributes of Christ, this effort will "become the tide that raises all boats in the harbor," as Elder Scott D. Whiting said.[37] One effort of improvement to develop a Christlike attribute can influence our development of all the other attributes the Savior possesses.

Now, a final word of caution. With our faith motivated and an increased desire to consider our ways, we sometimes seek to make massive changes or pick multiple areas we want to improve. But President Henry B. Eyring taught we are better off if we pick one small change we can work at consistently rather than trying to make significant, rapid changes in many areas. As mentioned in chapter 1, he said, "The best place to look [for improvement] is for small changes we could make in things we do often. There is power in steadiness and repetition. And if we can be led by inspiration to choose the right small things to change, consistent obedience will bring great improvement."[38]

Chris and I are working to change ourselves. With this book, we hope to offer ideas that expand your power and capacity to consider your ways so you too can become more of an enduring disciple of Jesus Christ. In all, this is a book about becoming greater disciples of the Savior through covenant keeping, repentance, and enduring to the end. We believe that as we do these things, we can receive more fully of the nature of God and experience the enabling power of Christ's Atonement to do greater works than we could if left to our own efforts. As we each seek to improve, we believe we can truly develop a more Christlike character.

---

37. Scott D. Whiting, "Becoming like Him," *Ensign* or *Liahona*, Nov. 2020, 14.
38. Henry B. Eyring, "The Lord Will Multiply the Harvest" (an evening with Elder Henry B. Eyring, Feb. 6, 1998), 3.

3

AN ENDURING DISCIPLE

MDM

"Unless a man shall endure to the end, in following the example of the Son of the living God, he cannot be saved."

—2 Nephi 31:16

When I was twelve years old, my Scoutmaster, Earl Woolley—a chemist at BYU—planned to take us on a fifty-mile backpacking trip in the Uinta Mountain Range of Utah. To prepare us for the long hike, Brother Woolley planned to have us walk fifty miles in town in one day. It was an endurance test. We would walk a route from our church, heading north for two and a half miles to a particular telephone pole, where we would then turn around and head back to the building. The goal was repeat the circuit ten times so we would reach fifty miles. To be honest, it wasn't very exciting for a teenage boy to walk between the church and telephone pole for what seemed like a million times, but maybe from a scientist's point of view, the math added up. In any case, we would have to learn to endure and get into shape if we wanted to participate in the fifty-mile backpacking trip later.

We began at 5:00 a.m. at the church. We all arrived, bright-eyed and bushy-tailed, thrilled we were going to walk fifty miles! There was a bounce in our step. We laughed and joked as we progressed back and forth from church to pole and back, time and again. As the hours passed, though, my enthusiasm waned. My feet hurt. My legs started aching. I was tired from being up so early, and like Esau, I was starving and ready to sell my birthright for a mess of pottage! At lunch time, I recall telephoning my mom, asking if she could bring me some food.

She found me on the street corner waiting for her. Then, she and I sat in the family car where I drank warm soup from a Mason jar and ate hot bread. As I sat there with her, I felt relief from all the pain of enduring the back and forth of our walk. My mother asked how I was doing.

"I'm tired, Mom. This is really hard," I said, probably putting on my best "tired boy" face to sell how miserable I was.

My mother is the kindest person I know. Her compassion runs deep. She looked at me with her consoling eyes and said words I will never forget: "Mark, you don't have to do this. You could come home."

Shocked by the realization, her message sunk into my little-boy heart. I thought, "You know, she's right. I could go home!" Sitting in the car, eating warm food, and talking to my comforting mother, I made a choice that troubled me for many years. I threw in the towel! Reluctantly at first, but gleefully in the end, I went home and abandoned my effort to walk the remaining miles. I think I rationalized, "It's just some stupid Scout thing. What does it matter anyway if I walk back and forth all day?"

When we got home, I quickly skipped down the stairs to my bedroom, having a surprisingly renewed spring in my step. I went to my bed to sleep, but sleep didn't come. It was like those days when you go house to house looking for someone to play with—I knocked and knocked on sleep's door, but it never answered. Looking up at the ceiling, I thought, "David Goodrich, Neil Hansen, and Paul Jaussi are all walking the path to success." My eyes remained open while my faith remained closed. My aching heart began to realize my shame. I had quit. *Run upstairs!* I thought. *Tell Mom you made a dumb mistake and beg her to take you back to the church!* But I'd be alone. They were all ahead of me, and I'd be all alone. I stayed there in bed and ignored the prompting. Feeling alone changes people. It shapes motivation and interferes with destiny.

While our roads may be different, the test is always the same. Will you abandon your cause because you feel alone? Will you turn around and forsake the thing you knew was right when you first started it?

Later, on a church bulletin board, I saw a picture of my friend David slouched over in a chair at the church, silhouetted by the dark outside. His exhausted face smiled at me with satisfaction. I can still see the confidence and success in his eyes. They were bright, and his slight smile revealed the joy inside. That face spoke volumes. He did it! He finished the fifty miles, and I could tell he felt great.

In church the following Sunday, our bishop called out the names of the young men who finished the walk, asked them to stand, and congratulated them. "These young men did something amazing yesterday. They walked fifty miles in preparation for a hike in the Uintas." After praising the finishers, he invited me to stand. "We would also like to recognize Mark Mason as our honorable mention. He walked thirty-five miles."

I didn't feel good despite the thirty-five miles I walked. In one day, a twelve-year-old walked thirty-five miles but was unable to celebrate his success. Why? Because I had quit.

I couldn't successfully blame my mother, although I tried to. I couldn't successfully blame my bishop either for the shame I felt when he had me stand in front of everyone. Both were simply responding as best they could to the choices I made. In fact, they were being kind. Mom would have just as easily left me at the church if I'd stood my ground: "No, Mom, I'm okay. I can do this." Had I said those words, she would have instantly turned on "motherly encouragement mode" and prodded me out of the car. Yet looking back, I see the influence of this event. I'm determined never to quit again. I have felt the lifelong significance of a moment that could have ended in success had I not quit.

Each of us face our "fifty-milers," those events that are so difficult yet laden with potential to create in us a better person. They prepare us for greater things if we willingly submit to their requirements. Each of us also fails at some point to rise to the occasion. Like Peter walking on the water, we sink from success into fear and despair when we take our eyes off of the Savior.[39] Yet like Joseph Smith, we might lose our 116 pages of God-given responsibility but learn a great lesson when we resolve, from our experience, "I made this my rule: when the Lord commands, do it."[40]

What I wish I knew at the age of twelve was something taught so clearly by Elder David A. Bednar—a quote that would have surely captured my attention back then. Speaking of the enabling power of Jesus Christ's Atonement, then-President Bednar of BYU–Idaho said, "I frankly do not think many of us 'get it' concerning this enabling and strengthening aspect of the Atonement, and I wonder if we mistakenly believe we must make the journey from good to better and become a saint all by ourselves through sheer grit, willpower, and discipline, and with our obviously limited capacities."[41]

I just didn't have the "grit" to pick myself up, ask my mom to drive me back to the church, and see if Brother Woolley would walk with me while I caught up to the rest of the guys. The thought never entered my mind. Of course, I did nothing to access the Savior's power to get me back on task. Back then, I would have thought Jesus didn't even care about me walking fifty miles.

How many times as teenagers, and even as adults, do we feel we face our challenges alone? What will it take for us believe the Savior when He said, "Come unto me, all ye that labour and are heavy laden, and *I will give you rest.* Take my yoke upon you, and learn of me; for

---

39. See Howard W. Hunter, "The Beacon in the Harbor of Peace," *Ensign*, Nov. 1992. Here president Hunter said, "Only when with wavering faith [Peter] removed his glance from the Master to look at the furious waves and the black gulf beneath him, only then did he begin to sink."

40. Joseph Smith, in *History of the Church*, 2:170.

41. David A. Bednar, "In the Strength of the Lord" (Brigham Young University devotional, Oct. 23, 2001), 3, speeches.byu.edu.

I am meek and lowly in heart: and *ye shall find rest* unto your souls. For my yoke is easy, and my burden is light" (Matthew 11:28–30, emphasis added). These words speak volumes to me. "I will give you rest" sounds so good when life is hard, but what does this rest look like? When it says "take my yoke upon you," the yoke refers to an implement of work. This rest is probably not what I would have thought it was as a teenager—I would have wanted the Savior to make walking easy and fun.

Maybe the Savior offers rest from feeling alone. I know there are at least two kinds of modern yokes. The first one is wooden beam with a U-shaped curved bar that wraps under the neck of the animal, allowing its neck to rest against the beam while holding it fast. It fits only a single ox. If this were the yoke the Savior described, He was inviting me to go to work pulling His load alone. I've seen an ox pull this way, and though it shoulders all the burden, it's never alone—the master always walks beside it. In this image, the Savior as the Master would walk beside me, directing me, giving me commands of when to start, stop, turn, pull hard, or rest. This image explains the Savior's enabling power as the one who guides and directs our efforts while we do the pulling. We're not alone doing His work because He's always beside us. The "rest" we receive is respite from being alone, because when we engage in His work, we are never alone.

I think there's another powerful image of yoking with Christ. The second kind of yoke a longer beam with two U-shaped bars, joining two oxen's necks together, allowing them to push against the beam as a single unit. This yoke binds two into one.[42] I often imagine this as "the Savior's yoke." It is a yoke made for two. What "rest" does this yoke offer us? Here, Jesus invites us to take His yoke upon us, where we are one of the "oxen" and Jesus is the second of the pair. If I take

42. While no physical examples of yokes exist from Jesus's day, the *Strong's Concordance* language dictionary defines the word used here, *zugos*, as "properly, a yoke; a wooden bar placed over the neck of a pair of animals so they can pull together; (figuratively) what unites (joins) two people to move (work) together as one." Thus, *Strong's Concordance* supports the idea of a united yoke.

His yoke upon me this way, then I am binding myself with Christ in His work. This powerful image leads me to see the Savior yoked beside me, increasing my power to accomplish His work. The "rest" I receive here is the fact that I'm not the only one pulling the load. I think this image describes best the Savior's power of grace, which enables me "to do good works that [I] otherwise would not be able to maintain if left to [my] own means."[43]

Why then would the Savior care about me walking fifty miles? How could that have been the work of God? In fact, had I better understood God's purposes, I would have recognized that so many of the tasks I had done when I was young were God's work, but I didn't realize it at the time. And I certainly didn't understand how the Savior had power to enable me to accomplish more with Him than I ever could have done on my own. God cares about our Christlike development, even if it's only a twelve-year-old walking to get ready for a hike in the mountains. He needs us to have faith. And we develop faith at the levels we are currently at. Before Peter could raise the lame man at the temple, he had to give up fishing to follow the Savior. Likewise, before I could accomplish greater acts of faith, I had to learn about commitment and dedication to a cause, even if it was simply walking in preparation for a long hike.

Elder Orson F. Whitney taught, "No pain that we suffer, no trial that we experience is wasted. It ministers to our education, to the development of such qualities as patience, faith, fortitude, and humility. . . . It is through sorrow and suffering, toil and tribulation, that we gain the education that we come here to acquire."[44] Regardless of what tasks we endure, God is there to help us. He can reach down from heaven to refine our souls, making us a little bit stronger and lifting us to new levels of determination as we learn from our moments of weakness. As we endure these trials through repentance, we become even better, gaining access to develop the character of Jesus Christ. When

---

43. Bible Dictionary, "Grace."

44. Orson F. Whitney, in Spencer W. Kimball, *Faith Precedes the Miracle* (Salt Lake City: Deseret Book, 1972), 98.

we fail to rise to the occasion, we can learn what we never want to experience again. His Spirit can come into us and change our repentant hearts to desire a better way.

I for one never want to be a "thirty-five-miler" again. That event, combined with my repentant heart, has fueled my determination many times when things were much tougher than walking a long distance. In fact, I've often considered the growth from that experience to be a great blessing.

Chris and I hope that applying what you learn in this book will give you greater strength to endure—not just in general but specifically along the covenant path to become an enduring disciple. We ourselves have felt the need for this added strength to endure as we have faced many problems in our lives, and in 2013, we felt the desire and need to write this book. As Chris said, since then we've experienced many challenges, and we've also learned of the challenges of others, all of which have tutored us about the value of enduring faithfully to the end as disciples of Jesus Christ. We'll share more about these experiences in future chapters.

Our Purpose: To Experience the Savior's Enabling Power

Like accomplishing a long hike, we have a purpose to fulfill in this life as members of The Church of Jesus Christ of Latter-day Saints, and more specifically, as disciples of Christ. This purpose is to keep our gospel covenants so that we might receive eternal life, the greatest of all the gifts of God (see Doctrine and Covenants 14:7). To obtain this gift, we need to endure to the end in following the example of Jesus Christ (see 2 Nephi 31:16, 20). Following His example is one of the many ways we can experience the Savior's enabling power. It shows us what we need to do and how we can rise above our challenges. God sent His only Begotten Son to earth to be our model, the perfect example of what our Father wants from us. Certainly, the Savior's life was one of amazing accomplishment, but He too faced serious challenges and tests. If we are to succeed along the covenant path as Jesus did, we need strength and stamina to rise above the challenges we face.

However, enduring along the covenant path is more than gritting our teeth and pushing through the difficulties. Facing one of the greatest tests of his life in Liberty Jail, Joseph Smith exemplified a model of what we must do to endure effectively.

Expelled from their homes during the cold months of November and December 1833, the Saints relocated to Far West, Missouri.[45] There the flames of persecution rekindled, this time with the Prophet Joseph Smith living among the Saints in Missouri. George M. Hinkle, a member of the Church and a Colonel in the Missouri state militia, betrayed the Prophet into the hands of his enemies, causing him to suffer in Liberty Jail for four months.

Feeling betrayed and suffering terribly, Joseph Smith cried out, "O God, where art thou? And where is the pavilion that covereth thy hiding place? How long shall thy hand be stayed, and thine eye, yea thy pure eye, behold from the eternal heavens the wrongs of thy people and of thy servants, and thine ear be penetrated with their cries?" (Doctrine and Covenants 121:1–2).

A response from the Lord came in words I'm sure the Prophet could never forget: "My son, peace be unto thy soul; thine adversity and thine afflictions shall be but a small moment; And then, *if thou endure it well*, God shall exalt thee on high; thou shalt triumph over all thy foes" (Doctrine and Covenants 121:7–8; emphasis added). The Savior's power enabled the Prophet to better understand the Lord's expectations. This kind of understanding can help us see how to access the Savior's power. From the Lord's response, we learn that getting through our adversity is not enough. The Lord expects that, through our adversities, we will become more like Him as we "endure it well."

---

45. See *Church History in the Fulness of Times Student Manual* (2003), 127–39.

Enduring Well

Enduring well leads us to become more converted to the Savior's way of living. We see this kind of change in Nephi when he faithfully responded to the Lord's command to Lehi to take his family into the wilderness. In contrast, when Laman and Lemuel learned of the Lord's command to leave their home, "they did murmur in many things against their father" (1 Nephi 2:11). According to Nephi, their lack of knowledge of God caused them to complain in this way. He explained, "I, Nephi . . . having great desires to know of the mysteries of God . . . did cry unto the Lord; and . . . he did visit me, and . . . soften my heart that I did believe all the words which had been spoken by my father; *wherefore, I did not rebel against him like unto my brothers*" (1 Nephi 2:16; emphasis added).

Surprisingly, Nephi admitted he too was feeling at least a little hard-hearted—maybe even a lot. Yet he had the faith to pray and ask God to teach him. This event led to a change in Nephi's heart so that he "did not rebel . . . like unto [his] brothers." This change of heart is a powerful example of Nephi experiencing the enabling power of Jesus Christ's Atonement. Apparently, the change did not come because Nephi had sinned and needed to repent. Rather, it came as Nephi exercised his faith and the Spirit came into his heart to lift him to a higher level. His faith led to spiritual greatness and a knowledge that likely aided him immeasurably when he faced problems like his broken bow. Nephi learned that rather than becoming bitter in his trials, he could rely on the Lord for strength. No doubt this condition led Nephi to become more humble, faithful, and obedient—all Christlike virtues.

Developing a Christlike Character and Attributes

Developing these virtues is evidence of God's influence in our lives, and they come as we experience the enabling power of the Savior. They are given to us not because of our diligent effort but as a reward when we have qualified to receive them.[46] Elder Neal A. Maxwell said, "Part of enduring well consists of being meek enough, amid our suffering, to learn from our relevant experiences. Rather than simply passing through these things, they must pass through us and do so in ways which sanctify these experiences for our good (see Doctrine and Covenants 122:7)."[47]

The Prophet Joseph Smith said, "I am like a huge, rough stone rolling down from a high mountain; and the only polishing I get is when some corner gets rubbed off by coming in contact with something else. . . . Thus I will become a smooth and polished shaft in the quiver of the Almighty."[48] With the attitude of enduring well, adversity can be a polishing experience that shapes our character. This polishing comes not just from our efforts to endure but also through the Savior as He empowers us.

In my life, this polishing has taken place in many ways. One of the most difficult trials I went through was my parents' divorce. It was hard. As a result of their divorce, I questioned many times my role in the Church and often felt like I didn't belong. Because of my father's alcoholism, we didn't have a good relationship. It wasn't until much later in life when he got sober that we truly became father and son. After working through all the difficulties, in my thirties I finally had the relationship I was looking for. Then one day, after "rolling along through life" for a while like Joseph Smith, I struck into "something hard." My dad called me in April 2006 to tell me he had been diagnosed with cancer. I was stunned. How was this possible? He was so healthy and vigorous. I'd waited all these years and had finally developed a relationship with him, only to now find out he had cancer.

At first, the doctors were optimistic, saying he would recover. "Prostate cancer is the most treatable kind," my dad would tell me. Yet by November 2006, he was gone.

---

46. See Scott D. Whiting, "Becoming like Him," *Ensign* or *Liahona*, Nov. 2020.
47. Neal A. Maxwell, "Enduring Well," *Ensign*, Apr. 1997.
48. *Teachings of the Prophet Joseph Smith*, sel. Joseph Fielding Smith (1938), 304.

With suffering like this, I too cried out, "O God, where art thou?" I felt numb. Throughout the process of coping with my father's death, my feelings were a jumbled mess. One minute I was fine, then I would think of something I wanted to talk to him about, and all the awful despair would return. I knew God loved me, but I couldn't understand why He would give me a father with so many problems, help me resolve those issues, and then take him from me.

My father was not a member of the Church. I had tried many times to share the gospel with him. I prayed for many years that his heart would soften and he would join the Church, but he didn't want it. I would feel so dejected every time he rejected my offers to learn about the restored gospel. I couldn't understand what was wrong. I had sufficient faith. My desires were pure. How could wanting my father to be a member of the Church be bad? When Dad died, I felt despair and a total loss. But as I prayed and fasted, I slowly began to feel trust in God again and develop a greater sense of understanding. I felt the Spirit help me recognize the miracles God had brought into my father's life and mine.

My dad was very rough around the edges (though I'll spare you the details). However, as I reflected, the Spirit began to point out to me that even though my father had many problems and didn't join the Church in this life, I could see his continued spiritual development. He started going to a church—not one of our faith, but he loved it. He loved singing hymns and joining Bible study groups. He started his own group and was sharing his testimony of God with others and was even bringing them to Christ. We prayed together. We talked about scriptures together. Eventually, he was baptized into a Christian church and his faith continued to grow. Little by little, as his faith developed, he was changing. By the time my father passed away, he fully believed in Jesus Christ with all his heart. The Spirit brought healing into my life by giving me an eternal perspective, even though my specific desire—to have my father at church with me, going to the temple together, and talking with each other about the Restoration and other glorious truths—did not happen during my father's lifetime on earth.

A year after his death, I went to the temple and performed saving ordinances for him. That day was life-changing for me. I believe it was for him as well. I began having feelings about my father that he was progressing in the spirit world. I wondered if my father would ever have accepted the restored gospel in this life had he continued to live on earth. What was clear was this: knowing the love he developed for Jesus Christ, I could imagine him in the next life realizing, "So . . . the only way I can be with Jesus is through the Mormons!" Then, I could hear him saying, "Alright, then tell me what I need to know, and I'll do it."

The Savior's grace and enabling power allowed me to change my perspective. Shifting from thinking about myself and what *I* wanted, I began to accept God's will, His way, and His timing. In God's wisdom, my father may have needed to go home to progress any further. In a strange way, I began to feel that my father's death was an unusual but powerful answer to the many years of prayer that he would join God's Church. I can't support these thoughts and feelings with scriptures and quotes—it's just a feeling I have. This change was about me developing greater trust in the Son of God and His almighty power, and believing with all my heart in the Resurrection and the afterlife. I have had to reach to heaven in prayer to believe that work for the dead is real—not just in my mind but to feel the change in my heart. I've had to have faith that the Savior's Atonement allowed Him to extend the opportunity for my dad to be healed spiritually and have his heart changed, even after he died.

In fact, I had not fully realized the level of change the Savior's Atonement was having on my faith until writing these words and accepting this outcome—I needed the Savior more than ever to change me. His power to transform my heart is real, and I am forever grateful for the light of truth I feel right now. My dad is not gone, and our relationship can continue. What hope! What resolution! And all of this is made possible through the Savior's Atonement.

For whatever reason, this kind of spiritual growth requires suffering. Elder Glenn L. Pace was a member of my ward and a close friend. One day, while talking about how difficult these changes are, Elder

Pace explained something so simple yet powerful: "Sanctification always requires suffering."

When I think about my experience with my father, Elder Pace's comment brings a deeper level of understanding. I now know more personally what the Savior endured in the Garden of Gethsemane and on the cross at Golgotha. He was purchasing for me the hope and power to heal me and my father. I also think that through my extreme difficulties, I learned to say with the Savior, "Thy will be done" (see Matthew 6:10). I believe life requires that we become polished and refined in this way. Maybe it's through this kind of suffering, as we more fully partake of the Savior's Atonement, that we can become more Christlike in our nature. I know I've certainly felt His enabling power as I've grown and developed a more eternal perspective through the things I have suffered.

Stephen E. Robinson explained how the difficulties, challenges, and trials of life can affect our faith. He spoke of us becoming more than "provisionally converted" in terms of a marriage relationship. Being provisionally married would be a marriage of convenience, which could be terminated when we "fall out of love" or find someone more attractive or to our liking. We need a stronger commitment to Christ, one that doesn't end when things get hard. Of this kind of relationship, Brother Robinson said the following:

> Just as such a [provisional] relationship would be unsatisfactory in [an eternal] marriage, so it is unsatisfactory in the spiritual marriage of the gospel. Such individuals need to become converted, to receive the witness of the Spirit and the conviction that accompanies faith. Just as partners in a truly celestial marriage say, "we are sealed, no matter what," so a truly converted member says: "I am a member of this church. My lot is cast with the Apostles and prophets—no matter what. Above all other issues, loyalties, agendas, and commitments, this is where I stand."[49]

In summary, because life is filled with so many challenges, and because each of us needs polishing to become more like Jesus Christ,

49. Stephen E. Robinson, "Enduring to the End," *Ensign*, Oct. 1992.

we can expect to face a variety of trials and difficulties along the covenant path. What we need to develop along the way is resilience. How we bounce back after trials is manifest by our faith in Christ when we feel crippling despair. It's when we want to quit. We've hit our thirty-five miles on this faith journey, and we feel like going home and not walking with Christ anymore. In a meeting I attended at a CES symposium years ago, Brother Robinson described this kind of experience like us being a compass.[50] When you shake a compass, the needle bounces all around, but eventually it points back to magnetic north. Like the compass, when we face trials, we need to realign ourselves with Jesus Christ—pointing again to true north.

It's through these kinds of refining experiences that we have to reevaluate our dedication. We recommit ourselves to following the one true path. Maybe it happens as we face our intellectual doubts about the Prophet Joseph Smith or a Church policy, and then in total submission and in a Christlike way, we say, "I just don't know how all these pieces fit together, and I feel so disoriented, but I know God lives and the Savior loves me. I can't explain why Joseph practiced plural marriage, but I know he was a prophet, and I know this Church is true. So I'm moving forward despite my doubts."

These moments of total submission bring us into the Savior's world of disoriented but firm faith. Compared with what the Son of God suffered, these moments are small in magnitude, but they're eternally meaningful in similitude with Christ when we "tremble because of pain" (Doctrine and Covenants 19:18). While we do not "bleed at every pore," we do "suffer both body and spirit" and pray to the Father with earnestness of heart to "not drink the bitter cup, and shrink" (verse 18). As we in our childlike way submit to the will of the Father and continue on our faith journey—not knowing all things but trusting in the Son of God and His infinite Atonement—we can understand the Savior's faith a little better when He was "suffering pains and

---

50. I don't recall in which CES symposium Stephen Robinson shared this metaphor, but it made a significant impact on me when he taught it.

afflictions and temptations of every kind" (Alma 7:11). Then, through His power, we gain strength to get up and try again.

What Follows Next

Throughout the remaining chapters, we plan to consider the following topics: baptism, the gift of the Holy Ghost, the oath and covenant of the priesthood, the sacrament, scripture study, the temple, the Atonement of Jesus Christ, and happiness. In each chapter, we seek to demonstrate how we can consider our ways and become enduring disciples. We'll do so using examples from our own lives and the lives of others, scriptural analysis, and the words of modern prophets. As we examine each topic, we invite you to prayerfully consider what you might need to do to begin applying what you learn, either by stopping things you should not do or starting things you should do. We know personally that this kind of repentance works. Most importantly, we feel these kinds of changes can only come as we seek to emulate the Savior Jesus Christ, for His grace is sufficient to lift us to a new level of discipleship.

4

BAPTISM

CRG

"One Lord, one faith, one baptism."

—Ephesians 4:5

My oldest daughter, Casey, was baptized in the fall of 2003. Around the same time, our family had the opportunity to attend a luncheon. It was held in appreciation for the work that employees for the Latter-day Saint Humanitarian Center had accomplished throughout the year. It had been a rough year. Natural disasters and other conflicts around the world, like an enormous earthquake in Algeria as well as a devastating heat wave in France, had kept the Humanitarian Center operating at an intense capacity.

Upon arriving at the picnic spot, I introduced my family to the manager of the Humanitarian Center, Bill Reynolds. When introducing Casey to him and his wife, I expressed that she would soon be baptized. Bill, while shaking her hand, looked her in the eyes and asked, "Are you sure you want to be baptized?" I remember some momentary anxiety over the question and worried how Casey would respond, but her innocent response not only surprised me but made me quite proud. Without any hesitation, she looked right back at Bill and said, "Of course. Don't you think it's the right thing to do?" I remember Bill standing straight up, smiling, and looking over at Tami and me and saying, "You raised her right!"

Although the desire to be baptized is one thing, it's another thing to fully understand the commitment involved and the covenant we make at baptism. When it comes to gospel principles, I have always used the "crawl, walk, run" methodology of teaching that I learned from my own parents, who learned it from their parents—teaching in a gradual way. For example, taking your children to see their friends and neighbors get baptized is a wonderful teaching opportunity. It generates gospel-oriented questions from them and offers a perfect time for parents to conduct personal interviews with their children to address those questions. It also is a good opportunity to teach them by the Spirit in their own language and understanding.

Many times, prior to my own children's baptisms, they would ask, almost nervously, "Why is baptism important, Daddy?" Or, perhaps fearing the worst, "You won't let me drown, will you Daddy? I'm scared to go under the water." After some brief explanations, my children would insightfully ask questions like "Why did the Savior need to be baptized?" and "Why do we need to follow the Savior's example?"

In order to answer these questions correctly, we need to understand the ordinance of baptism, what it is, why it's so important, what we do after we make the covenant of baptism, and how it can help us achieve a spiritual rebirth that results in true discipleship.

Baptism as a Saving Ordinance

For each of us, starting on the covenant path toward exaltation and eternal life, while partnering with our Father in Heaven, begins with faith, repentance, and then ultimately baptism (see Articles of Faith 1:4). These three steps come first, and baptism is the first saving ordinance that we must do to return and live with Him. Because our

Savior understood this, He was baptized to show us "the straitness of the path, and the narrowness of the gate, by which [we] should enter" (2 Nephi 31:9). "Notwithstanding he being holy, he showeth unto the children of men that, according to the flesh he humbleth himself before the Father, and witnesseth unto the Father that he would be obedient unto him in keeping his commandments" (2 Nephi 31:7). Because He was a perfect example to each of us, and because He was perfectly obedient to His Father in Heaven, is there any question why He began His mortal ministry in this way?

> Then cometh Jesus from Galilee to Jordan unto John, to be baptized of him. But John forbad him, saying, I have need to be baptized of thee, and comest thou to me? And Jesus answering said unto him, Suffer it to be so now: for thus it becometh us to fulfil all righteousness. Then he suffered him. And Jesus, when he was baptized, went up straightway out of the water: and, lo, the heavens were opened unto him, and he saw the Spirit of God descending like a dove, and lighting upon him: And lo a voice from heaven, saying, This is my beloved Son, in whom I am well pleased. (Matthew 3:13–17)

Additionally, our Savior emphasized the importance of baptism in His final and closing words here on earth: "Go ye therefore, and teach all nations, *baptizing them* in the name of the Father, and of the Son, and of the Holy Ghost: Teaching them to observe all things whatsoever I have commanded you: and, lo, I am with you always, even unto the end of the world. Amen" (Matthew 28:19–20; emphasis added).

From these scriptures, we learn that baptism is very important to our Savior Jesus Christ, which means it should be just as important to all of His followers today.

How vividly I remember when I was participating as an actor in the Church's musical production of *Savior of the World.* This charge given by the Savior to His Apostles to teach and baptize others is one of the last scenes in the production. It was a very spiritual and personal experience for me, and I can recall the chills I had while I imagined that I was actually there in the Holy Land, receiving this mandate from our Lord. How thrilled those Apostles must have felt!

If we want to become like our Savior, then we should be baptized. It is part of our Father in Heaven's plan of happiness for us.

Baptism as a Covenant

It's important to understand that Heavenly Father works with *all* His children through covenants, for instance covenants that *we* make as His sons and daughters and covenants that *He* has made with us. Simply put, a covenant is a pact or agreement between two or more parties. These divine covenants we make are significantly different from worldly covenants, however. For example, worldly covenants are negotiated (like what we would see in a legal document, employee contract, a homeowner association agreement, etc.), but our Father in Heaven's covenants are imposed by Him.

For example, from the beginning, Heavenly Father's relationship toward us has been defined by certain requirements and promises. God tells His children what is required of them and also what will happen when His commands (or covenants) are met with obedience. These covenants are stipulated to us in the scriptures. Interestingly, the word *testament* comes from the Latin word *testamentum* or *testamenti*, which means covenant.[51] So, the Bible is a covenant document, with the New and Old Testaments literally translating to new and old *covenants*.

As His sons and daughters, we make covenants with our Father in Heaven, and He, in turn, makes covenants with us. And if we are true and faithful to the promises (or covenants) we make, He will bless us. As the Doctrine and Covenants teaches, "There is a law, irrevocably decreed in heaven before the foundations of this world, upon which all blessings are predicated—And when we obtain any blessing from God, it is *by obedience* to that law upon which it is predicated" (Doctrine and Covenants 130:20–21; emphasis added).

---

51. According to the Latdict website (Latin Dictionary and Grammar Resources, latin-dictionary.net), the English translation of the word *testamentum* or *testament* means (1) a covenant and (2) a will or testament.

There is much comfort in understanding that we *will* be blessed as we obey the principles and ordinances that our Father in Heaven has given to us. Making and keeping sacred covenants will result in a life of pressing forward in Christ and adhering to the covenant path. Conversely, if we do not understand covenants, we cannot fully understand the issue of baptism, because baptism is a covenant ordinance. As mentioned earlier, it is so important that even our Savior, Jesus Christ, participated in this sacred ordinance. President Spencer W. Kimball taught that "to be baptized is to enter into a covenant [with God] . . . to *do,* not merely to refrain from doing."[52] President Kimball later goes on to say that our covenant of baptism is also "to work righteousness as well as to avoid evil."[53] Later in this book, we will discuss how the covenant of baptism can help and motivate us to avoid evil.

By reading Doctrine and Covenants 20:37 and Mosiah 18:8–10, we can understand that we make the following covenants with the Lord when we are baptized. We:

- enter into the Church of Jesus Christ;
- are called after His name;
- are willing to serve God and keep His commandments;
- are willing to serve others and bear one another's burdens; and
- will always be a witness for Jesus Christ and His Church.

Sounds a lot like the sacrament prayer, doesn't it? In return, conditional upon our obedience to the baptismal covenant, the Lord promises that He will:

- forgive us of our sins;
- provide the guidance of the Holy Ghost for us;
- bring us forth in the First Resurrection; and
- give us eternal life, the greatest of all the gifts of God (see Doctrine and Covenants 14:7).

---

52. Spencer W. Kimball, *The Miracle of Forgiveness* (1969), 96; emphasis added.
53. Spencer W. Kimball, *The Miracle of Forgiveness*, 94.

Baptism as a Symbol

The Lord uses symbols to help us understand eternal truths. The ordinance of baptism is particularly rich with symbolism, and it would be to our benefit to reflect and ponder upon its meaning. The more we do so, the more these symbols (especially that of baptism) will begin to make sense to us. President Russell M. Nelson explained, "We are taught in the Master's way. His way differs from modes of others. His way is ancient and rich with symbolism. We can learn much by pondering the reality for which each [baptismal] symbol stands."[54] It has often been said that baptism is an outward testimony of what has occurred inwardly in a believer's life. Additionally, baptism illustrates a person's identification with Jesus Christ's death, burial, and resurrection.

There is a reason why the Lord uses symbols to help with His teachings. Symbols bring color and strength to language while deepening and enriching our understanding. Even Adam, our first parent, needed help in understanding the symbolism of sacrifice (see Moses 5:7). So we too may need help in understanding the "ancient and rich" method the Lord uses with regards to baptism.

For instance, going under the water represents dying and being buried with Christ. The action of coming out of the water represents Christ's resurrection over death. It also symbolizes our willingness to accept Him into our life by terminating our "old life," cleansing and washing it away in favor of a "new life" that the Savior has promised to those who accept Him. This "new life" is the start of the covenant path and of gaining greater access to Jesus Christ and using His Atonement to help make us better than we are.

Baptism also represents the individual's commitment to a life in Christ, being born of God and thus born again of the water and of the Spirit.[55] It is a step toward complete obedience—publicly declar-

---

54. Russell M. Nelson, "Personal Preparation for Temple Blessings," *Liahona*, July 2001, 38.

55. See Romans 6:3–6; Mosiah 18:13–14; Moses 6:59–60; and Doctrine and Covenants 128:12–13

ing faith in Jesus Christ and a commitment to Him. It clearly states from the Book of Mormon that our baptism is a covenant to "stand as witnesses of God [and His kingdom] at all *times* and in all *things*, and in all *places* that ye may be in, even until death, that ye may be redeemed of God, and be numbered with those of the first resurrection, that ye may have eternal life" (Mosiah 18:9; emphasis added).

Baptism as a Motivator to Live a More Committed Life

As wonderful and fulfilling as baptism is, we need to understand that it is not a "free ticket" into the celestial kingdom. It is the first ordinance that we need to complete along our covenant path. This doesn't mean that we'll never sin again, because sin has a way of coming back to our lives, but it does mean, like Paul said, that we should no longer be slaves to sin (see Romans 7:14). We certainly know and understand that we will all sin again, and that "no unclean thing can enter into his kingdom; therefore nothing entereth into his rest save it be those who have washed their garments in my blood, because of their faith, and repentance of all their sins, and their faithfulness unto the end" (3 Nephi 27:19). After baptism, we should make every effort to ensure that sin no longer dominates or controls our lives as we strive to be holy, even as He is holy (see 1 Peter 1:15–16).

As in all principles and doctrines that our Savior taught, unless true conversion comes first, then baptism is just a meaningless ordinance. Taking upon us His name is one of the most significant experiences we can have in life. Oftentimes, the outward act of baptism is emphasized, but it's the inward change that we truly need to focus on. Many times, we pass through this experience without a full understanding of what it truly means. Missionaries and members of the Church who are helping bring others into the "fulness of the gospel" must also understand that "baptism and confirmation is not the end goal. It is the missionary's [and member's] privilege and responsibility to teach investigators that there are additional covenants and ordinances they may receive in the house of the Lord."[56]

Most of us are familiar with the catchphrase "to be *in* the world but not *of* the world" (see John 17:11, 14–17). It's important for us to understand as children of a loving Heavenly Father that our mortal existence is necessary to fulfill our Father in Heaven's plan of salvation. This means, literally, that we live *in* this world, but also that we must live not *of* this world because of all the worldly influences that are ever before us. Elder Robert D. Hales, of the Quorum of the Twelve Apostles, once taught, "Each week in sacrament meeting we promise to remember the atoning sacrifice of our Savior as we renew our baptismal covenant. We promise to do as the Savior did—to be obedient to the Father and always keep His commandments. The blessing we receive in return is to always have His Spirit to be with us."[57]

The "new lifestyle" that follows conversion is what we usually call sanctification, or the lifelong process of becoming free from sin, pure, clean, and holy through the Atonement of Jesus Christ (see Moses 6:59). This is another area where synergism ("working together") is required. In sanctification, both the accountable mortal human and the divine (the Holy Ghost) must work together simultaneously. For example, in the Book of Mormon, it says, "Nevertheless they did fast and pray oft, and did wax stronger and stronger in their humility, and firmer and firmer in the faith of Christ, unto the filling their souls with joy and consolation, yea, even to the purifying and the sanctification of their hearts, which sanctification cometh because of their yielding their hearts unto God" (Helaman 3:35).

The ability to "yield" our hearts to God is no easy task and takes a lifetime of work and effort. However, we do know that our Father in Heaven has made this possible through the Atonement, and that we should work out our salvation with "fear and trembling" (Philippians 2:12). I do want to point out, though, that many people fail to see what

---

56. *Missionary Preparation Teacher Manual* (2005), 87.

57. Robert D. Hales, "The Covenant of Baptism: To Be in the Kingdom and of the Kingdom," *Ensign*, Nov. 2000, 8.

is written in the very next verse, which says, "For it is God which worketh in you both to will and to do of *his* good pleasure" (Philippians 2:13; emphasis added). So the question is, how can we, as accountable mortal humans, get God to work *within* us so that we, together as a team, can do what He pleases at the same time?

The power of His word is especially moving and can motivate us to change and will us into action. Therefore, the key lies in two attributes: (1) knowledge, which leads to (2) motivation. The scriptures say:

> But be ye doers of the word, and not hearers only, deceiving your own selves. For if any be a hearer of the word, and not a doer, he is like unto a man beholding his natural face in a glass. For he beholdeth himself, and goeth his way, and straightway forgetteth what manner of man he was. But whoso looketh unto the perfect law of liberty, and continueth therein, he being not a forgetful hearer, but a doer of the work, this man shall be blessed in his deed. (James 1:22–25)

As this passage indicates, it's not enough to be just "hearers of the word, but doers also." We must hear, and then go do. That's the wonderful blessing of the gospel of Jesus Christ. Being part of this gospel, we must, by default, teach it to others—whether it be by formal assignment or by example. Teaching the gospel powerfully convicts us and moves our hearts and wills into action. It also can reprove us at times, correct us, and instruct us further in what we need to do to be more like Him. As indicated earlier, if we don't understand the reason we are baptized—if we lack the knowledge—it can't motivate us to become better. It's a lot like having a house wired for electricity but not knowing how to turn on the lights or use the appliances powered by that electricity.

Personally, I have discovered that it's easy to be educated about a gospel principle but much more difficult to turn that education into a motivation to do better. This may happen because we get so caught up in teaching sound doctrine about faith, repentance, and baptism (though all of these are necessary) that we forget about the heart and will of the individual. In other words, we fail to motivate. We can become very shortsighted. We work hard to motivate an investigator to be baptized, teaching them sound doctrine, but then we neglect to lead that convert to the complete commitment of lifelong obedience that he or she has now accepted.

Unfortunately, "it is not easy to become a member of this church. . . . It means setting aside old habits, leaving old friends and associations, and stepping into a new society which is different and somewhat demanding."[58] Therefore, there needs to be some "post-conversion" experience that can help the new convert feel in their heart the impact of accepting the gospel of Jesus Christ and be moved to a higher level of spirituality, love, and commitment. Regarding this, President Gordon B. Hinckley said the following:

> They [the missionaries] still have an obligation to nurture and help those they have baptized—to befriend them, to write to them, to give them encouragement. But greater than that is your responsibility, my brethren, as bishops, as stake presidents, as elders quorum presidents, to put your arms around these people and make them feel comfortable and at home and warm and happy. It is an imperative.
>
> What does it profit the missionary to baptize someone who leaves the Church within six months? Nothing is accomplished; in fact, damage is done. We have pulled them away from their old moorings and brought them into the Church, only to have them drift away.[59]

So, it would seem that the power and potential to move to this deeper level of covenant-keeping, or pressing forward in Christ, has been there all along, but the motivation to live it simply needs a "jump start." It breaks my heart when I hear of people that are preoccupied by the "things of this world"—they are not necessarily in "transgression" for being that way, but certainly they can be in "diversion," which

58. Gordon B. Hinckley, "Every Convert is Precious", *Liahona*, Feb. 1999.

59. Woods Cross Utah Regional Conference, Jan. 10, 1998, taken from "Messages of inspiration from President Hinckley," *Church News*, Apr. 1, 2000.

consequently can cause them to waste "the days of their probation" (2 Nephi 9:27). Regardless, many of these people claim that they proudly live "without God in the world" (Alma 41:11), and the gates and doors to their hearts are unfortunately locked from the inside!

Baptism as a Way Back Home

Oftentimes the term *baptism* is synonymous with the ideas of "renewal" or "the way back home." There can be very tender memories of those who made a conscious decision to "come back home" and subsequently felt the love of our Father in Heaven and Savior Jesus Christ when they were baptized. For example, I recall the joy often experienced by those who were baptized in my own mission. One of the converts I helped bring into the Church was so excited for this momentous occasion that he couldn't sleep the night before. I don't believe that is an isolated experience.

For others, this can be a very frightening decision. For example, maybe they fear the isolation or loneliness they might feel as a new members, or perhaps they were baptized as a means of testing the Lord to see if they get healed from an aliment (sign-seeking) and are worried what will happen. These fears are perpetuated by the adversary. This new family that you become part of—this family of Christ—is where we all belong. It changes us forever.

For me, becoming part of a new family, where I didn't know a soul but was so warmly received and valued, reminds me of a couple of experiences I had several years ago while participating in *Savior of the World* at the Conference Center.

As we finished the Christmas 2004 production run, I had the opportunity to thank all my many friends and fellow cast members, telling them how much I would miss them and how much I looked forward to seeing them again. One of the ladies I had gotten to know in the costuming department—a sweet older lady named Suzy—said something to me that really made me stop and think. As I was saying goodbye to her, my emotions came to the surface and I even shed some tears. I recall that she was putting some clothing racks on the elevator with our costumes, and she turned to me and said, "This must be what it was like at the veil."

I asked her what she meant by that, so she expounded. "We all have friends here in this cast that we will miss terribly," she said. I nodded in agreement. She continued, "We all had friends in the pre-earth life that we were most likely better friends with—people whose companionship, company, and spirit we would miss. So, when the time came for us to part, and to begin our mortal life, there were probably tears shed at the veil as we parted for a time."

As I have thought about this, I feel in my heart she is correct. I had only worked with those cast members for four months, but when the time came to say goodbye, tears were shed. I wonder how many more tears were shed when the time came for me to say goodbye to my friends in premortality (who I had known for an eternity) as I left my heavenly home to begin my mortal life. I bet it was very emotional for me.

The following year, at the end of our 2005 production run, I wrote the following thought in my journal:

> During our last performance of *Savior of the World*, 2005, I again had the distinct privilege of saying goodbye to the hair and make-up lady, Suzy. I have gotten to know Suzy really well during our seasons together (particularly this season as I had to wear an artificial beard and mustache during the entire run), and she is a complete joy to be around. But like last season, her parting words to me again stirred my soul and have caused me much reflection. As I was leaving the make-up room, with tears in my eyes, I turned to her and told her how much we loved her. She looked at me and said, "Come back home to us, Chris."
>
> Those words "come back home" have a deeper meaning to me since doing *Savior of the World*. I imagine that we all had the opportunity to say goodbye to our friends in the pre-earth life where many of them most likely said the same thing Suzy said to me: "Come back home to us, Chris." For some reason, this statement just stirs my heart and causes me to reflect on my life and do some pondering. Is my life in harmony with His teaching so that I *can* return home to live with Him? Am I doing all I possibly can? I

> can't help but feel that I have heard this statement before. I wonder now if my Father in Heaven said something similar to me as I was leaving the pre-earth life. Sometimes people can say such profound things.

What do these experiences from my own life teach me about the covenant and ordinance of baptism? They teach me that I need to be in the world but not of the world. They remind me that I am to stand as a witness of God (and His kingdom) at all times and in all things and in all places (see See Mosiah 18:9).

Like baptism, being in those productions changed my life and helped me and my family establish an allegiance to the kingdom of God. For me, when I think of my own baptism, or when I think of my part of portraying an Apostle of Jesus Christ in *Savior of the World*, it helps me to remember who I am serving, why I am serving Him, and the promises I have made to Him—to do all I can to return and live with Him with my family and all the friends I have made here who want the same thing I do.

Oftentimes, we think of baptism as a once-in-a-lifetime event, which it is in the sense that it only takes place once in a member's lifetime. However, the covenant we make during baptism is for our entire lifespan. This covenant is to be remembered and cherished each and every day of our lives. Because of this, the sacrament should have much more meaning and significance than just partaking of bread and water—it is meant to help us remember, each and every week, those covenants that we made at baptism. As a result, the baptismal covenant can remain an active part of our daily life and spiritual progression long after the actual ordinance and will lead to much greater spiritual power in our individual lives. It will enable us to get to know our Lord and Savior Jesus Christ and open the door to additional promises and blessings.

I feel such gratitude and appreciation for my Savior and my baptism into The Church of Jesus Christ of Latter-day Saints. I am grateful for my baptism as a saving ordinance, covenant, symbolism, and motivator to a more committed lifestyle. And I am thankful for goodly parents, siblings, and teachers who have helped me along my path. I invite you to ponder and reflect upon the sacred ordinance and covenant of baptism as the gateway into His kingdom. How might you do better to cherish the choice of baptism you made to be part of His kingdom?

5

THE GIFT OF THE HOLY GHOST

CRG

"The Holy Ghost shall be thy constant companion, and thy scepter and unchanging scepter of righteousness and truth; and thy dominion shall be an everlasting dominion, and without compulsory means it shall flow unto thee forever and ever."

—Doctrine and Covenants 121:46

During the summer of 2005, my two oldest sons, Conrad and Caleb, were on a Young Men's whitewater river trip adventure in Moab, Utah. While they were going down the fast currents of the Colorado River, a strong storm stopped their adventure. As many people know, the weather in southern Utah can become very extreme and dangerous at times. The party soon became separated. The leaders were further downriver and out of sight, but Conrad and Caleb, as some of the oldest of the young men, felt they needed to bring up the tail end of the group and ensure that all were okay.

The boys made the decision to beach the rafts and take cover from the hail under a nearby tree close to shore. While they were under this tree, the sky got darker, the hail got worse, and the wind significantly increased. The young men that were with Conrad and Caleb were getting a little frightened at this awesome display of nature and began to question if they were safe or not. At this exact point, Caleb felt that a prayer would be appropriate, and Conrad volunteered to say it on behalf of all present. According to Conrad, during the prayer, the memory of our most recent family home evening came to his mind, with the added thought to put into practice what they had been taught during that lesson. As a result, Conrad felt to voice in his prayer that they "would be able to adapt to their individual circumstances." Shortly afterward, the storm was over, and they were able to rejoin their group further downriver with no injuries or trauma—just a riveting memory to share with their friends.

The family home evening that Conrad had remembered was held just a few days before they left on their river trip. My youngest son, Collin, had shared some points of interest on a talk by Elder David A. Bednar titled "In the Strength of the Lord."[60] One particular point was the idea of adapting to each trial we have rather than asking for it to disappear. This way, our dependence on the Lord increases and we grow in strength and faith.

The amazing thing is that our children were actually listening! More importantly, both boys had received impressions or feelings from the Holy Ghost during a very stressful time and acted upon them—with Caleb suggesting to say a prayer with the group and Conrad recalling the recent lesson. They had learned from this family home evening lesson, and ultimately they prayed to be able to endure rather than to have the trial go away.

One of the purposes of the Holy Ghost is to be able to bring to mind lessons we've learned from our lives that can help us grow and develop as children of our Father in Heaven. Learning to recognize

---

60. See David A. Bednar, "In the Strength of the Lord" (Brigham Young University devotional, Oct. 23, 2001), speeches.byu.edu.

these promptings from the Holy Ghost is not just a one-time experience. For my sons, they had learned the gospel from a very early age, and then, on their river trip, all that celestial schoolwork was applied in a real-life situation.

After we make the conscious decision to be baptized, we are given the gift of the Holy Ghost through proper priesthood authority. What is this "unspeakable gift" (Doctrine and Covenants 121:26) that is given to us? How can this gift help us press forward in Christ and stay on the covenant path?

As each of my own children has received the ordinance of baptism, it was my privilege to confer upon them the gift of the Holy Ghost. Like with baptism, this decision to receive the Holy Ghost was not an arbitrary choice for any of them. It was intentional, purposeful, and anticipated. It was an honor to speak with each of my children prior to being baptized and receiving the gift of the Holy Ghost in order to help them understand the answers to these questions:

1. What is the purpose of the Holy Ghost?
2. What is meant by the word "Comforter" spoken of in the scriptures?
3. How does the Holy Ghost teach us truth and gospel principles and help us remember things that can strengthen our faith and testimony?

When the Savior led his disciples into the Garden of Gethsemane for the last time, I'm positive that His eleven Apostles sensed, but perhaps could not fully understand, that something monumental and epic was happening. Earlier, Jesus had spoken of leaving them. These Apostles suspected that the man they had worked with, lived with, been taught by, and loved was going somewhere, but they did not know precisely what this meant. Maybe they just didn't want to believe He could leave them after all the amazing things He had done. Yet they had heard Him say, "I will not leave you comfortless. . . . But the comforter, which is the Holy Ghost, whom the Father will send in my name, he shall teach you all things, and bring all things to your remembrance, whatsoever I have said unto you" (John 14:18, 26). This was said at a time when confusion and misunderstandings were so evident among the Apostles, and I feel like this statement brought reassurance and great comfort to these remaining men.

As a child, I found the doctrine of the Holy Ghost to be somewhat frightening. For some reason, in my mind, a word association with *ghost* gave me the impression of haunted houses, spooks, and things that go bump in the night. That could not have been further from the truth! For this reason, I wanted to make sure that my own children, while they were growing up, understood exactly who the Holy Ghost is and how He can truly be a Comforter when needed.

The Holy Ghost is the third member of the Godhead. He is a personage of spirit and bears witness to all truth. Although there are many scriptural references to Him, most of the references call him a comforter (a title I have come to tenderly love), a revelator (one that reveals the will of our Father in Heaven), or a teacher. When the Savior visited the people of Nephi, receiving the Holy Ghost was the one thing they most desired.[61] Likewise, in our own lives, it should be something that we desire above all other things.

The Purpose of the Holy Ghost

In order to answer what the purpose of the Holy Ghost is, we need to start with what it says in the scriptures. John says, "But when the Comforter is come, whom I will send unto you from the Father, even the Spirit of truth, which proceedeth from the Father, *he shall testify of me*" (John 15:26; emphasis added).

The Holy Ghost does testify of the reality of our Father in Heaven and Savior Jesus Christ. He reveals truth. I experienced this as a young missionary in Brisbane, Australia.

Before my mission, I grew up in a devoted Latter-day Saint home. My parents expressed love and freely talked about the gospel. Family prayer, family home evening, and church participation were

61. See 3 Nephi 19:9: "And they did pray for that which they most desired; and they desired that the Holy Ghost should be given unto them."

encouraged. My mom and dad would quite often testify to me and my siblings that the Church was true. I would often ask them how they received their testimony and when they knew for themselves that the Church was true. I can vividly remember how passionate they felt about personal prayer. These lessons were taught in my youth and stayed with me all throughout my teenage years. Yet despite all of this being available to me as a young man, I had never taken the time to actually pray about the Church or discover for myself if it was true. My parents would say that the Church was true; therefore, *I* would say that the Church was true. I leaned heavily on my parent's testimony while growing up; that is, until I had a life-changing experience early on my mission.

I had been out in the mission field for less than a week when my companion and trainer, Elder Paul L. Clark, and I unknowingly knocked on the door of a Pentecostal minister. He welcomed us into his home but immediately began to attack our beliefs. He made it very clear that he had no intention of ever becoming a member of the Church. It appeared that all he wanted to do was destroy our faith and tell us how "misguided" we were. He felt it was his duty to try to "save" us. He asked us questions we did not have the answers to and debated points of doctrine with us. Elder Clark tried to do the best he could, knowing that I was a new missionary and that he was responsible for my training.

I had never experienced anything like this before in my life, and unfortunately, I made the mistake of being shaken up by his words. After several minutes, it was evident to all of us that this conversation was going nowhere, and we promptly left. Nevertheless, I was still troubled by many of the points the minister had brought up, and they kept going through my mind over and over again. After several minutes, in despair, I finally stopped riding my bike. Elder Clark came over, instinctively knowing that something was amiss, and asked, "What's wrong?" I responded, "I need to go back to our flat and spend some time alone." Elder Clark, being so attentive to the Spirit, could sense the need I had and allowed me some personal time.

When we got back to the apartment, I immediately went into a private room where I could kneel in prayer and finally ask what I should have asked my Father in Heaven years earlier: Was the Church true? Were there *really* prophets and apostles on the earth today? Was the Book of Mormon real, and did Joseph Smith see what he said he saw?

I began to quote from memory Moroni 10:3–5 just to remind Him that I was sincere in my quest for knowing. Before I had even finished the quote, I knew. It was so powerful. The Spirit testified to me that it was true—all of it.

When I left that bedroom, I knew something that the Pentecostal minister didn't know. I knew that the doctrines taught in the Church were true. I knew that priesthood power had been restored to the earth again. I knew that the Book of Mormon was the word of God and had been divinely translated by Joseph Smith. I knew that my Father in Heaven loved me and knew who I was.

The Holy Ghost testified to me of truth in a way that I could understand and build upon. And the best news of all is that this was not an isolated experience. It happened to me over and over again on my mission, especially at times I really needed it. And it continues to happen in my life today as I live worthy of His companionship. The Holy Ghost will testify to all. It is a key part of enduring discipleship.

The Holy Ghost can also soften hearts. For example, this is something that happened to Nephi shortly after leaving Jerusalem with his family: "And it came to pass that I, Nephi . . . having great desires to know of the mysteries of God, wherefore, I did cry unto the Lord; and behold he did visit me, and did *soften my heart* that I did believe all the words which had been spoken by my father; wherefore, I did not rebel against him like unto my brothers" (1 Nephi 2:16; emphasis added).

Nephi says that the Lord did "soften" his heart. Does that imply that he too had some difficulty and reservations accepting the teachings of his father Lehi at first? Would he have had some initial doubts or some fear perhaps? It appears so. But because Nephi decided to press forward in Christ, despite the hardships he and his family were facing, the Holy Ghost, through the Savior Jesus Christ, softened his heart.

President Boyd K. Packer, President of the Quorum of the Twelve Apostles, explained that the Holy Ghost speaks with a voice that you *feel* more than you *hear*. It is described as a "still small voice." And though we speak of "listening" to the whisperings of the Spirit, most often one describes a spiritual prompting by saying "I had a feeling."[62] President Packer taught at another time that "the Holy Ghost communicates with the spirit through the mind more than through the physical senses. This guidance comes as thoughts, as feelings, through impressions and promptings. It is not always easy to describe inspiration. The scriptures teach us that we may 'feel' the words of spiritual communication more than hear them, and see with spiritual rather than with mortal eyes (see 1 Nephi 17:45)."[63]

Also, President Spencer W. Kimball taught, "The gift of the Holy Ghost grows with worthiness. If you are baptized when you are eight years old, of course you are a child, and there is much you would not be expected to know. But the Holy Ghost comes to you as you grow and learn and make yourselves worthy. It comes a little at a time as you merit it. And as your life is in harmony, you gradually receive the Holy Ghost in a great measure."[64]

So, how does a person know when he or she truly has received a manifestation of the Holy Ghost? They will know it by how they feel.

What Is Meant by "Comforter"?

The book of John does a good job explaining what is meant by the term *Comforter*. It says, "But the Comforter, which is the Holy Ghost, whom the Father will send in my name, he shall teach you all things, and bring all things to your remembrance, whatsoever I have

62. Boyd K. Packer, "Personal Revelation: The Gift, the Test, and the Promise," *Ensign*, Nov. 1994, 60.
63. Boyd K. Packer, "Revelation in a Changing World," *Ensign*, Nov. 1989, 14.
64. *The Teachings of Spencer W. Kimball*, ed. Edward L. Kimball (1982), 114.

said unto you" (John 14:26). As in the story of Conrad and Caleb, these feelings that come from the Holy Ghost can provide comfort at times of great need. I cannot think of a more appropriate title than Comforter when referencing the Holy Ghost.

The term *comfort* is generally something we all think of as being sorely needed during trials and tragedies. As indicated earlier in this chapter, comfort was something that our Savior's Apostles were genuinely looking for after His crucifixion. They received that comfort when the Savior appeared to them, as recorded in Luke 24.

There are numerous other examples found in the scriptures of people receiving comfort during times of grief. One such example is when our beloved prophet Joseph Smith was a prisoner in the Liberty Jail. I can only imagine the heartache he must have been feeling knowing that his people were being wronged in every imaginable way. The members of the Church at the time were being mocked, ridiculed, robbed, plundered, cheated, and in some cases, murdered, while he spent time in this cold, dark, damp, dreary, rat-infested dungeon. Joseph's health had taken a turn for the worse. He himself had been poisoned, abused, starved, and beaten. Finally, at a time when he could take it no longer, the comforting words came: "My son, peace be unto thy soul; thine adversity and thine afflictions shall be but a small moment; And then, if thou endure it well, God shall exalt thee on high; thou shalt triumph over all thy foes" (Doctrine and Covenants 121:7–8).

I have a very personal experience of receiving comfort when I needed it most. Like many during the pandemic, I had parents who died from COVID-19. I vividly remember my dear mother calling me on Thanksgiving Day in 2020 and telling me that she and my dad had been exposed to COVID. Despite prayers and fasting in their behalf, she passed away at her home eight days later. Exactly three weeks later, my dear father, who had always been so robust and active, passed away at home as well. It was a difficult time for me to see them deteriorate and not be able to do anything about it.

I was on the road traveling when I got word of my father's passing. Interestingly, I felt a great sense of peace knowing that Mom and

Dad were together in eternity. In fact, the lyrics of a song kept going through my mind from the Broadway musical *Annie* called "I Don't Need Anything but You." Specifically, the part of the song that kept going through my mind was this:

> Together at last! Together forever!
> We're tying a knot, they never can sever! . . .
> They're two of a kind, the happiest pair now
> Like Fred and Adele, they're floating on air now . . .
> Yesterday was plain awful—you can say that again
> Yesterday was plain awful, but that not now, that's then.[65]

I'm grateful that my mother and father are together again—forever. It does not mean that I don't have my difficult days, especially on Mother's Day and Father's Day. But I am so grateful for the added knowledge I have as a member of The Church of Jesus Christ of Latter-day Saints, and the reassurance from the Comforter who has testified to me numerous times of the truthfulness of the gospel and of the plan of salvation. The Comforter has helped when I've needed Him the most. But remember that He can also come at times other than when we're grieving. As explained earlier, He comes to testify of truth, which in and of itself is a great comfort.

How Does the Holy Ghost Work?

Revelation from the Holy Ghost can come to us in many ways. Usually, however, revelation comes through thoughts, impressions, or feelings in our hearts. The Prophet Joseph Smith taught that revelation may come as "sudden strokes of ideas."[66] Have you ever had an experience when an idea just popped into your mind, or you remembered a detail at just the very moment you needed to?

---

65. Andrea McArdle, Reid Shelton, and Sandy Faison, "Annie: I Don't Need Anything But You," track #14 on *Annie (Original Broadway Cast Recording)*, Masterworks Broadway, 1977, compact disc.

66. *Teachings of the Prophet Joseph Smith*, sel. Joseph Fielding Smith (1976), 151.

While attending a ward leadership meeting during the summer of 2013, we were discussing ways we could reach out and help others who may have chosen a different path and fallen into church inactivity. Most of these good people were located within one specific area of the ward boundaries. The bishop, Kevin C. Christensen, decided to say a special prayer that we would be able to determine what course of action our Father in Heaven wanted us to take. Time was then set apart to ponder over the idea and generate some thoughts. After some time, Brother Jeff Bingham, who was serving as a counselor in the bishopric, said rather enthusiastically, "I have an idea!" He indicated that a thought had just come into his mind, and he wanted to share it with all who were present.

That is the way the Holy Ghost can prompt us if we take the time to listen. It will come to us as sudden ideas. Sometimes, if we are not listening, the impressions we get can be so subtle, so delicate, that the lessons the Holy Ghost is trying to teach us may be overlooked.

I love to use this example when I teach Sunday school classes, especially when I am teaching the youth. So many times, perhaps in their hastiness, some youth have said they have never felt the Spirit. But nothing could be further from the truth. My experience has led me to believe that many times, the youth *have* been inspired by the Spirit to do or say something, but they need to have these pivotal moments pointed out to them to help them understand that this is the Holy Ghost working through them. As teachers of the gospel, it is important that we help those we teach make connections between what they are learning in class and the experiences they are having in their lives, tying the two together.

In November 1996, during a BYU devotional, Sister Sally T. Taylor gave a great explanation of how the Holy Ghost works in each of us and helps us learn:

> As our teacher, the Holy Ghost can do three things for us in our efforts to learn. First, he can reveal new knowledge. The Doctrine and Covenants says, "If thou shalt ask, thou shalt receive revelation upon revelation, knowledge upon knowledge, that thou mayest know the mysteries and peaceable things" (Doctrine and Covenants

> 42:61). If we do our part and can do no more, the Holy Ghost will add that "line upon line" to our understanding. We may even receive new insights that the world could not give. A second thing the Holy Ghost can do is to help us make connections. Like a chemist putting two different familiar elements together to create something new, we can be guided in our studies to make connections that will open up an entirely new possibility. A third way that the Holy Ghost can teach us is to bring to our mind forgotten things."[67]

Strive to recognize these promptings, and more importantly, learn to follow them. As Elder Marvin J. Ashton taught, "Small voices are heard only by those who are willing to listen."[68]

Adversarial Imitations of the Gifts of the Spirit

In March 2013, one of my sons—who was serving a mission in California at the time—indicated to me in several emails that he was worried that many of his friends back home in Utah were being deceived by false imitations of the Spirit and leaving the Church. Many of his friends had recently gone through some trials and tremendous personal tragedies. As a result, they said they would see things they couldn't explain, and subsequently they were being gradually led away from the gospel. Their testimonies—and all they had come to know about the gospel of Jesus Christ—were being challenged, despite the great missionary effort and comfort provided by the Holy Ghost.

My son asked me what he should do about it and how he could best help them. How I wish I could have spoken to him in person about this topic, but I knew he was doing what he was supposed to at the time and place he was supposed to be doing it. A letter would have to suffice for now—this was prior to the approval of doing weekly phone calls with missionaries.

---

67. Sally T. Taylor, "The Holy Ghost: Our Infallible Guide" (Brigham Young University devotional, Nov. 5, 1996), 3, speeches.byu.edu.
68. Marvin J. Ashton, "There Are Many Gifts," *Ensign*, November 1987, 21.

After much pondering and prayer, I was able to write my response. My son told me after the fact that this had been very helpful to him and his companion. Below are excerpts from the letter I wrote him:

> I am sure that [your friends'] interests and motives are pure. [They] have had some significant events in [their] lives that may explain why they do what they do. When people are exposed to tragedy, they instinctively are drawn into things that may or may not help them deal with their grief.
>
> I certainly don't know all of the circumstances surrounding [your friends'] lives or even their character. I only know them from what you have told me about them. But what I do know is that some time ago, they were baptized as members of the Church and given the gift of the Holy Ghost, which is a wonderful blessing. I hope they understand this.
>
> As you know, following baptism, each of us had hands laid on our heads by proper priesthood authority to receive the gift of the Holy Ghost. If we are faithful, we can have His influence continually with us. Through Him, each of us can be blessed with certain spiritual powers called gifts of the Spirit. These gifts are given to those who are faithful to Christ. "All these gifts come from God, for the benefit of the children of God" (Doctrine and Covenants 46:26). They help us know and teach the truths of the gospel. They will help us bless others. They will guide us back to our Heavenly Father. To use our gifts wisely, we need to know what they are, how we can develop them, and how to recognize Satan's imitations of them.
>
> As you know, there are many gifts of the Spirit. Most notable are the gift of tongues, the interpretation of tongues, translation, wisdom, knowledge, teaching wisdom and knowledge, believing the testimony of others, and knowing that Jesus Christ is the Son of God.[69]
>
> It is up to each of us to develop these gifts ourselves, sometimes with the help of others. To develop our gifts, we must find out which gifts we have. We do this by praying and fasting. We should seek after the best gifts (see Doctrine and Covenants 46:8). Sometimes

---

69. See Doctrine and Covenants 46:9–26 for a more thorough list of gifts that are active in the Church today. There are literally too many to list on a single sheet of paper

patriarchal blessings will help us know which gifts we have been given. We must be obedient and faithful to be given our gifts. We then should use these gifts to do the work of the Lord. They are not given to satisfy our curiosity or to prove anything to us because we lack faith. Of spiritual gifts, the Lord said, "They are given for the benefit of those who love me and keep all my commandments, and him that seeketh so to do" (Doctrine and Covenants 46:9).

In these last days, Satan does all he can to satisfy our cravings for spiritual experiences. At times, people will do desperate things because they feel compelled to do them. Satan uses this to his advantage and feeds upon the gullibility of people. Satan can also imitate the gifts of tongues, prophecy, visions, healings, and other miracles. Moses had to compete with Satan's imitations in Pharaoh's court (see Exodus 7:8–22). Satan wants us to believe in his false prophets, false healers, and false miracle workers. They may appear to be so real to us that the only way to know is to ask God for the gift of discernment. The devil himself can even appear as an angel of light (see 2 Nephi 9:9) or, as in [your friends'] cases, allow us to believe that we are hearing the voices of departed loved ones through "white noise" or another form of media.

Satan wants to blind us to the truth and keep us from seeking the true gifts of the Spirit. Mediums, astrologers, fortune tellers, and sorcerers are inspired by Satan, even if they claim to follow God. Their works are abominable to the Lord (see Isaiah 47:12–14; Deuteronomy 18:9–10). We should avoid all associations with the powers of Satan.

One thing we need to remember is the sacred nature of these gifts. Many people like to talk freely about experiences they have had with the Spirit. That can be a great blessing to many people. However, there is a line between what is appropriate to discuss and what is not. For example, the Lord said, "A commandment I give unto them, that they shall not boast themselves of these things, neither speak them before the world; for these things are given unto you for your profit and for salvation" (Doctrine and Covenants 84:73). We must remember that spiritual gifts are sacred (see Doctrine and Covenants 6:10). There are other scriptures that I can show to you as well if you should ask about not talking openly about sacred events or experiences in our lives.

In return for giving us these gifts, the Lord asks that we "give thanks unto God in the Spirit for whatsoever blessing [we] are blessed with" (Doctrine and Covenants 46:32).

President Joseph F. Smith once said the following in general conference, which may give you some additional insight:

"From the days of Hiram Page (Doctrine and Covenants 28), at different periods there have been manifestations from delusive spirits to members of the Church. Sometimes these have come to men and women who because of transgression became easy prey to the Arch-Deceiver. At other times people who pride themselves on their strict observance of the rules and ordinances and ceremonies of the Church are led astray by false spirits, who exercise an influence so imitative of that which proceeds from a Divine source that even these persons, who think they are 'the very elect,' find it difficult to discern the essential difference [Matthew 24:24]. Satan himself has transformed himself to be apparently 'an angel of light' [2 Corinthians 11:14; 2 Nephi 9:9].

"When visions, dreams, tongues, prophecy, impressions or any extraordinary gift or inspiration conveys something out of harmony with the accepted revelations of the Church or contrary to the decisions of its constituted authorities, Latter-day Saints may know that it is not of God, no matter how plausible it may appear. Also they should understand that directions for the guidance of the Church will come, by revelation, through the head. All faithful members are entitled to the inspiration of the Holy Spirit for themselves, their families, and for those over whom they are appointed and ordained to preside. But anything at discord with that which comes from God through the head of the Church is not to be received as authoritative or reliable.

"The gifts of the Spirit and the powers of the holy Priesthood are of God, they are given for the blessing of the people, for their encouragement, and for the strengthening of their faith. This Satan knows full well, therefore he seeks by imitation-miracles to blind and deceive the children of God. Remember what the magicians of Egypt accomplished in their efforts to deceive Pharaoh as to the divinity of the mission of Moses and Aaron."[70]

I am glad that [your friends] feel close enough with you that they can confide these matters to you. I hope this answers your

---

70. *Teachings of Presidents of the Church: Joseph F. Smith* (1998), 117.

question to some degree. Please write and ask if you need further clarification. I love you.

Dad

How grateful I am for this wonderful and important gift that our Heavenly Father provides for each of us. How thankful I am that through the Holy Ghost, we can know with assurance that our Father in Heaven lives, that Jesus is the Christ, and that the priesthood and His church have been completely restored to the earth.

Conversely, without the Holy Ghost in our lives, we would be filled with doubt, we would not be able to have peace or be comforted, and we would not be able to pray effectively. We would also not be able to testify and help bring others into the gospel of Jesus Christ. We would stagnate and atrophy in our personal growth and spiritual development.

It is my prayer that each of us will live our lives in such a manner that we can enjoy the full comfort, reassurance, protection, and numerous gifts that the Holy Ghost can provide for us all.

6

THE OATH AND COVENANT OF THE PRIESTHOOD

CRG

"God, for his part, declares with an everlasting oath that all who receive the priesthood and obey the covenants that pertain to that priesthood shall receive 'all that [the] Father hath.'"

—President Boyd K. Packer[71]

Several years ago, while my Dad was struggling with a variety of different cancers throughout his body, he asked my brother Clay and I to come over to his house and give him a blessing. He was beginning to experience pain from a kidney stone attack, and he was also fending off the effects of a robust chemotherapy treatment plan that left him exhausted and weak. I was asked to anoint, and Clay was asked to be

71. Boyd K. Packer, "What Every Elder Should Know—and Every Sister as Well," *Ensign*, Nov. 1994.

voice. Up to that point, Dad had been given many blessings, so Clay expressed some worry prior to the blessing that he would not be in tune enough to "hear" what the Lord wanted him to say. I explained to Clay that we should never feel this way because the scriptures teach us that the Spirit will tell us at the "very moment, what ye shall say" (Doctrine and Covenants 100:6) if we are worthy.

I know that Dad received a beautiful and comforting blessing from our Heavenly Father that evening. We never talked about it, but we didn't need to. My brother and I, as well as my father, had accepted the will of the Lord in this case, regardless of what might happen.

I also remember that Dad was struggling to breathe at that time and had an oxygen line hooked up and running into his nose. At the time we were giving the blessing, I remember hearing Dad struggling for breath and thinking to myself, "This poor man needs relief, if just for a few hours." His struggle for breathe continued throughout the blessing. Once we were done, Clay and I stepped back, away from Dad, and his breathing returned to normal as well as the coloring in his face. I thought for a moment that my brother and I were literally seeing a modern-day miracle. But once we came to our senses, we realized that while we were giving the blessing, I had inadvertently stepped on his air hose, thus cutting off my father's air intake and making it quite difficult for him to breathe. In typical Dad fashion, however, he decided not to say anything about it at the time, preferring instead to just "endure" through it. We get a good laugh about this now. Dad never complained, and that is one of the Christlike qualities that I truly admired about him and which he demonstrated to me on a daily basis while he was alive.

Although this story may be humorous to our family, there have been numerous times when our lives have been blessed tremendously from the priesthood. For example, in 2009, my wife had a memorable learning experience when she needed it most, and it strengthened her testimony of the power of the priesthood. She was going through some significant health issues at the time, and despite the best medical care, her doctors were perplexed. They couldn't answer why she was feeling the way she was and also losing so much weight so quickly. She had gone through enormous amounts of medical testing and spent hours with her physicians, but despite their best efforts, they could not identify her condition. We were all a little anxious and worried that her health would continue to deteriorate.

I spoke with a great mentor and friend of mine, H. Kaye Chandler, who suggested that Tami and I come over to his home one evening so he and I could give her another priesthood blessing. I had always been drawn to Brother Chandler because of his great wisdom, insight, spiritual strength, and knowledge. (He passed away in 2017 but left a lasting impression on me that will stay with me for the rest of my life.) At the time, I felt that perhaps I could learn something from this great man, and indeed I did! The date was arranged, and Tami enthusiastically agreed to do this.

On the designated day, and with Tami's permission beforehand, I had asked Brother Chandler to act as voice. For me, it is a great privilege to hear people I highly esteem pray and give blessings, and this was no exception. I wanted to hear what Brother Chandler would say and learn from it. There was no question I was being taught by a man who was intimately familiar with the workings of the Spirit.

As Brother Chandler laid his hands on top of Tami's head, I could feel the effort he was putting into his wording to make sure he was saying exactly what he was supposed to be saying. It became less of a blessing and more of a deeply personal prayer between Brother Chandler and the Lord. I was so honored to have been part of this. I vividly remember him pleading with the Lord, in our behalf, that a "miracle" would take place in our life. More specifically, he asked for a "miracle of healing to take place immediately in order for Tami to continue to function as a wife and mother, and that the medical professionals would not be confused about which course of action they should pursue." Brother Chandler was speaking with the Lord in our behalf in a very personal way, which is almost beyond my ability to write about. It was one of those experiences where you needed to be there to fully understand its significance, rather than just hearing about it.

Within days of Tami receiving this blessing, her health slowly returned to normal, and the drastic weight loss that had concerned so many people and medical professionals stopped. We had gotten our "miracle" that Brother Chandler had prayed for. And I had learned a lesson about faith and the power of prayer.

This experience reminded me of when the Savior's Apostles could not cure and cast out an unclean spirit from an individual despite their best efforts. They had seen it done by the Master over and over again, yet they lacked the preparation and understanding to do it themselves. "And when he was come into the house, his disciples asked him privately, Why could not we cast him out? And he said to unto them, This kind can come forth by nothing, but by prayer and fasting" (Mark 9:28–29). I learned a valuable lesson that day—one that I will cherish for the rest of my life.

The Oath and the Covenant

In section 84 of the Doctrine and Covenants, it indicates that the oath and covenant of the priesthood is made up of two parts. The *oath* portion is the part that *we* commit to do, requirements *we* need to meet, or conditions/obligations that *we* must satisfy as mortal children of our Father in Heaven to press forward along the covenant path. Conversely, the *covenant* portion is what the *Lord* promises to us individually once those certain commitments (or oaths) have been made.

Let's have a closer look at what section 84 says about the oath and covenant of the priesthood:

> For whoso is faithful unto the obtaining these two priesthoods of which I have spoken, and the magnifying their calling, are sanctified by the Spirit unto the renewing of their bodies.
>
> They become the sons of Moses and of Aaron and the seed of Abraham, and the church and kingdom, and the elect of God.
>
> And also all they who receive this priesthood receive me, saith the Lord;

> For he that receiveth my servants receiveth me;
> And he that receiveth me receiveth my Father;
> And he that receiveth my Father receiveth my Father's kingdom; therefore all that my Father hath shall be given unto him.
> And this is according to the oath and covenant which belongeth to the priesthood.
> Therefore, all those who receive the priesthood, receive this oath and covenant of my Father, which he cannot break, neither can it be moved. (Doctrine and Covenants 84:33–40)

Upon careful observance of this section, there are clearly some beautiful blessings available to us—truly wonderful things that will enable us to press forward in Christ in these difficult times.[72] Now let's discuss each of these points more in depth.

The Oath Portion (What *We* Commit to Do):

In the *oath* portion of the oath and covenant of the priesthood, our obligations are as follows. We commit to:

- receive the Aaronic and Melchizedek Priesthoods;
- magnify our calling;
- be faithful in obeying the commandments; and
- receive the servants of the Lord.

1. To Receive the Aaronic and Melchizedek Priesthoods in Good Faith

First, we must receive God's priesthoods based on the recommendations of proper authority through being faithful. It is not a "rite of passage"—it is entirely contingent on diligence, obedience, and honoring the knowledge you have. Then, based on those qualities, those with proper priesthood authority will recommend worthy men for confirmation and ordination.

---

72. Many of these ideas came from a sacrament talk given by Gregory Scot Collins on Sunday, May 21, 2006, while he was serving as the ward young men secretary.

While serving as a ward and stake executive secretary for many years, I set up appointments for many parents of youth and other individuals who expressed to me disappointment and shock that their child or themselves were being "held back" or "not getting advanced in the priesthood," thinking that priesthood advancement was a "rite of passage" just because they had reached a certain age. As I indicated earlier, a careful reading of the 84th section of the Doctrine and Covenants makes it abundantly clear that advancement is conditional upon worthiness and faithfulness. For example, "For whoso is *faithful* unto the obtaining these two priesthoods of which I have spoken . . . are sanctified by the Spirit" (Doctrine and Covenants 84:33; emphasis added). I am so grateful for good bishops and stake presidents who, through the Spirit, have the gift of discernment and can determine worthiness.

2. To Magnify Our Calling

Second, we covenant to magnify our calling. Elder David A. Bednar said that the priesthood is "the means whereby the Lord acts through men to save souls."[73] This is a call to action, not inaction. It means we are to work on our various callings and capacities and not expect things to be done for us. It is a call "to act for [ourselves] and not to be acted upon" (2 Nephi 2:26).

President Marion G. Romney, a former member of the First Presidency, once taught that "ordination to the priesthood is a prerequisite to receiving [blessings], but it does not guarantee them. For a man actually to obtain them, he must faithfully discharge the obligation which is placed upon him when he receives the priesthood."[74]

Further, President Gordon B. Hinckley once said the following while addressing a gathering of Aaronic Priesthood holders:

> That word *magnify* is interesting. As I interpret it, it means to enlarge, to make more clear, to bring closer, and to strengthen. . . .

---

73. David A. Bednar, "The Powers of Heaven," *Ensign* or *Liahona*, May 2012, 48.
74. Marion G. Romney, in Conference Report, Apr. 1962, 17.

> All of you, of course, are familiar with binoculars. When you put the lenses to your eyes and focus them, you magnify and in effect bring closer all within your field of vision. But if you turn them around and look through the other end, you diminish and make more distant that which you see.
>
> So it is with our actions as holders of the priesthood. When we live up to our high and holy calling, when we show love for God through service to fellowmen, when we use our strength and talents to build faith and spread truth, we magnify our priesthood. When, on the other hand, we live lives of selfishness, when we indulge in sin, when we set our sights only on the things of the world rather than on the things of God, we diminish our priesthood.[75]

I love the special knowledge that as long as we magnify our callings, we in turn are magnified. When we diminish that calling, we shrink to being less than what we are capable of being. What a powerful thought!

3. To Obey the Commandments

Another thing we commit to do is to be faithful in keeping the commandments. Faithfulness is a prerequisite for one to minister and officiate in the priesthood. That faithfulness and obedience to our Father in Heaven's commandments must continue in order to reap the full blessings He has in store for us. If you obey only a few commandments, you will only receive a few blessing. Conversely, if you obey all of His commandments, you will be given all of His blessings. The Lord instructs that we must "be faithful, and yield to no temptation" (Doctrine and Covenants 9:13). Paul taught this truth to the Corinthians in these words: "Let a man so account of us, as of the ministers of Christ, and stewards of the mysteries of God. Moreover it is required in stewards, *that a man be found faithful*" (1 Corinthians 4:1–2; emphasis added).

How can we be faithful? We must "put on the whole armour of God, that [we] may be able to stand against the wiles of the devil" (Ephesians 6:10–18). "And take the helmet of salvation, and the sword

75. Gordon B. Hinckley, "Magnify Your Calling," *Ensign*, May 1989, 46–47.

of my Spirit, which I will pour out upon you, and my word which I reveal unto you . . . and be faithful until I come, and ye shall be caught up, that where I am ye shall be also" (Doctrine and Covenants 27:18).

This goes back to the gate idea presented in the introduction of this book. As a reminder, our Father in Heaven requires everyone who enters into the gate leading to eternal life to begin a journey along a path that is narrow, helping us to develop as we press forward in Christ. We become something better through these mortal challenges and experiences as we stay true to the covenant path. On the other hand, the path that leads away from eternal life, the way the world is traveling, is a broad path, attractive in its appeal, and has several distractions to keep our minds off who we are, where we came from, and where we want to go.

In our limited, mortal understanding, we may mistakenly think that the broad road is easier to travel, but it isn't. It's easier to get *on* that broad path because the gate to sin is wide and open to all, and sin is so easy to fall into. But ultimately, this broad path makes us more distant from our Father in Heaven, and we are less likely to hear His voice and follow the path He has set for us. As a result, we can have many difficulties in our life that are brought on by our own selfish indulgences. Hence, it might be *easier* to get on that broad path, but as we travel on it, we are subject to more destructive behaviors that hinder our spirituality.

We need to be sensitive to the fact that the tactics of the adversary are very cunning and clandestine. He starts with small things, which, unless recognized and stopped, will lead to bigger things—and he knows it. But from the scriptures, we also learn that God too works through small things, for "out of small things proceedeth that which is great" (Doctrine and Covenants 64:33). This verse is followed by another insight: that "the Lord requireth the heart and a willing mind" (verse 34).

So, why are "small things" so important to the Lord, and what do they have to do with "the heart and a willing mind"? One explanation is found in the Book of Mormon: "Nevertheless they did fast and pray oft, and did wax stronger and stronger in their humility, and firmer and firmer in the faith of Christ, unto the filling their souls with joy and consolation, yeah, even to the purifying and the sanctification of their hearts, which sanctification cometh because of their *yielding their hearts unto God*" (Helaman 3:35; emphasis added).

The answer is quite simple: Through consistently doing the "small things," we yield our hearts and minds to God. And this, in turn, purifies and sanctifies us.

Satan works hard to get us to compromise by working on each of us slowly, yet consistently, to transgress. He and his legions attempt to get us to stop doing these "small things" because he is aware that obedience to the small things helps protect us, prepares us for becoming something better, and leads to us receiving more blessing from our Father in Heaven. As the Book of Mormon teaches:

> And others will he pacify, and lull them away into carnal security, that they will say: All is well in Zion; yea, Zion prospereth, all is well—and thus the devil cheateth their souls, *and leadeth them away carefully down to hell.* And behold, others he flattereth away, and telleth them there is no hell; and he saith unto them: I am no devil, for there is none—and thus he whispereth in their ears, until he grasps them with his awful chains, from whence there is no deliverance. (2 Nephi 28:21–22; emphasis added)

Greater blessings are bestowed upon the faithful. We can learn about some of those blessings in our patriarchal blessings. However, those blessings are contingent upon faithfulness. Additionally, we read that when a person "shall prove himself faithful in all things that shall be entrusted unto his care, yea, even a few things, he shall be made ruler over many" (Doctrine and Covenants 124:113). If we "keep the commandments of God . . . [we] are blessed in all things, both temporal and spiritual" (Mosiah 2:41), and "God will support, and keep, and preserve us, so long as we are faithful unto him, and unto our faith, and our religion; and never will the Lord suffer that we shall be destroyed except we should fall into transgression and deny our faith" (Alma 44:4).

What great promises are ours if we are faithful and diligent. Truly, we need to "consider [our] ways" (Haggai 1:7) when it comes to the oath and covenant of the priesthood and pressing forward in Christ. When trials and tribulations of the world seem to reach out and envelop us, it is wise to "consider our ways." Like the people of Haggai's days, we may discover that it's actually our disobedience or casual, flippant attitude that is blocking blessings from our Father in Heaven.

To summarize Elder and Sister Tad R. Callister, understanding true doctrine, which comes from obeying the commandments, provides protection and perfects us. The Apostle Paul taught us to "take heed unto thyself, *and unto the doctrine*; continue in them: for in doing this thou shalt both save thyself, and them that hear thee" (1 Timothy 4:16; emphasis added). It is difficult, if not impossible, to study and ponder the gospel of Jesus Christ—the doctrine as He taught it—while simultaneously thinking or doing evil. This gospel truth was taught by Nephi: "Whoso would hearken unto the word of God, and then would hold fast unto it, they would never perish; neither could the temptations and the fiery darts of the adversary overpower them" (1 Nephi 15:24).[76]

4. To Receive the Servants of God

Lastly, we commit to receive God's servants, for the Lord taught that "he that receiveth my servants receiveth me; And he that receiveth me receiveth my Father" (Doctrine and Covenants 84:36–37).

An interesting fact that is evidenced by scriptural and modern-day examples is that it has been easier to accept, believe in, and follow a dead prophet than a living one. Moses was rejected of the Hebrew slaves who insolently proclaimed, "Who made thee a ruler and a judge?" (Acts 7:35). Ironically, the Jews later murmured of Christ, "We know that God spake unto Moses: as for this fellow, we know not from whence he is" (John 9:29). From Adam to Moses to Jesus to

76. See Tad R. Callister and Kathryn S. Callister, *Teaching with Power: Drawing Your Family and Others to Christ* (Salt Lake City: Deseret Book, 2021), 58.

Joseph Smith to our living prophet, all have been rejected and at times murdered by the people.

When prophets have said, "Thus saith the Lord," their words subsequently become scripture. However, we know through the scriptures that if people would not receive the prophets at they time they were alive, interestingly, many of those prophets were received by those who lived afterwards. These prophets were then honored, and sometimes the people even built monuments to them. Summarizing this point, President Hugh B. Brown wrote, "How is it that you build monuments to the dead prophets and crucify the living?"[77]

Jesus denounced this lack of respect, declaring, "Woe unto you . . . because ye build the tombs of the prophets, and garnish the sepulchers of the righteous, And say, If we had been in the days of our fathers, we would not have been partakers with them in the blood of the prophets. Wherefore ye be witnesses unto yourselves, that ye are the children of them which killed the prophets. Fill ye up then the measure of your fathers" (Matthew 23:29–32).

Furthermore, look at what happened to Stephen. He rebuked the combative Jews in the synagogues, saying, "Which of the prophets have not your fathers persecuted? and they have slain them which shewed before of the coming of the Just One; of whom ye have been now the betrayers and murderers" (Acts 7:51–52). Additionally, Samuel the Lamanite rebuked the wicked Nephites with these words:

> Wo unto this people, because of this time which has arrived, that ye do cast out the prophets, and do mock them, and cast stones at them, and do slay them, and do all manner of iniquity unto them, even as they did of old time.
>
> And now when ye talk, ye say: If our days had been in the days of our fathers of old, we would not have slain the prophets; we would not have stoned them, and cast them out.
>
> Behold ye are worse than they; for as the Lord liveth, if a prophet come among you and declareth unto you the word of the Lord, which testifieth of your sins and iniquities, ye are angry with

77. Hugh B. Brown, *An Abundant Life* (Salt Lake City: Signature Books, 1988), 334.

> him, and cast him out and seek all manner of ways to destroy him; yea, you will say that he is a false prophet, and that he is a sinner, and of the devil, because he testifieth that your deeds are evil. (Helaman 13:24–26)

God has taught us that "whether by mine own voice or by the voice of my servants, it is the same" (Doctrine and Covenants 1:38). Regarding these servants, He has said, "Wo unto that house, or that village or city that rejecteth you, or your words, or your testimony concerning me" (Doctrine and Covenants 84:94). On the other hand, He has said that "who receiveth you receiveth me. . . . And who receiveth you as a little child, receiveth my kingdom; and blessed are they, for they shall obtain mercy" (Doctrine and Covenants 99:2–3).

Those who receive the servants of the Lord must do so as little children—not as masters or as critics. Children are willing to learn; they are confiding, eager to be assisted, and full of trust and hope for the future. That is the spirit in which to receive the servants of God.[78]

The Covenant Blessings (What the Lord Promises to Do for Us)

As for the *covenant* portion of the oath and covenant of the priesthood, the promises our Heavenly Father bestows upon us are listed as follows. We are promised that He will:

- sanctify us by the Spirit;
- renew our bodies;
- make us the sons of Moses and of Aaron;
- make us the seed of Abraham;
- make us the church and kingdom and the elect of God; and
- give us all that He has.

78. Hyrum M. Smith and Janne M. Sjodahl, *Doctrine and Covenants Commentary* (Salt Lake City: Deseret Book, 1972), 629.

1. Be Sanctified by the Spirit

First, the Lord promises us sanctification, which means the process of becoming holy. Additionally, it means becoming clean, pure, and free from sin. This process occurs through the Atonement of Jesus Christ. Paul taught the Hebrews that this sanctification comes through the sacrifice of the body and blood of Christ (see Hebrews 10:10; 13:12; Doctrine and Covenants 76:41). And Mormon, in abridging the book of Helaman, wrote that "sanctification cometh because of their yielding their hearts unto God" (Helaman 3:35; see also Doctrine and Covenants 20:31).

After baptism, we receive the gift of the Holy Ghost, which grants us the reception of the Holy Ghost into our lives. Only after we truly receive the Spirit through our righteousness and faithfulness do we qualify to be sanctified (see 3 Nephi 27:20; Moses 6:59–60).

Becoming sanctified and pressing forward in Christ aligns us with the mind and will of God. This sets us apart from the rest of the world to the point that people will begin to recognize this. Alma taught the crafty, outspoken lawyer Zeezrom about one of the effects that complete sanctification has on people, stating that "after being sanctified by the Holy Ghost, having their garments made white, being pure and spotless before God, [they] could not look upon sin save it were with abhorrence" (Alma 13:12).

2. Receive a Renewal of Body

Next, the Lord promises the faithful "the renewing of their bodies" (Doctrine and Covenants 84:33). In a letter to the Church in Rome, Paul wrote, "If the Spirit of him that raised up Jesus from the dead dwell in you, he that raised up Christ from the dead shall also quicken your mortal bodies by his Spirit that dwelleth in you" (Romans 8:11).

Expounding on this point, Elder Bruce R. McConkie taught, "This renewal is real. It comes by the power of the Holy Ghost, and it comes as the individual himself gives grace or service to others."[79] Continuing, Elder McConkie explained that "to be sanctified is . . . to become a new creature of the Holy Ghost, one whose body has been renewed by the rebirth of the Spirit."[80]

This renewal of body is evidenced in latter-day prophets who are often found with surprising physical stamina and mental clarity, allowing them to continue their service into well-advanced years. I think of President Spencer W. Kimball who, despite significant health issues, had incredible stamina and mental clarity while he served as President of the Church. Several others also come to mind, including President Russell M. Nelson. Interestingly, it is not necessarily that the body is visibly transformed (though this could be the case at times) but that the positive effects of the Spirit support and invigorate physical and mental well-being.

In connection with the oath and covenant of the priesthood, the renewal of the body refers to an eternal effect as well as a mortal one. Since our present bodies are mortal and corruptible, they must be renewed in order for us to inherit the mansions which the Father has prepared for us, for "no unclean thing can inherit the kingdom of heaven" (Alma 11:37).

3. Become the Sons of Moses and of Aaron

The next blessing the Lord promises is that those who are ordained to the priesthood become the sons of Moses and Aaron. In the Old Testament, we learn that Moses and Aaron were Levites and, as such, held the rights to officiate in the priesthood. Moses held the higher, or Melchizedek, priesthood while Aaron held the lesser, or Aaronic, priesthood.

Elder Orson Pratt identified one of the great privileges that will befall the bearers of these two priesthoods in the last days. He said:

---

79. Hyrum L. Andrus, *The Glory of God and Man's Relation to Deity* (Salt Lake City: Deseret Book, 1964), 31.

80. Bruce R. McConkie, *Mormon Doctrine*, 2nd ed. (1966), 675.

> When the Temple [in New Jerusalem] is built the sons of the two Priesthoods, that is, those who are ordained to the Priesthood of Melchizedek, that Priesthood which is after the order of the Son of God, with all its appendages; and those who have been ordained to the Priesthood of Aaron with all its appendages, the former called the sons of Moses, the latter the sons of Aaron, will enter into that Temple . . . and all of them who are pure in heart will behold the face of the Lord . . . for he will suddenly come to his Temple. . . . In doing this, he will purify not only the minds of the Priesthood in that Temple, but he will purify their bodies until they shall be quickened, renewed and strengthened, and they will be partially changed, not to immortality, but changed in part that they can be filled with the power of God, and they can stand in the presence of Jesus, and behold his face in the midst of that Temple.
>
> This will prepare them for further ministrations among the nations of the earth, it will prepare them to go forth in the days of tribulation and vengeance upon the nations of the wicked, when God will smite them with pestilence, plague and earthquake, such as former generations never knew. . . .
>
> When they are prepared, when they have received a renewal of their bodies in the Lord's temple, and have been filled with the Holy Ghost and purified as gold and silver in a furnace of fire, then they will be prepared to stand before the nations of the earth and preach glad tidings of salvation in the midst of judgments that are to come like a whirlwind upon the wicked.[81]

4. Become the Seed of Abraham

Another promise from the Lord is that the faithful will become "the seed of Abraham." Through careful study of the scriptures, especially the Old Testament, we can learn many helpful truths about this topic.

It is fitting that we should be called the seed of Abraham, for he is known as "the father of the faithful" (Doctrine and Covenants 138:41). Whether we are literal descendants or adopted into Abraham's lineage makes no difference. Both groups are heirs of the Abrahamic

81. Orson Pratt, in *Journal of Discourses*, 15:365–66.

covenant through obedience to the laws and ordinances of the gospel of Jesus Christ.[82]

God covenanted with Abraham and his seed forever, bestowing great blessings upon them because of his faithfulness. In the New Testament, we read of Abraham in Romans and the promise made to him: "He staggered not at the promise of God through unbelief; but was strong in faith, giving glory to God; And being fully persuaded that, what he had promised, he was able also to perform. And therefore it was imputed to him for righteousness" (Romans 4:20–22).

Today, as the current seed of Abraham, we inherit the blessings and obligations of that same covenant, the basics of which are described in the book of Genesis in these words: "And I will make of thee a great nation, and I will bless thee, and make thy name great; and thou shalt be a blessing: And I will bless them that bless thee, and curse him that curseth thee: and in thee shall all families of the earth be blessed" (Genesis 12:2–3). And also, "By myself have I sworn, saith the Lord . . . That in blessing I will bless thee, and in multiplying I will multiply thy seed as the stars of the heaven, and as the sand which is upon the sea shore; and thy seed shall possess the gate of his enemies; And in thy seed shall all the nations of the earth be blessed; because thou hast obeyed my voice" (Genesis 22:16–18).

So, to fulfill that covenant, we must bless all the families of the earth. How is this to be accomplished? Quite simply, it's accomplished through the three-fold mission of the Church: proclaiming the gospel, perfecting the Saints, and redeeming the dead through temple work.

Additionally, we read in Galatians that "even as Abraham believed God, and it was accounted to him for righteousness. Know ye therefore that they which are of faith, the same are the children of Abraham. And the scripture, foreseeing that God would justify the heathen through faith, preached before the gospel unto Abraham, saying, In thee shall all nations be blessed. So then they which be of faith are blessed with faithful Abraham" (Galatians 3:6–9).

---

82. See Bible Dictionary, "Seed of Abraham."

5. Become the Church and Kingdom and the Elect of God

Next, as we keep our covenants, we are promised that we will become God's "church and kingdom, and the elect of God" (Doctrine and Covenants 84:34). From the sound of this blessing, this can initially appear daunting given all the circumstances of mortality. However, the church and kingdom of God consists of all nations and people, and it is a type for the heavenly kingdom the faithful will inherit if we press forward in Christ despite these hard times.

But who are these elect? "The elect are those who love God with all their hearts and live lives that are pleasing to him. Those who live such lives of discipleship will one day be selected by the Lord to be among his chosen children."[83] Being elect is not a status—it does not make one superior to another. It is an election of service and obedience. President Spencer W. Kimball wrote, "The elect of God! A moment's reflection ought to convince us that no sacrifice would be too great if a man and woman and their family could qualify to be the elect of God! These promises of great blessings are conditional, however; I know of none that are not—even the resurrection, for each of us had to qualify in the premortal existence to receive the blessing of an immortal body. All blessings, then, are conditional upon faithfulness."[84]

Elder Bruce R. McConkie also explained, "These are the portion of church members who are striving with all their hearts to keep the fullness of the gospel law in this life so that they can become inheritors of the fullness of gospel rewards in the life to come."[85] Dave Ramsey is credited in saying that we should live like no other so that one day we can live like no other. Although he was talking about finances, it is certainly true from a gospel perspective as well!

---

83. Guide to the Scriptures, "Elect," scriptures.ChurchofJesusChrist.org.

84. Spencer W. Kimball, "The Example of Abraham," *Ensign*, June 1975, 3.

85. Bruce R. McConkie, *Mormon Doctrine*, 2nd ed. (1966), 217.

6. Receive All That the Father Hath

Finally, the Lord promises that "all that my Father hath shall be given unto [the faithful]" (Doctrine and Covenants 84:38). What an incomprehensibly wonderful promise is extended to those who prove worthy, for what more could the Father give to His faithful than all that He has? In our mortal and sinful state, we can't even begin to comprehend what that "all" entails, for as Paul said, "Eye hath not seen, nor ear heard, neither have entered into the heart of man, the things which God hath prepared for them that love him" (1 Corinthians 2:9). However, by faith, righteous living, and pressing forward in Christ, the curtains of eternity are pulled back, even if only slightly, to reveal glimpses of what is in store for those who love and obey God. Faith and obedience are essential to the process, for the Lord has said:

> Come unto me, O ye house of Israel, and it shall be made manifest unto you how great things the Father hath laid up for you, from the foundation of the world; and it hath not come unto you, because of unbelief. Behold, when ye shall rend that veil of unbelief which doth cause you to remain in your awful state of wickedness, and hardness of heart, and blindness of mind, then shall the great and marvelous things which have been hid up from the foundation of the world from you. . . . be unfolded in [your] eyes. (Ether 4:14–16)

There are many things that lead us away from persevering and remaining steadfast and immovable on the covenant path. These can include (but are certainly not limited to) disbelief, wickedness, a hard heart, and a blind mind. We know that "all things which are good cometh of God; and that which is evil cometh of the devil" (Moroni 7:12). So, once again we see Satan trying to keep us from all that the Father has in store for us and from achieving our true potential. As we read in the Doctrine and Covenants:

> Satan seeketh to turn their hearts away from the truth, that they become blinded and understand not the things which are prepared for them. Verily, verily, I say unto you, ye are little children, and ye have not as yet understood how great blessings the Father hath in

> his own hands and prepared for you; And ye cannot bear all things now; nevertheless, be of good cheer, for I will lead you along. The kingdom is yours and the blessings thereof are yours, and the riches of eternity are yours (Doctrine and Covenants 78:10, 17–18)

I love how the Brethren were inspired to change some of the wording in the temple recommend questions in 2019 to reflect the word *striving*. To me, striving means earnestly attempting or trying. What a great comfort it is to know that the Lord is on our side as we *strive* to live righteously! Blessings will come to us as we *strive* to press forward in Christ. Perfection is pending, as President Russell M. Nelson taught.[86]

A knowledge and understanding of the things of eternity is certainly attainable in this life, but we must have faith and be obedient before the Lord will reveal them to us. These revelations will then come line upon line, little by little, as we are ready to receive them and accept the further responsibilities that always attend additional knowledge. God has said, "No man receiveth a fulness unless he keepeth his commandments. He that keepeth his commandments receiveth truth and light, *until* he is glorified in truth and knoweth all things" (Doctrine and Covenants 93:27–28; emphasis added).

We must remember that our Father in Heaven will *always* keep his promises; therefore, the blessings in the oath and covenant of the priesthood depend on our individual faithfulness. We are the ones responsible for our own faithfulness. The Lord has declared, "I, the Lord, am bound when ye do what I say, but when ye do not what I say, ye have no promise" (Doctrine and Covenants 82:10).

It is my prayer that we will ever live worthy and faithful to the oath and covenant of the priesthood so that we may be crowned with great glory in the kingdom of God at the last day.[87]

---

86. See Russell M. Nelson, "Perfection Pending," *Ensign*, Nov. 1995.
87. See also Psalm 8:5 and Hebrews 2:7. Searching the Church's website for "glory" can also give reveal added insights and scriptures related to being given a crown of glory.

7

THE SACRAMENT

CRG

When President Marion G. Romney would take the sacrament each week, he would say to himself as the bread and water came to his lips, "I do remember thee."[88]

During the summer of 1978, and as a brand new "Tenderfoot" Boy Scout and new deacon in the Aaronic Priesthood, I had the great opportunity of climbing to the top of Mount Whitney in central California with my Boy Scout troop, which enabled me to get the coveted "fifty-miler" patch for my uniform. Mount Whitney is the highest mountain in the contiguous United States, with an impressive elevation of over 14,500 feet. As part of that experience, we were able to attend a sacrament meeting at a local church prior to our climb.

Under normal circumstances, I probably would not have remembered this experience, as I was still learning what the Spirit felt like and working toward growing my very young and developing testimony. I

---

88. Marion G. Romney, "Reverence," *Ensign*, Oct. 1976, 2–3.

certainly did not have the understanding I have now of what it means to take the sacrament and renew the covenants I have made with the Lord. However, I do remember the experience of taking the sacrament in this little branch of the Church. I remember the holders of the Aaronic Priesthood coming to me with the bread, and instead of having traditional bread, there were croutons! How clearly I remember hearing the "crunch, crunch, crunch" of people eating the croutons.

The crunching noise from eating the croutons somewhat detracted from the reverence of the sacrament, but what I remember the most was that taking the sacrament was important enough to my Scout leaders that they made this side trip to do it. Many years later, I discovered that it really didn't matter that it was croutons that we were using at the time. As the scriptures teach, "It mattereth not what ye shall eat or what ye shall drink when ye partake of the sacrament, if it so be that ye do it with an eye single to my glory—remembering unto the Father my body which was laid down for you, and my blood which was shed for the remission of your sins" (Doctrine and Covenants 27:2).

When the Church was originally organized in April 1830, it was common practice to use wine instead of water for the sacrament. And "while the Church did not adopt the custom of using water exclusively in the Sacrament at that early time, yet it was from this time that water was used as a substitute for wine, which had been used principally because of its resemblance to blood. Today throughout the Church water is used in the Sacrament in remembrance of the blood of Jesus Christ which was shed for the remission of sins in behalf of all who repent and accept the Gospel."[89]

How Does the Sacrament Help Us Press Forward in Christ?

So, how does the sacrament help us in our enduring discipleship and help us to remember Him? How can it help us to "consider our

---

89. *Church History and Modern Revelation*, 2 vols. (1953), 1:132.

ways" and press forward in Christ despite the hardships we face here on earth?

I have discovered that the older I get, the more I value and cherish the time I spend taking the sacrament and renewing my covenants. Why is this? Because I've realized how powerful this experience can be. Once, during my personal studies, I read something very insightful that really resonated with me: "In many ways, the Gospel of Jesus Christ is one of the best-kept secrets in the Church. I refer not necessarily to the knowledge and understanding associated with the gospel but rather to the gospel as an experience, as 'the power of God unto salvation' (Romans 1:16). We are too often prone to be content with traveling about in twilight when we could walk and talk in the glorious light of the noonday sun."[90]

The reason this resonates with me is because we have the powers of God within such easy reach, but because of preoccupation or distraction, we fail to allow such powers into our life. In doing so, we limit ourselves and our potential for growth here upon the earth. Partaking of the sacrament each week enables us to remember Him and motivates us to live a more Christlike life.

I love this quote from Elder Marion D. Hanks, a former member of the First Quorum of the Seventy. He explained:

> "Our religion is not a weight; it is wings. It can carry us through the dark times, the bitter cup. It will be with us in the fiery furnace and deep pit. It will accompany us to the hospital room and to the graveside. It can assure us of the presence of a captain on the rough voyage. It is, in short, not the path to easy disposition of problems, but the comforting assurance of the eternal light by which we may see and the eternal warmth that we may feel. All of this comes to us through the love of Christ.[91]

---

90. Robert L. Millet, *Steadfast and Immovable* (Salt Lake City: Deseret Book, 1992), 153. See also Doctrine and Covenants 95:5–6.

91. Marion D. Hanks, *Bread upon the Waters* (Salt Lake City: Bookcraft, 1991), 34.

What this tells me is that as we move ahead in life, press forward in Christ, and earnestly strive to stay on the covenant path, we can be steadfast and immovable in the gospel of Jesus Christ. And as we come to live by every word of God, we come to know Him. We come to know our Lord by study and by faith. The sacrament is a consistent reminder for us to "consider our ways" and press forward in Christ.

In my opinion, the sacrament can help us achieve five things, which I'll discuss in the remainder of this chapter. This list is certainly not all-inclusive, and each person can add to it based on the whisperings of the Spirit they receive in their own life. However, this may be a good start for your personal and individual study of the sacrament. By partaking of the sacrament each week, we can:

1. come to treasure up His word by learning His gospel more fully and being able to teach it through the Spirit;
2. become an "example of the believers, in word, in conversation, in charity, in spirit, in faith, in purity" (1 Timothy 4:12);
3. support and sustain His servants;
4. come to love our Savior and others more fully, serve them more genuinely, and become more expressive in our gratitude; and
5. learn to trust and rely on the Lord more completely.

In order to answer the question of *how* the sacrament empowers us to press forward in Christ despite hardships, Elder David A. Bednar had this to say:

> That we might more fully keep ourselves unspotted from the world, we are commanded to go to the house of prayer and offer up our sacraments upon the Lord's holy day (see Doctrine and Covenants 59:9–12). Please consider that the emblems of the Lord's body and blood, the bread and the water, *are both blessed and sanctified*. . . .
>
> To sanctify is to make pure and holy. The sacramental emblems are sanctified in remembrance of Christ's purity, of our total dependence upon His Atonement, and of our responsibility to so honor our ordinances and covenants that we can "stand spotless before [Him] at the last day."
>
> The ordinance of the sacrament is a holy and repeated invitation to repent sincerely and to be renewed spiritually. The act of

> partaking of the sacrament, in and of itself, does not remit sins. But as we prepare conscientiously and participate in this holy ordinance with a broken heart and a contrite spirit, then the promise is that we may *always* have the Spirit of the Lord to be with us. And by the sanctifying power of the Holy Ghost as our constant companion, we can always retain a remission of our sins.[92]

But how do we know if we are worthy to take the sacrament each week? Elder John H. Groberg once shared what it means to partake of the sacrament worthily:

> If we desire to improve (which is to repent) and are not under priesthood restriction, then, in my opinion, we are worthy. If, however, we have no desire to improve, if we have no intention of following the guidance of the Spirit, we must ask: Are we worthy to partake, or are we making a mockery of the very purpose of the sacrament, which is to act as a catalyst for personal repentance and improvement? If we remember the Savior and all he has done and will do for us, we will improve our actions and thus come closer to him, which keeps us on the road to eternal life.
>
> If, however, we refuse to repent and improve, if we do not remember him and keep his commandments, then we have stopped our growth, and that is damnation to our souls.
>
> The sacrament is an intensely personal experience, and we are the ones who knowingly are worthy or otherwise.[93]

Like I mentioned earlier, taking the sacrament is something that I look forward to each week, and it has increasingly meant more to me after each passing year. I see it now as critical to my success in this life, and I'll go out of my way to take it as well as be worthy of it. The COVID-19 pandemic helped me to appreciate taking the sacrament much more and has made it more personal to me. Taking the sacrament helps me to "remember Him" as it did for President Marion G. Romney (see the introductory quote of this chapter). I have also

---

92. David A. Bednar, "Always Retain a Remission of Your Sins," *Ensign* or *Liahona*, May 2016, 61–62; emphasis added.
93. John H. Groberg, "The Beauty and Importance of the Sacrament," *Ensign*, May 1989, 38.

discovered that during those moments when I am taking the sacrament, the Spirit whispers to me those things that I need to improve, and this experience gives me the motivation to press forward for another week, despite how hard my life's circumstances may be at the time.

Now, let's examine more in depth the five ways the sacrament can help us.

1. We Come to Treasure Up God's Word

First, through the sacrament, we come to treasure up God's word by learning His gospel more fully and being able to teach it through the Spirit.

Chapter 8 of this book is entirely dedicated to the topic of scripture study. My associate, Mark Mason, has done a wonderful job listing the things we need to look for, feel, and apply in our own life through scripture study, as well as what we need to do to take our scripture study to the next level. Partaking of the sacrament is a great way to improve gospel study. It not only enhances our ability to understand the scriptures, but it also reminds us how important it is to "treasure up His word" (Doctrine and Covenants 84:85) in our own life.

In a recent one-on-one priesthood interview I had with a new elder's quorum president, we spoke at length about the importance of getting instructors to specifically teach the gospel of Jesus Christ, by treasuring up His word as well as instructing by the Spirit. Why do you suppose we talked about this for so long?

How many times have you been in a meeting or class where strange or controversial subjects are brought up by the facilitators, the lessons take a giant swing left, and before you know it, a different spirit is brought into the meeting? Instead of being edified by the Spirit, people become confused and they leave the class concerned, troubled, or worried. Unfortunately, much time is spent on subjects that are not in the approved curriculum. And oftentimes, it becomes a public forum by the instructor to "demonstrate" just how knowledgeable they are by referencing obscure books or out-of-context statements that have no bearing at all on the subject and are not faith-promoting. Instead of using the scriptures and helping others to "treasure up His word," it has a reverse effect and can potentially keep others from feeling the Spirit.

Doctrine and Covenants 50:19–20 says, "And again, he that receiveth the word of truth, doth he receive it by the Spirit of truth or some other way? If it be some other way it is not of God." Elder Bruce R. McConkie expounded on this principle:

> If you teach the word of truth—now note, you're saying what is true, everything you say is accurate and right—by some other way than the Spirit, it is not of God. Now what is the other way to teach than by the Spirit? Well, obviously it is by the *power of the intellect.*
>
> Suppose I came here tonight and delivered a great message on teaching, and I did it by the power of the intellect without any of the Spirit of God attending. Suppose that every word that I said is true, no error whatever, but it was an intellectual presentation. The revelation says: "If it be by some other way it is not of God" (Doctrine and Covenants 50:18).
>
> That is, *God did not present the message through me because I used the power of the intellect instead of the power of the Spirit.* Intellectual things—reason and logic—can do some good and they can prepare the way, and they can get the mind ready to receive the Spirit under certain circumstances. But conversion comes and truth sinks into the hearts of people *only* when it is taught by the power of the Spirit.[94]

I love this quote from President Boyd K. Packer: "True doctrine understood, changes attitudes and behavior. The study of the doctrines of the gospel will improve behavior quicker than a study of behavior will improve behavior."[95]

There is great safety and wisdom in treasuring up the word of the Lord. Doing so—in conjunction with taking the sacrament each week—invites the Spirit of the Lord into our life, strengthens our testimonies, and helps us to cherish the scriptures, This motivates us

---

94. Bruce R. McConkie, *The Foolishness of Teaching* (pamphlet, 198[illegible]), 9; emphasis added.
95. Boyd K. Packer, "Little Children," *Ensign*, Nov. 1986, 17.

to love our Father in Heaven and Savior Jesus Christ more and shows them our love through our obedience to the principles of the gospel (see John 14:15). The sacrament then becomes a more meaningful and impactful ordinance for us and develops into a priority for us and something we look forward to each week, and having this weekly ordinance becomes a priority in our life.

2. We Become an Example of the Believers

Second, through the sacrament, we become an "example of the believers, in word, in conversation, in charity, in spirit, in faith, in purity" (1 Timothy 4:12).

President Russell M. Nelson taught that Paul's counsel to be an "example of the believers" applies equally to members of the Church: "Each member can be an example of the believers. Brethren [and sisters], as followers of Jesus Christ, each of you can live in accord with His teachings. You can have 'a pure heart and clean hands'; you can have 'the image of God engraven upon your [countenance]' (Alma 5:19). Your good works will be evident to others (see Matthew 5:16; Alma 7:24). The light of the Lord can beam from your eyes (see Doctrine and Covenants 88:11)."[96]

Through the power of our faith and our righteous example, we have the ability to influence the entire world. Think about that for a moment. That is an incredibly powerful statement that President Nelson is making. Each of us has the ability to make a difference in the world, reach outside our own spheres of influence, and leave behind us a legacy of faith and an example of pressing forward in Christ.

I think of the example and legacy that President Thomas S. Monson showed in his lifetime. His biography, *To the Rescue*, is so appropriately named. There are myriad examples from his personal life that show how the power and example of one can influence others to make righteous choices and subsequently live fuller lives. Are we in a position currently to come "to the rescue" of those around us?

---

96. Russell M. Nelson, "Be Thou an Example of the Believers," *Ensign* or *Liahona*, Nov. 2010, 48.

Passing on his lessons learned, President Monson gave excellent counsel on how we can be an "example of the believers" (1 Timothy 4:12). He said, "Make every decision you contemplate pass this test: What does it do to me? What does it do for me? And let your code of conduct emphasize not, 'What will others think?' but rather, 'What will I think of myself?' Be influenced by that still, small voice. Remember that one with authority placed his hands on your head at the time of your confirmation and said, 'Receive the Holy Ghost.' Open your hearts, even your very souls, to the sound of that special voice which testifies of truth."[97]

In my own life, I have been blessed to associate on a personal level with many great people who have been an "example of the believers" to me, who have lived such a life that their legacy and example continues to resonate with me today. My first son, Conrad, was named for one such example of the believers. While serving as a missionary in Brisbane, Australia, I had the honor of getting to know a fellow missionary, Elder Con B. Fox, who unfortunately was killed in a car accident while serving. When I speak with my son, I can't help but think of this wonderful person he was named after and the example he left in this world. I learned so much from him. I learned the value of a sense of humor and being able to laugh at yourself as well as the importance of hard work.

Others have come into my life as well and have taught me important life lessons from their own examples. I think often of President Jeffery L. Schofield, who served in the Clearfield Utah Stake presidency for many years. Despite his health issues, and prior to his passing, he taught me the value of maintaining a positive attitude, trusting in the Lord, and faithfully serving in all our callings regardless of what they are. He also taught me that the Lord will not forget our faithful service even though others may.

Additionally, I was richly blessed with "goodly parents" (1 Nephi 1:1), Jerry and Judy Greenwood. The many lessons they left with me

---

97. Thomas S. Monson, "Be Thou an Example," *Ensign* or *Liahona*, May 2005, 113.

are deeply woven into my life and are too numerous to explain. I am and will always be eternally grateful for them. Several months prior to them both passing away from COVID-19, I had the privilege of telling them how much they meant to me. We had a wonderful conversation about some of the lessons they taught me and what wonderful parents they were to me and my siblings.

Most of us, when we think about it, have had mentors and examples who have left indelible spiritual impressions in our life. My life has been deeply enriched by these "examples of the believers." They have truly taught me what it means to press forward in Christ despite hardships, and they have made taking the sacrament so much more impactful for me.

3. We Sustain and Support His Servants

Third, partaking of the sacrament each week empowers us to sustain and support the Lord's servants.

In order to understand how the sacrament can do this, it is first necessary to understand what it means to "sustain" someone. When we raise our arm to sustain someone, we are promising our Father in Heaven, our Savior Jesus Christ, and all those around us that we *promise* to support the person called while we do our part as well. It's not just submissively raising our hand because everybody else is; it is, first, consenting to the proposal and, second, manifesting our commitment with a promise to support whoever or whatever is proposed. We have the privilege of doing this in wards and stakes each week.

In 1919, Elder George Albert Smith, who later became President of the Church in 1945, spoke of sustaining: "The obligation that we make when we raise our hands . . . is a most sacred one. It does not mean that we will go quietly on our way and be willing that the prophet of the Lord shall direct this work, but it means . . . that we will stand behind him; we will pray for him; we will defend his good name, and we will strive to carry out his instructions as the Lord shall direct."[98]

---

98. *Teachings of Presidents of the Church: George Albert Smith* (2011), 64.

President Russell M. Nelson recalled the following experience from his life when he sustained Spencer W. Kimball as President of the Church:

> Well do I remember my most unique "deed" to sustain a prophet. As a medical doctor and cardiac surgeon, I had the responsibility of performing open-heart surgery on President Spencer W. Kimball in 1972, when he was Acting President of the Quorum of the Twelve Apostles. He needed a very complex operation. But I had no experience doing such a procedure on a 77-year-old patient in heart failure. I did not recommend the operation and so informed President Kimball and the First Presidency. But, in faith, President Kimball chose to have the operation, only because it was advised by the First Presidency. That shows how he sustained his leaders! And his decision made me tremble!
>
> Thanks to the Lord, the operation was a success. When President Kimball's heart resumed beating, it did so with great power! At that very moment, I had a clear witness of the Spirit that this man would one day become President of the Church![99]

When we take the sacrament, we promise God that we're willing to keep His commandments, and that includes supporting His divinely called servants. When we understand why we do this sustaining each week in our wards and stakes and in general conferences, it makes it more meaningful and impactful in our own lives. What a great blessing to participate in this!

4. We Come to Love Our Savior and Others More Fully

Fourth, the sacrament can help us love the Lord and others more fully, serve them more genuinely, and become more expressive in our gratitude.

Several years ago, prior to a church meeting, I saw the following statement written on a whiteboard: "No Jesus, no Heaven." Then, underneath it was written, "Know Jesus, know Heaven." Though this may be a cute play on words, the reality of the statement is powerful.

---

99. Russell M. Nelson, "Sustaining the Prophets," *Ensign* or *Liahona*, Nov. 2014, 74.

When we come to know our Savior more fully, we begin to experience a change of heart.

Sometimes the scriptures call this a mighty change, but for most of us, the experience of acquiring a change of heart is incremental and takes many years. Afterward, when we look back on our change, that's when we see that is has been truly mighty. As we experience this change, we begin to look at our friends and neighbors as our brothers and sisters and feel genuine love for them. It impacts the way we treat them and respond to them. We become more patient with them and want to serve them more. Our motives become more pure and Christlike. We begin to see others as our Savior sees us, and we become more grateful.

The words that I read on that whiteboard are true. If we choose a path where there is no Savior in our life, there will be no reward for us. We become stagnant and complacent. Conversely, if we take the time to truly get to know our Savior, He molds and shapes us, and we become perfected through this work, which in turn allows us to approach the throne of God with confidence. It makes taking the sacrament each week more meaningful for us.

5. We Learn to Trust and Rely on the Lord

Finally, the sacrament helps us learn to trust and rely on the Lord more fully.

This step has come to me incrementally, line upon line over many years. Truly trusting in Him is a process that comes through devotion and "always remembering him," as said in the sacrament prayer (see Moroni 4:3; 5:2). However, trusting in the ways of the Lord cannot come without revelation in our lives, and as revelation becomes a part of us, we learn to trust more. If we seek to learn the things of God solely by reason alone, we are certain to stop short of our final goal—that of eternal life. Why? Because to learn the things of God, and to learn to trust in Him, we need faith and revelation. This will lead us to the Living Water (see John 4:13–14) and help us following the counsel in Proverbs 3:5–6: "Trust in the Lord with all thine heart; and lean not unto thine own understanding. In all thy ways acknowledge him, and he shall direct thy paths" (Proverbs 3:5–6).

I have a friend who shared with me the following dream he had. For him, it was an eye-opening experience that helped him know how he was doing with trusting the Lord at that time. With his permission, but without including his name, I'd like to share this powerful lesson here:

> In my dream I saw a wide, swift river. I was walking along the river bank. Looking in the river, I saw a multitude of different people at various depths. It was revealed to me that the river represented the current flow of celestial spirituality. All the people were headed in the same direction, but some were moving faster than others. Some who were further out were bobbing in the water, which was over their head, and as a result were following the current and not resisting it. Other people were in up to their waist, their legs, or their calves and were moving along in the river as quickly as they could. Finally, other people were only in the water up to their ankles and moving at their own leisurely pace. All of the people in the river were moving in the same direction, but the deeper in they were, the quicker they moved because of the current.
>
> I noticed that those who were in the deepest part of the river and were letting the current move them along had on a life jacket. It was revealed to me that the life jacket represented the Savior Jesus Christ. We often find ourselves in deep water, but the Savior will not let us drown. These people understood that principle, and as a result, *they trusted the Lord*; they were willing to let the current carry them to where they needed to go, and they got to their destination quickly. They would get there faster than those who were walking and those who were in the current only up to their waist or legs.
>
> Regardless of how hard some of the people tried, if they were only in the spiritual water up to their ankles, legs, or waist, they still could not move as fast as those who had completely yielded themselves to the water and trusted in the Lord to guide them to wherever they needed to go.
>
> I saw all of this at once and understood it completely. The interpretation was very clear to me. The water represented the current of spirituality each of us can be part of. It's up to us how much we want to trust the Lord to get us to our destination. Even

though we all may be going the same direction, it's up to us how much we desire His assistance to get there. We can either trust in Him and let the current carry us, or we can try to get there ourselves, on our own merits, working only partially with Him, which ultimately will take much longer and is more difficult and strenuous.

Additionally, I also saw where I myself was in this spiritual river, and the thought came to me that I was in up to my waist but not entirely willing to "go the distance" and let the current carry me according to the will of the Lord. I'm not yet entirely trusting in Him. That is a sad state for me, and I need to reevaluate why I am doing that.[100]

Questions to Ask Ourselves

Lastly, I wanted to share the counsel of Elder Peter F. Meurs of the Seventy, who suggested several questions we might ask ourselves to make the sacrament more meaningful to us. They are as follows.

First, "What will I do this week to better prepare for the sacrament?"[101]

When I personally think of this question, I am reminded that even Nephi, as stalwart and diligent as he was, was often at times beset with personal struggles and challenges (see 2 Nephi 4:18). I love how in the "psalm of Nephi" (2 Nephi 4), Nephi opens himself up very vulnerably in his writings, exposing the things of his soul in a powerful collection of verses (see 2 Nephi 4:15–35). These are some of the most beautiful writings in all of scripture. Interestingly, in verse 17, Nephi writes, "O wretched man that I am! Yea, my heart sorroweth because of my flesh; my soul grieveth because of mine iniquities." Then we get to verse 18: "I am encompassed about, because of the temptations and sins which do so easily beset me." Nevertheless, he still found strength in the Lord "in whom I have trusted" (verse 19).

---

100. Email in possession of the author, dated July 10, 2018.

101. Peter F. Meurs, "The Sacrament Can Help Us Become Holy," *Ensign* or *Liahona*, Nov. 2016, 87.

Like Nephi of old, we need to press forward along the covenant path in our attempt to work toward righteousness, despite our weaknesses, problems, or obstacles. "Let us lay aside every weight, and the sin which doth so easily beset us, and let us run with patience the race that is set before us, Looking unto Jesus the author and finisher of our faith" (Hebrews 12:1–2). As Elder Meurs suggests, asking ourselves what we can do to better prepare ourselves for the sacrament each week enables us to reach out to our Savior and helps us to press forward in Christ despite the difficult times we live in. And for me personally, it also allows me to realize that others are struggling as much as I am, which in turns motivates me to help others. If Nephi can do it, so can we—if we trust the Lord as Nephi did.

Next, Elder Meurs suggestions the following questions: "Could I contribute more to the reverence and revelation that can accompany the beginning of sacrament meeting?" and "What doctrine was taught in the sacrament hymn?"[102]

Sometimes, reading the lyrics of the hymn during the sacrament brings a spirit of peace and helps us reflect more precisely on what our Savior did for us. As a former cast member of the Church's musical, *The Savior of the World*, I don't think I can ever hear the song "Jesus, Once of Humble Birth" without thinking of the experiences I had while performing in that production, and how it conveyed to me the reality of what the Savior did for me personally. That song has so much more meaning for me now. Oftentimes, I will read the lyrics of that song and think of my experiences portraying an Apostle of the Lord Jesus Christ and having the Savior appear to us and show us His wounds.

Finally, Elder Meurs recommends we ask ourselves "What did I hear and feel as I listened to the sacrament prayers?" and "What did I think about as the sacrament was passed?"[103]

As part of my *Come, Follow Me* study for the Doctrine and Covenants, I belonged to a study group, and one evening we discussed

102. Peter F. Meurs, "The Sacrament Can Help Us Become Holy," 87.

103. Peter F. Meurs, "The Sacrament Can Help Us Become Holy," 87.

at length the meaning, applicability, and differences of "the *arm* of the Lord" and the "*hand* of the Lord," as used in the scriptures.[104] It was a fascinating discussing. In summary, what we learned from each other is that in most cases, when the "arm of the Lord" is mentioned, it is symbolic of our loving Savior, Jesus Christ, reaching out toward us, opening up His arms in love. It's representative of His extending His power, covenant, and love to each of us. In this context, it's easy to envision the Savior saying, "Come, follow me," as he extends His arms to us.

Conversely, when the phrase "hand of the Lord" is used, it generally means that the Savior is executing either justice or mercy. This can be broken down even further. For example, when the Savior is using His right hand, He is generally delivering blessings, benefits, mercy, and grace. When He is using His left hand, He is generally executing justice, judgement, or some sort of punishment. Interestingly, it is now procedure to take the sacrament with our right hand when possible, according to the recent changes in the Church's handbook.[105] Certainly, the partaking of the sacrament is a blessing and benefit to us individually.

The bottom line is that the Lord is extending His arms to us by allowing us to partake of the sacrament each week. This enables us to feel His love, power, and mercy each week, which in turn makes the Atonement of Jesus Christ more impactful in our lives. Additionally, taking the sacrament each week motivates us to pause for a moment, think about what we are doing, consider our ways, and press forward in Christ despite hard times. We can be like President Marion G. Romney who, as mentioned earlier, would say to himself as the

104. There are many scriptures found in the Doctrine and Covenants that specifically differentiate between the "arm of the Lord" (e.g., see Doctrine and Covenants 1:14; 90:10) and the "hand of the Lord" (e.g., see Doctrine and Covenants 61:6; 76:3; 84:119). Although arguments could be made indicating one way or the other, in my research, most of the scriptures actually distinguish between what the "arm" may represent or what the "hand" may represent.

105. *General Handbook: Serving in The Church of Jesus Christ of Latter-day Saints*, 18.9.4, ChurchofJesusChrist.org.

sacramental bread and water came to his lips, "I do remember thee."[106] What a tremendous blessing it is to take the sacrament.

---

106. Marion G. Romney, "Reverence," 2–3.

8

SCRIPTURE STUDY

MDM

"For my soul delighteth in the scriptures."

—2 Nephi 4:15

When I was twelve, I began to read the Book of Mormon on my own for the first time. Though I didn't finish the whole book—not even making it past 1 Nephi—I still felt the Spirit burning in my heart. As I began reading 1 Nephi 8, I started highlighting verses. Strong feelings continued until I reached chapter 12 or 13. I was marking every verse in every chapter!

Thinking back on this experience, it's funny how unhelpful my highlighting was. One day in church, a quorum adviser saw what I was doing and said, "You know, you're not supposed to highlight *everything*. You're supposed to mark a verse or two so they stand out." He didn't realize at the time what was happening to me, and neither did I. Much later when I reflected on my experience, I realized my 12-year-old heart was feeling the Spirit, and that is why I was marking every verse.

I wish I would have understood then what I know now, something I'm sure all of us have felt at times. We see our past experiences through more mature eyes. Now, this early experience has become a powerful testimony to me that the Book of Mormon is true. The Spirit filled my heart as I read God's word. And I am so grateful for that because not long after, great trials and tests came into my life. Because of what I had done at age twelve, I already began forging a testimony. At the very least, I knew God was real and The Church of Jesus Christ of Latter-day Saints was His church on earth. And I knew the Book of Mormon was true.

This first experience with personal study helped me begin to feel what Nephi described: "For my soul delighteth in the scriptures" (2 Nephi 4:15). Since then, I've felt the same power of scripture study growing throughout my life as I've learned to devote myself to feasting on the words of Christ and have become more aware of the meaning of what I read and feel.

I went through some very serious faith trials as a young man. I was inactive from the age of fifteen to nineteen. Yet through all my struggles, because of my early childhood experience with the scriptures (and also my patriarchal blessing), I always knew the Church was true. And when it finally came time to decide if I would return to God and His Church, I could rely on my young testimony, which was powerful enough to strengthen my resolve to come back. Truly, like David wrote so long ago, I too can say, "Thy word is a lamp unto my feet, and a light unto my path" (Psalm 119:105). My testimony was founded on the study of the Book of Mormon with my family, at church, and on my own. My faith led me through darkness and back to Christ and His love. The beauty of the gospel is that this faith is available to all who seek it. Scripture study is central to developing deep and abiding faith in Christ that will allow us to endure through all of life's challenges.

Scripture Study Brings Great Power to Endure

Why is studying the scriptures so vitally important to our receiving the power of Jesus Christ? How does the power of scripture study help us endure faithfully? What can we do to approach the scriptures with greater purpose and conviction? And how can studying the scriptures help us become better disciples of Jesus Christ?

When Joseph Smith faced his moments of "serious reflection and great uneasiness" (Joseph Smith—History 1:8) in his youth, he turned to the scriptures. As we know, he came across the passage of James 1:5–6. What stands out to me is the impact that reading this passage had on young Joseph. "Never did any passage of scripture come with more power to the heart of man than this did at this time to mine. It seemed to enter with great force into every feeling of my heart. I reflected on it again and again, knowing that if any person needed wisdom from God, I did; for how to act I did not know" (Joseph Smith—History 1:12).

Notice how the study of scripture led Joseph to "consider his ways." He reflected on the verses, felt a power drawing him into the scriptures like they were written to him personally, and felt deeply convicted that he needed to ask God about what was troubling him. A power from heaven came to him so impressively that he could not stop pondering the words as he considered his situation. Young Joseph knew he must act in faith because of what he read.

As we know, the culmination of this event brought Joseph to conclude, "I must either remain in darkness and confusion, or else I must do as James directs, that is, ask of God" (Joseph Smith—History 1:13). As Joseph acted in faith, he made his way to the grove of trees and prayed. With the appearance of the Father and the Son, great power flowed into the young Prophet's life. With each successive act of obedience after this experience, greater power came, enabling him to do a work he never could have accomplished on his own.

Joseph's faithful seeking of the Savior infused his life with divine light. Because it's vitally important that we receive this same power from God to help us in *our* lives, we too need to faithfully study the scriptures. As we ponder them, they will lead us to revelation. As we in turn act in faith, the Lord will reveal more to us, helping us grow line upon line. Each of these successive acts of seeking and faithful obedience will lead us to the power to overcome the trials of our faith and grow toward perfection.

I imagine Jesus's sermon on the Bread of Life in John 6 presented a significant faith trial for Peter and the Apostles. Previously, Jesus fed the five thousand, and as a result, many followed Him—"not because [they] desire to keep my sayings, neither because [they] saw the miracles, but because [they] did eat of the loaves, and were filled" (Joseph Smith Translation, John 6:26 [in John 6:26, footnote *a*]). In response to their somewhat misguided devotion, the Savior taught them not to labor for "the meat which perisheth, but for that meat which endureth unto everlasting life" (verse 27). Jesus was the meat that endures. He was the Bread of Life they should have been seeking, meaning His teachings and way of life could bring sustaining power to help them endure—as significantly as if they were fed with physical bread or meat.

After teaching His disciples, Jesus then instructed them to eat "my flesh" and drink "my blood" (John 6:54). This saying caused many to be offended, saying, "Who can hear it?" (verse 60), or in our words, "Who can follow such strange teachings?" Then, many "walked no more with him" (verse 66).

After their departure, the Savior directed His words to the Apostles. "Will ye also go away? Then Simon Peter answered him, Lord, to whom shall we go? thou hast the words of eternal life" (John 6:67–68). To his credit, Peter remained spiritually connected to the Savior, despite confusion and what may have seemed like a mass exodus of Christ's followers. What brought Peter such strength of testimony? It was Christ's words—what we today call His scriptures. This connection to the Savior's words gave Peter power to overcome adversity—even a potential faith crisis that could have caused him to walk away from the gospel as others did. With Christ's word in his heart, Peter rose to face his challenges.[107]

John the Beloved taught that Jesus was "the Word" (John 1:1). This title has many meanings, and one of them has to do with divine investiture. Divine investiture means that "in all His dealings with the human family Jesus the Son has represented and yet represents Elohim His Father in power and authority."[108] This means Christ speaks for the Father. He is God's word to us. Furthermore, Jesus embodies the word of God through His actions. His life, character, and attributes represent the prime example of how the Father lives. Thus, Jesus Christ shows us what we should know and do both in word and in deed. Jesus is the message of the scriptures. He is the main character. As He once said to the Apostle Thomas, "I am the way, the truth, and the life: no man cometh unto the Father, but by me" (John 14:6). As we study His word, we know what to focus on: learning of Christ.

Nephi also described the power of Christ's word. First, he taught that we need to "press forward with a steadfastness in Christ" and that by following Jesus we would gain a "perfect brightness of hope, and a love of God and of all men" (2 Nephi 31:20). In other words, following Christ leads to the development of hope, one of the Savior's primary virtues, and this hope gives us power to press forward. Nephi concluded, "Wherefore, if ye press forward, feasting upon the word of Christ, and endure to the end . . . thus saith the Father: ye shall have eternal life" (2 Nephi 31:20). Thus, through feasting on Christ's word—that is, through scripture study—we can learn to follow Jesus.

The Savior has said, "Whosoever receiveth my word receiveth me" (Doctrine and Covenants 112:20). Through studying the scriptures, we learn *His* words. We see *His* manner of living. And we gain strength to press forward and become more like *Him* as we act in faith on what we learn. His words become the source of instruction for our daily walk (see Doctrine and Covenants 33:16). We increase our

107. To study other examples of people overcoming through Christ's word, see Matthew 4:1–11; 2 Nephi 4:15–35; Mosiah 2–5; Mosiah 12–17; Alma 17:2–3; Alma 18:13–43; Alma 19:1–36; and Doctrine and Covenants 121–23.

108. *Teachings of Presidents of the Church: Joseph F. Smith* (1998), 359.

power to overcome sin (see Matthew 22:29). We learn to believe in Christ and increase in His wisdom (see John 2:22; Alma 33:12). Truly, the scriptures become "a lamp" guiding the course of our path, and as we continue along that path, we can become more "at one" with the Son of God, developing His thoughts, feelings, and intentions.[109]

In many ways, this relationship of coming unto Christ is how we experience the Atonement—or at-one-ment—with Christ. The power that flows into a person's life *is* Christ. The scriptures are the words of life, and life is Jesus. We learn of Him and the way He lives. We act like Him, and His power flows into us. We become like Him as He transforms our nature to overcome the fallen, natural man and become a disciple, a spiritual person. We are led to Him—by Him—to become more like Him.[110] This is scripture study in its finest and purest form of personal development.

Greater Purpose in Scripture Study: To Become like Jesus

President David O. McKay taught, "Spirituality, our true aim, is the consciousness of victory over self, and of communion with the Infinite. Spirituality impels one to conquer difficulties and acquire more and more strength. To feel one's faculties unfolding and truth expanding in the soul is one of life's sublimest experiences."[111]

I take this quote to mean two important truths. First, spirituality involves communication with God. I think this part is what many people consider religion to be. It involves reading the scriptures to know God's word and praying to understand personally what He would have us know. It involves listening to talks in sacrament

109. See David O. McKay, "Something Higher Than Self" (Brigham Young University devotional, Oct. 12, 1965), speeches.byu.edu.

110. See Doctrine and Covenants 35:20. Here, I take the phrase "mine own bosom" to mean that we develop the Savior's thoughts, feelings, and intentions. Thus, if we take the scriptures into our hearts, minds, and actions, we are becoming more "at-one" with Christ.

111. David O. McKay, "Something Higher Than Self," 4.

meeting and general conference. In short, any form of spiritual communication from God makes us more spiritual people.

However, the second portion of the quote suggests a more action-focused meaning to spiritual growth. The victory over self implies our ability to put into practice what we learn through divine communication. King Benjamin explained this well when he said, "For the natural man is an enemy to God, and has been from the fall of Adam, and will be, forever and ever, unless he yields to the enticings of the Holy Spirit, and putteth off the natural man and becometh a saint through the atonement of Christ the Lord" (Mosiah 3:19).

I believe King Benjamin taught here the power of listening to the Spirit to align our lives with God's desires. Thus, we are "spiritual" people when we act according to the Spirit. Our spirits tell our bodies what to do rather than the other way around. Think of someone addicted to drugs—their body tells them what to do. Or someone addicted to pornography—their passions overcome their spirit. When we direct our lives spiritually, we rise above temptations and sins. We shape our lives around the teachings and example of Jesus. Hence, we overcome the "natural," "earthly," or "worldly" man or woman and become the Christ-centered, spirit-led person we want to be.

Of course, we do not achieve this kind of development by our own efforts. We do so through the Atonement of Jesus Christ. His grace empowers our ability to change as we hearken to the Spirit. Then, we gain power to put off the natural man. While this is a simplified explanation for the process of we are discussing, at least we can see the essence of the kind of change we are looking for.

For these reasons, reading the scriptures—as well as all other forms of spiritual communication—is good, because this communication brings us closer to God. But studying them—really feasting upon them—is far better. If we want to develop our lives in full and increases our purpose and conviction to follow Jesus Christ, then we will need to exert ourselves beyond just communicating with God. We will need to begin the process of conquering ourselves through considering our ways, repenting, and seeking more to emulate Jesus.

Six Essential Scripture Study Skills

While all these thoughts may sound good, it might still happen that we start our next scripture study with excitement and a dutiful heart only to realize when it's over, "I have no idea what I just read! I mean, I can check a box that says 'I've finished,' but it really wasn't very meaningful." One problem many people face, at least those who shared their concerns with me, is not knowing what to do while studying the scriptures so they can draw closer to Christ. They read them, sometimes even consistently, but they feel little power from the experience and often fail to connect with what they read. Yet the problem can be even more complex. For example, some people learn scripture study skills and *still* have problems. We can find out the context of a passage, define the keywords, look at footnotes, and mark important verses, but we still may fail to experience the personal growth we desire.

One way we overcome this problem is by examining the Lord's instructions within the scriptures regarding scripture study. If we choose study skills from a scripture, we know we have connected to God's commandments about His word. What follows are what I think are the essentials skills we need, including examples to increase our power to use them.

Keep in mind you will need to practice these skills to develop the power you want. So, spend individual time incorporating them into your study. It's worth the extra effort as you deepen your relationship with the Savior. With this emphasis, you can use each skill as a gateway to knowing Him better. Thus, these skills are not simply tools to understand a text but methods to find and understand the Son of God, His plan of salvation, and your role in it.

There are six skills we will examine: being diligent in our study, spending sufficient time, searching the word, pondering what we read, likening it to ourselves, and acting on what we think and feel. In this way, we will increase our power to receive revelation, which will help us endure to the end. We will examine our lives and develop a closer relationship with Jesus Christ.

Each of these skills builds on the others and likely could be happening all at once rather than in a piecemeal, stepwise process. They interrelate with each other to create an outcome. The outcome is learning to build a relationship with God, knowing what He expects from us, obeying Him, and becoming more like Him.

Being Diligent

"They had searched the scriptures diligently, that they might know the word of God" (Alma 17:2).

In this verse, Mormon described Ammon and his brethren, the sons of Mosiah, and what made them powerful teachers and minsters for Christ. Here, I want to address their dedication to search the scriptures *diligently*. Certainly, to be diligent implies engaging in something consistently, and the word *engage* also suggests a *feeling* about what we are doing. It is enthralling. We love it and we choose to do it willingly.

When I think of engagement, I think of my wife when we she was my fiancée. All I could think of was my bride-to-be. She filled my every thought. I longed to be near her, talk to her, and know what was going on in her day. For me, this feeling was heightened because I had taken a job before we met, requiring my relocation to Jacksonville, Florida, for the summer. This separation lasted until the week before our wedding day. With my fiancée in Provo the entire time, the separation was painful, but we needed the money. I longed to be near her, and this kind of longing for someone is precisely the feeling of a diligent learner.

The word *diligent* in Latin claims its roots from *diligere*, meaning "love" or "take delight in" something or someone.[112] This definition aligns perfectly with President Gordon B. Hinckley's plea for us to develop a relationship with the Lord as we study His word. He said, "I am grateful for emphasis on reading the scriptures. I hope that for you this will become something far more enjoyable than a duty; that,

---

112. *Oxford English Dictionary*, 2nd ed. (Oxford: Oxford University Press, 2004), s.v. "diligent."

rather, it will become a love affair with the word of God. I promise you that as you read, your minds will be enlightened and your spirits will be lifted. At first it may seem tedious, but that will change into a wondrous experience with thoughts and words of things divine."[113]

Moses captured this feeling of love for the word of God when he wrote, "And thou shalt teach [the words of God] diligently unto thy children, and shalt talk of them when thou sittest in thine house, and when thou walkest by the way, and when thou liest down, and when thou risest up" (Deuteronomy 6:7). We certainly won't develop this kind of relationship through casual reading or listening to His word occasionally or sporadically.

That said, I think it's important for us to accept the hand that life can deal us at times. When I finished my graduate degree, I was so spent mentally, emotionally, and physically that I couldn't bring myself to read anything. That included scripture. My close friend Michael asked something about my scripture study, and I said, "I never read the scriptures, Michael. I can't stand reading *anything* right now." He laughed awkwardly as if saying, "What's wrong with you? Have you lost your testimony?"

"I'm okay. I haven't lost my testimony," I replied. "Right now, I can barely function after what I've been through. I do listen to the scriptures daily—not much or for very long—but that has to be good enough for now. I just don't have anything to give."

Such events can happen in our lives for many reasons. Sometimes during our trials, we have the drive to drink deeply from God's words and find solace, but other times, we read one verse and just pray for help to continue. The key here is that we love God. If we don't, we can't move forward. The first commandment is to "love the Lord thy God" (Luke 10:27). While I only listened to His word at that difficult time of life, I loved the Savior's presence. Just hearing His words lifted and strengthened me. In love, I offered my few loaves of bread and fish, and thankfully the Lord multiplied my scanty meal. He strengthened me through that difficult time. But such behavior cannot become our

113. Gordon B. Hinckley, "The Light Within You," *Ensign*, May 1995, 99.

normal routine. This was an acute situation I resolved over time. If such behavior becomes our chronic condition, we may not be able to draw adequately on the powers of heaven to receive sufficient help.

Of course, during this time I maintained my relationship with God and continued to "pray always" so that I would "not faint" (2 Nephi 32:9). Prayer, even when listening to scripture, is essential. Prayer opens the pathway to God and helps us maintain our love for Him.

Speaking of how to develop this kind of diligent, loving, prayerful relationship with the scriptures, President Howard W. Hunter said, "Those who delve into the scriptural library . . . find that to understand requires more than casual reading or perusal—there must be concentrated study. It is certain that one who studies the scriptures every day accomplishes far more than one who devotes considerable time one day and then lets days go by before continuing."[114] Thus, diligence implies consistency over time. Yet, as we have seen, to search the scriptures diligently means more than putting in the time; our hearts are involved, and we can't bear to be away from His word.

Just as love within a couple grows, so too does love for God's word develop over time. My experiences with scripture today bring much more into my life than when I was a young man diligently reading to prepare for my mission. Yet the time I spent with the scriptures as a young man was perfect for my development then. Scripture study really does reflect our relationship with God. Our connection with God's word grows as we become more connected to Him. As we become more engaged with the Lord and His word over time, our love for Him will grow richer and deeper.

Spending Time

"You shall let your time be devoted to the studying of the scriptures" (Doctrine and Covenants 26:1).

In this verse, the Lord invited the Prophet Joseph Smith, Oliver Cowdery, and John Whitmer to spend more time studying the

114. Howard W. Hunter, "Reading the Scriptures," *Ensign*, Nov. 1979, 64.

scriptures. I realize they had sacred callings, and this likely explains why the Lord encouraged them to spend more time in the word. Yet the question of how long we study is one everyone ought to consider.

We are all busy people. The fact we are so busy suggests we need to look for ways to improve our lives, both in efficiency and effectiveness. This is most likely why you're reading this book. Despite our busy schedules, scripture study isn't something we should consistently hurry through.[115]

President Howard W. Hunter said, "It would be ideal if an hour could be spent each day; but if that much cannot be had, a half hour on a regular basis would result in substantial accomplishment. A quarter of an hour is little time, but it is surprising how much enlightenment and knowledge can be acquired."[116] Why is the amount of time so important? Because it takes concentrated effort to feel the Spirit when we are reading. It takes time to engage in and perfect the skills we are discussing here. The key is to set a goal for an amount of time we are going to read.

Of course, what we *get* out of the time we spend depends on our *goal* for reading. If, for instance, our desire is to learn the story, because we have never read a particular book of scripture before, our time might be spent asking questions like, "What happened in this book? What is the meaning of this chapter?" If our purpose is to understand a particular doctrinal topic, we might search for keywords

---

115. Here, I'm not speaking to someone who is just starting a habit of reading the scriptures. If this is you, there's nothing wrong with starting small. I love James Clear's book *Atomic Habits*. In it, he shares the idea of just "showing up." This idea is to make any new goal so simple that you can't fail at it. That way, you consistently show up every day to do what you set out to do. It's the idea of small, incremental change. If you are just beginning to read the scriptures, then your goal may be just to read for a few minutes. I've seen people change from reading just one minute of scripture every day. It doesn't sound like much, but one minute can make all the difference for someone who has never had the habit, or for someone who has broken the habit and needs to rekindle what they've lost. The key is to make the goal so simple that you can't fail. By doing this, you start to gain traction and can then work on improving your goal.

116. Howard W. Hunter, "Reading the Scriptures," 64.

and phrases, define important words, and make connections between key concepts.

At some point, we need to develop a relationship with the Lord during the time we study. We might ask questions like, "Why are these events important to me? What about these people's actions is relevant to my life? How could knowing these stories, connections, and doctrines help me come closer to Heavenly Father and Jesus Christ?" Regardless of our purpose, we need to spend enough time to feel the power of the Savior's words. We will have to decide how much time we have available in our schedules, balancing all our needs.

The value of studying slowly is easily seen in the following example. In a priesthood calling, I once worked with a young man who was struggling with issues in his life. He was preparing to serve a mission and very excited to leave, but his difficulties were weighing him down and slowing his progress. Together we identified that one of his problems was he felt disconnected from God's word. We spoke often as he tried to overcome the issues in his life. I recommended that he read relevant scriptures that were focused on his concerns.

Knowing he needed some practice with scripture study, I asked if we could read the scriptures together. The first time we did this, he quickly read the verses I asked him to read, as if he was checking them off a list of things to do. I stopped him. "Slow down, please," I said. "Think about what you are reading. See if you can feel the power of the words." As he slowed down, his countenance visibly changed. I saw light in his eyes. He obviously felt the words. They became meaningful to him. He remarked, "This is the first time I've read that slowly. It felt so much better."

The issue of spending enough time in God's word is essential if we are going to feel their power. Elder D. Todd Christofferson said, "It is a good thing sometimes to read a book of scripture within a set period of time to get an overall sense of its message, but for conversion, you should care more about the amount of time you spend in the scriptures than about the amount you read in that time."[117] If we want greater power in the word, it's important to spend more time reading slowly so we can feel God's power.

Searching

"Search the scriptures . . . which testify of me" (John 5:39).

In John 5:39, Jesus commanded a group of Jews to search the scriptures with a particular aim in mind: to find testimonies of His life. Likewise, when *we* read, it is important that we are searching for something.

An experience my wife had showed me what searching can look like. After a ward activity, she was wiping off the windshield that was covered with newly fallen snow. She did not have a window scraper or gloves, so she used her bare hands. When she finished, she shook her hands to remove the cold water, and her wedding ring flipped off her finger into the snow in the church parking lot. She was desperate to locate it, and soon others joined in the search. It was impossible to find the ring in the snow, so a concerned neighbor got his snow shovel from the bed of his truck and began scooping snow from the parking lot near where my wife had been. He filled the bed of his truck with snow, hoping the ring was in it. Because it was a spring snowstorm, he thought the weather would turn warm again soon and melt the snow, and with luck, the ring would be in the bed of his truck. As we all hoped, after a day or so, he brought the ring to our home. All of us were grateful for its safe return.

What drove my wife and the many other people who helped in her search was the value of the ring. Likewise, we should be motivated to search the scriptures because of the tremendous value they hold. Coming to know Jesus is precious to us—far more precious than diamonds or gold. As we begin to search through verses of scripture, we need to search for *Him*, expending the necessary effort to find Him

117. D. Todd Christofferson, "When Thou Art Converted," *Ensign* or *Liahona*, May 2004, 11.

and the precious truths of the gospel that will become like treasure to us. This kind of reading requires effort and intention.

I remember one of the first times I began to see the Savior in the scriptures in a place where I had never seen Him before. It was the story of Moses and the parting of the Red Sea. As I pondered the story, I realized that Israel was surround by death. On one side, the Egyptians were riding upon them coming to destroy them, and on the other side were the waters of the Red Sea, which the Israelites surely would have drowned in without divine intervention. But by the power of God, the sea was parted, and Israel walked through "death" and came out on the other side unscathed.

With this realization, the story became a testimony to me of the Lord Jehovah, Jesus Christ, who parted the sea of death for all of us through His Atonement. I have often thought how terrifying those moments would have been to face Pharoah's army on one hand and towering waves on the other. The walk across that sea would have humbled me. Now, when the death of loved ones has come, I can reflect on the parting of the Red Sea and witness the power of Jesus delivering all of us from death.

The parting of the Red Sea, though, reflects more than just overcoming death. If Jesus can part the Red Sea, what problem *can't* He solve? Seeing Him in these events touches my heart to feel His power in all aspects of my life. Thus, when we search for Him and find Him in unexpected ways, we can develop a stronger testimony of His powerful love for us. This is just one example of searching for Christ while studying.

Another way I search the scriptures is by taking my problems to the word of God. I pray about my problems before I read and then search the verses looking for answers. I have often found comfort and direction this way. Looking at footnotes helps as well. Many times, they unlock passages. I also study with a dictionary. I prefer Webster's 1828 dictionary for the Doctrine and Covenants and Book of Mormon because it was published around the same time both books were compiled in English. I refer to a Hebrew concordance for the Old Testament and a Greek one for the New Testament. All these resources can unlock key passages. Often, I look at the Scripture Citation Index, a website that cites every instance a scripture is referenced in general conference.[118] This tool can be powerful because it shows how General Authorities understand and use verses of scripture. These are some resources that may help you in your study as you search the scriptures. There are many other resources too, but no matter which sources we utilize, the most important thing is that we *search* in order to understand God's word.

Likening

"For I did liken all scriptures unto us, that it might be for our profit and learning" (1 Nephi 19:23).

While quoting the words of Moses, Nephi suggested that he did "liken" them to his people. One of the powerful moments of Nephi likening scripture to himself was in 1 Nephi 3 and 4. While trying to get the brass plates from Laban, he and his brothers seemed to be failing. Laman and Lemuel questioned whether God could deliver the plates into their hands. Nephi responded, "Let us be strong like unto Moses; for he truly spake unto the waters of the Red Sea and they divided hither and thither, and our fathers came through, out of captivity, on dry ground" (1 Nephi 4:2). As Nephi sought to fulfill God's commandments, he saw himself like Moses who also sought to fulfill God's commands. Nephi knew that if God could defeat Pharoah and his armies for Moses, He could defeat Laban and his fifty for him.

Likening is what we do to improve our reading and transform it into scripture study. This kind of study brings us closer to Christ as we see ourselves in the scriptures and see how He can strengthen and help us. Recently, I was teaching about Doctrine and Covenants 110 in a religious class. Trying to help my students understand what it means to liken the scriptures, I asked them to read verse 7 to see if they could put themselves into the verse and make it about their lives. One young woman read it like this: "For behold, I have accepted [your life], and my name shall be [on it]; and I will manifest myself unto [you] in

118. The Scripture Citation Index can be found at scriptures.byu.edu.

mercy [because of how you are living your life]." We discussed how powerful it is to see ourselves in the scriptures and how her perspective expanded the meaning of the verse for each of us.

I noticed that another young woman appeared moved by the conversation. I asked her if she'd be willing to share what she was feeling. Very quietly, in a humble voice, she said, "The verse says the word *mercy*. As we read it, I thought maybe God could have mercy on me. I felt like He would accept me." This was an important moment for her. She had shared with us openly that she struggled with self-image, depression, and anxiety. Her comment reflected someone deeply moved by what she had learned about herself and the Savior's acceptance of her. Later I talked with her about this moment, and she said, "I can still feel His love for me right now. If I were alone, I would be crying." She had an experience right in front of us that changed her life. To hear her sweet testimony lifted us all and especially changed her. It came from putting herself in the scriptures.

Thus, likening means to put ourselves into the scriptures. And when we understand the context of a passage, likening becomes even more powerful. For instance, as we studied Doctrine and Covenants 110:7, we also emphasized that "this house" referred to the Kirtland Temple. As we continued our conversation, a young man drew the connection that we each could "build a house"—meaning our lives were like a house built unto God—and then present it as an offering to Him. Someone else suggested that our bodies are temples, and by living righteously, we are presenting a sacrifice to the Lord by keeping ourselves clean and pure like the temple.

While verse 7 teaches that the Saints could go to the Kirtland Temple to experience the Savior manifesting Himself to them, in a broader application, *we* can go to *any* temple and experience the Lord's blessings. Further still, we can make our lives living temples, which the Lord might accept and bless with His presence. Both the literal and the figurative meanings of the verse are powerful. Go to the temple and see God manifest, or become a temple to God and also see His power in your life. Studying brings power to understand what the prophet meant when he received the revelation, but likening opens the door to see what the scriptures might mean for us personally as we deepen our relationship with the Savior.

We can practice likening simply by asking, "What might this verse mean in my life?" We can also insert our name into the verse. We might ask, "Why would the Lord say these words to me? How could I gain access to the power of these verses in my personal life?" One way I have found power to liken is to first look for keywords and phrases, circling or underling them. Then I construct those keywords and phrases into a statement of truth—the main idea taught in the verses—and ask, "Why is this truth relevant in my life?" Whatever you do while studying, prayerfully seeking to liken the scriptures to your life can bring great power into what you are studying.

Pondering

"I sat in my room pondering over the scriptures . . . [and] the eyes of my understanding were opened, and the Spirit of the Lord rested upon me" (Doctrine and Covenants 138:1, 11).

In these verses of scripture, President Joseph F. Smith recounted his experience struggling with the death of his son, the Apostle Hyrum Mack Smith. Turning to the scriptures for comfort, as President Smith studied, he began to ponder the verses he had read. As he pondered, the Spirit revealed things he had never known before, and he received a new revelation for the Church.

Pondering the scriptures can bring powerful results. President Henry B. Eyring defined pondering this way: "Reading, studying, and pondering are not the same. We read words and we may get ideas. We study and we may discover patterns and connections in scripture. But when we ponder, we invite revelation by the Spirit. Pondering, to me, is the thinking and the praying I do after reading and studying in the scriptures carefully."[119] For me, this act of pondering means reflecting not only on the words and their meaning but how they relate to me. Typically, some impression from the Spirit touches me while reading. A fleeting thought emerges of a past event or a current

119. Henry B. Eyring, "Serve with the Spirit," *Ensign* or *Liahona*, Nov. 2010, 60.

problem. When I ponder, I prayerfully connect the dots between these gentle impressions and what I have just read. For instance, the Spirit begins to fill in the gaps between Nephi's, Joseph Smith's, or Elijah's experience and what I am going through currently.

Further, Elder D. Todd Christofferson added some technical details of what pondering might look like:

> [Consider] reading a few verses, stopping to ponder them, carefully reading the verses again, and as you think about what they mean, praying for understanding, asking questions in your mind, waiting for spiritual impressions, and writing down the impressions and insights that come so you can remember and learn more. Studying in this way, you may not read a lot of chapters or verses in a half hour, but you will be giving place in your heart for the word of God, and He will be speaking to you.[120]

Sometimes this pondering requires me to talk to someone about what I am feeling and thinking. I need someone to listen to me, and as I talk about my concerns with them, I see my situation in a new light. Talking about problems is part of our covenant to "mourn with those that mourn . . . and comfort those that stand in need of comfort" (Mosiah 18:9). We can continue pondering as we discuss what we read and listen to others' thoughts.

Finally, I find I cannot ponder well unless I write down my thoughts. I use a notebook and a plain graphite pencil so I can easily erase what I write down as I ponder. I use my electronic scriptures to take notes and regularly formulate my thoughts. And I also use a journal—actually, multiple journals: one on paper and one electronic. For example, I keep my electronic journal by me when I pray about the scriptures after studying them. I often need to pause the conversation with the Lord and ask His permission to write down the thoughts He gives me. This kind of pondering brings me closer to the Lord as I study His word. Pondering is power.

---

120. D. Todd Christofferson, "When Thou Art Converted," 11.

Acting

"I will go and do the things which the Lord hath commanded" (1 Nephi 3:7).

As Lehi received the Lord's commandments, he invited his sons to obey. Scripture represents the commandments the Lord gives to His prophets. Therefore, like Nephi, we need to study the Lord's commandments and then receive them through obedience. This process is not always easy or straightforward. As Nephi and his brothers sought to obtain the brass plates, their efforts failed multiple times. Finally, Laman and Lemuel were ready to return home, but Nephi responded, "As the Lord liveth, and as we live, we will not go down unto our father in the wilderness until we have accomplished the thing which the Lord hath commanded us" (1 Nephi 3:15). This kind of determined response when facing opposition is what we all need when problems come and our faith is tested. Then, like Nephi, we may find ourselves out of good ideas, having to move forward while simply being "led by the Spirit, not knowing beforehand the things which [we] should do" (1 Nephi 4:6).

This kind of sightless faith—not seeing beforehand but acting regardless of our limited understanding—provides the Lord with an opportunity to reveal Himself to us. When we successfully arrive at the other side of such experiences, we may faithfully conclude, "There is no way I could ever have accomplished that on my own. Only with God's help could I have done what I just did."

Elder David A. Bednar described this kind of faith-produced knowledge. He explained it using the events of the priests carrying the ark of the covenant into the promised land (see Joshua 3:7–17). As the priests approached the river Jordan, Joshua prophesied that the water would part as the priests stepped into the river; Israel would cross into Jordan led by the Lord, just as they had crossed the Red Sea after Moses led them out of Egypt. Of this event, Elder Bednar said, "Interestingly, the waters did not part as the children of Israel stood on the banks of the river waiting for something to happen; rather, the soles of their feet were wet before the water parted. The faith of the

Israelites was manifested in the fact that they walked into the water before it parted."[121]

One truth the Israelites may have learned that day was the power of God to lead them into the promised land. Yet they could not have learned that lesson without faith. This wasn't just something they gleaned from scripture study—they could only learn this lesson as they obeyed the prophet's words and acted in faith.

We too can learn this way. The Lord has described it as learning "by study and also by faith" (Doctrine and Covenants 88:118). As we have outlined here, we can learn by study as we diligently spend time in the scriptures, searching and pondering God's word, and likening what we learn to our lives. Yet that is not enough. We must then, through our faith, put into practice the truth we have received.

As we seek to apply what we learn in the scriptures, we gain an additional kind of knowledge. Nephi described this knowledge as God led him and his family across the desert to the promised land. He said, "For the Lord had not hitherto suffered that we should make much fire, as we journeyed in the wilderness; for he said: *I* will make thy food become sweet, that ye cook it not" (1 Nephi 17:12; emphasis added). Notice the Lord stating that He would do something for Nephi and his family that they could not do for themselves. The Lord continued, "And *I* will also be your light in the wilderness; and *I* will prepare the way before you, if it so be that ye shall keep my commandments; wherefore, inasmuch as ye shall keep my commandments ye shall be led towards the promised land; and *ye shall know* that it is by me that ye are led" (verse 13). Notice again that the Lord did what they could not do for themselves, but here He also states that, as a result, "[they] shall know" what God did for them. Finally, the Lord concluded, "After ye have arrived in the promised land, *ye shall know* that I, the Lord, am God; and that I, the Lord, did deliver you from destruction; yea, that I did bring you out of the land of Jerusalem" (verse 14).

---

121. David A. Bednar, "Seek Learning By Faith," *Ensign*, Sept. 2007, 63.

This account of Nephi's life encapsulates the kind of faith-produced knowledge we all need. As we obey God, He does for us things we cannot do for ourselves. As we continue in our obedience, we gain a sure knowledge that God is real, that He loves us, and that He is working to bring about our salvation as we obey Him. This kind of knowledge is what the Savior described when He said, "If any man will do his will, he shall know of the doctrine, whether it be of God, or whether I speak of myself" (John 7:17). We know God and His doctrine in an entirely different way by our obedience than we could ever learn by study alone. This, in my opinion, is one of the most powerful ways the Savior manifests Himself unto us and how we come to know Him personally.

Searching for Doctrines and Principles

As we develop greater skills with studying God's word, we need to focus our attention on the doctrines and principles of Christ's teachings, whether from His own words or the words of His prophets. Boyd K. Packer taught, "True doctrine, understood, changes attitudes and behavior. The study of the doctrines of the gospel will improve behavior quicker than a study of behavior will improve behavior."[122] I think the reason this is true is because His doctrines are at the heart of the plan of salvation. So by learning true doctrine, we are learning Christ's plan for us.

As we study the Savior's doctrines, we come to know what is at the center of His heart. I take President Packer's quote to mean that we can either (1) focus on what we do wrong in our lives and try to change it by ourselves, or (2) consider what Christ thinks and feels about our situation, develop a relationship with Him, and then together change our nature. Through His teachings, we learn what He thinks, how He feels, and why He acts the way He does. As we understand the scriptures at this level, they help us more deeply love the Savior and desire to live His plan. When we understand the truths of

---

122. Boyd K. Packer, "Little Children," *Ensign*, Nov. 1986, 16.

God's plan, we can place our behavior in the context of God's desires. These realizations that come from studying doctrine become powerful motivators for us to change our lives.

David A. Bednar defined doctrine when he said, "Doctrine refers to the eternal, unchanging, and simple truths of the gospel of Jesus Christ. There are several key words in that definition: eternal, unchanging, simple, and truth. Doctrines are never altered. They never vary. They will always be the same. You can always count on them."[123] For example, a doctrine would be the Atonement of Jesus Christ. This central teaching of the gospel is infinite and eternal and allows all of God's children to understand how to overcome their sins (see 2 Nephi 9:6–8). Christ's doctrine answers the question *why*, such as why we need to believe certain teachings and subsequently do certain things in the gospel. People search their whole lives looking for answers as to why they are here on earth. The Savior's doctrine answers this question.

Further, Elder Bednar explained, "Doctrine answers the *why* questions of our lives. Principles provide us with direction about the *what* and the *how*."[124] This quote emphasizes our need to search the scriptures looking for principles.

Principles within Christ's teachings grow out of His doctrine. For instance, in Doctrine and Covenants 18, the Savior taught of His Atonement and how it relates to the worth of souls. He said, "Remember the worth of souls is great in the sight of God; For, behold, the Lord your Redeemer suffered death in the flesh; wherefore he suffered the pain of all men, that all men might repent and come unto him" (verses 10–11). What the Savior then invites us to do in verse 15 is to "labor all your days in crying repentance" to everyone

123. David A. Bednar, "Teach Them to Understand" (Ricks College Campus Education Week devotional, June 4, 1998).

124. David A. Bednar, "Teach Them to Understand"; emphasis added. Furthermore, Quentin L. Cook explained, "Doctrine usually answers the question 'why?' Principles usually answer the question 'what?' Whenever we emphasize *how* to do something without reference to *why* we do it or *what* we do, we risk looking beyond the mark" (Quentin L. Cook, "Looking beyond the Mark," *Ensign*, March 2003, 44).

we can. Christ's *doctrine*—His intense love for us, so much that He would give His life for us—leads us to discover a *principle:* labor all your days calling others to repent.

When we truly understand doctrine, we feel deeply connected to the Savior's way of living—love your neighbor by sharing the gospel. As the Savior connected our salvation experience to sharing the gospel, it's as if He was saying, "You know how good you feel when you experience my love and my Atonement? Wouldn't you want to share that love with everyone? It would not only make them feel good, but in heaven you would be with them. Like me, you will become a savior of sorts, bringing my salvation to them. It would be the greatest joy you could imagine. I know because it's the love I feel for them, and I want to share that love with you too."

Of course, in this manufactured dialogue, Jesus would have been speaking from personal experience. He endured the Atonement and felt the pains of all people. He witnesses the powerful changes that come into people's lives because of His love. So, when He invites us to engage in this work, He knows precisely how it feels to see others experiencing relief from sin. When we feel His redeeming love, we want others to feel this redemptive power too. Thus, our understanding the doctrine of Christ's Atonement gives rise to the principle of sharing the gospel.

As for *how* we share the gospel, this becomes a matter of personal application that we negotiate through prayer and faith. The particulars come as we understand the doctrine and principles and seek through the Spirit to know how to act on them. Clearly, as we share the gospel, we become more like Christ in bringing salvation to others, and we gain increased power to face life challenges. Our sense of purpose develops in deep, rich ways. With the joy of sharing with others comes the power to rise above our personal challenges.

There are many additional scripture study skills we could utilize to bless our experience with God's word. I did not intend to create a comprehensive list here; rather, I wanted to spark in each of us the desire to try a little harder to create a more meaningful experience with the word of God.

As Alma taught, we each need to "experiment" with the word of God and plant it—the seed—in our hearts (see Alma 32:27–28).[125] As we do so, we will draw closer to Jesus Christ, for He is God's Word. As we allow the Savior greater access to our hearts, we will feel His great power in our lives. What Elder Bruce R. McConkie described can then come to pass for us. He said, "Each pronouncement in the holy scriptures . . . is so written as to reveal little or much, depending on the spiritual capacity of the student."[126] He then described the different responses people may have: some may get nothing from their study, others may receive more, and finally some who "have the mind of Christ" (1 Corinthians 2:16) will receive effulgent rays of celestial light.

If we are going to make it through all of life's challenges, we will need to continually improve in our ability to find and understand God's will through the scriptures. We can accomplish this aim by spending more time diligently studying the scriptures, searching for the Savior, pondering His word, likening what we read to our lives, and acting on what we learn. As we study this way, we then can go forward with faith that God will show us how to return and live with Him again. He will help us overcome our challenges and eventually receive eternal life.

---

125. See also Jeffrey R. Holland, *Christ and the New Covenant* (Salt Lake City: Deseret Book, 1997), 166–69.

126. Bruce R. McConkie, *A New Witness for the Articles of Faith* (Salt Lake City: Deseret Book, 1985), 71.

9

THE TEMPLE

MDM

"They found him in the temple."

—Luke 2:46

As a young man preparing to serve a full-time mission, I also prepared to receive my temple endowment. Living in San Francisco while my family still resided in Utah, I planned to come to Salt Lake to attend the temple there. Early in the morning on a cold day in February 1990, my mother, stepfather, and I arrived at the Salt Lake Temple. Anxious and excited, I didn't know what to expect. As I passed through the temple doors, I felt something that to me was remarkable. There was a sensation of warmth and love that surrounded me. In fact, I felt as if a blanket of spiritual warmth enveloped me. I said nothing to anyone in my party, but I thought to myself, "Did everyone feel that way as they walked into the temple?"

The feelings remained with me throughout my experience that day. As we concluded our worship in the temple, I found myself sitting in the celestial room in hushed reverence reflecting on all I had seen, felt, and begun to learn. As I looked at the amazing architecture and contemplated what I had witnessed, my experience transcended my physical surroundings. I asked myself, "Why does everything seem so bright in here?" The effect did not come from the ambient light streaming through the windows or the artificial light coming from electric bulbs. What I perceived was a heavenly glow in the room that caused me to exclaim in my mind and heart, "What a wondrous place this is!" I consider that day to be one of the pillars of my testimony.

At some point later, when I was studying the Doctrine and Covenants, I encountered section 109, which records the dedicatory prayer for the Kirtland Temple. In that prayer, the Prophet Joseph Smith asked the Lord to bless the temple and all who entered it, "that thy glory may rest down upon thy people . . . and that all people who shall enter upon the threshold of the Lord's house may feel thy power, and feel constrained to acknowledge that thou has sanctified it, and that it is thy house, a place of holiness" (Doctrine and Covenants 109:12–13). While the Prophet Joseph Smith offered the dedicatory prayer specifically for the Kirtland Temple, the blessings he asked for that day can be manifest in any temple. God fulfilled that promise for me when I felt the sacredness of His holy house, as many people certainly have felt as they have entered the temple.

I learned that day that the temple connects us to another "world" even though we are here on earth. It acts as a sacred doorway into the heavenly presence where God can introduce feelings and ideas to elevate us, even spiritually transport us beyond the understanding of this world. It truly is "otherworldly" in its nature.

Why do we need the temple? How can it help us in our journey on earth, allowing us to endure to the end and receive the full blessings of the Savior's Atonement? These questions bring with them sacred answers, all of which we cannot fully discuss in this chapter; not only because there wouldn't be enough space but also because there are some truths God reserves to teach Himself. God intends for us to learn these truths in the temple, and we are asked not to write about or discuss them outside of the temple for fear of profaning their sacredness. Because of this, we will not discuss the sacred lessons of the temple here. Rather, I seek to create a framework to help us better understand the role of the temple as found in scripture and the words of modern prophets. In this way, a spiritually sensitive person can draw their own conclusions based on personal experience, scripture study, revelation, and continued temple attendance.

Sacred Doorways

The first part of this framework for understanding the temple is to see our gospel experiences as sacred doorways that God desires for us to pass through. The gospel of Jesus Christ presents many sacred doorways on our journey to the celestial kingdom, and the scriptures present multiple examples of these doorways. The first heavenly transition to consider comes from Abraham 3. There we learn that we spent our pre-earth life as "intelligences" with God where He presented us with our destiny: an earth where we would live and prove whether we would "do all things whatsoever the Lord [our] God shall command [us]" (verse 25).[127] By choosing to follow Heavenly Father's plan, we stepped through this first doorway.[128]

The account of Adam and Eve reveals the effects of passing through this first doorway, where those who accepted God's plan in the pre-earth life received physical bodies created in the image of God (see Genesis 1:26–27). Passing through this doorway, Adam and Eve

---

127. I realize there is some debate about what an intelligence is—whether as an intelligence we were individuals, or whether intelligence is merely the stuff God organized us from. For purposes of this book, I assume the position that an intelligence is an individual. For a deeper study of this topic, please see James E. Faulconer and Susannah Morrison, "The King Follett Discourse, Pinnacle or Peripheral?," *BYU Studies*, vol. 60, no. 3 (2021), 88–89.

128. I believe our argument for this proposition is as follows. In Abraham 3, Abraham described those who kept their first estate. In the Webster's 1828 dictionary, the word *estate* is defined as one's "status" or "standing." Thus, those who kept their status or standing in the pre-earth life were added upon; that is, they came to earth and received physical bodies. Verse 28 suggests Lucifer did not keep his first estate; therefore, he was not "added upon." He did not receive the sacred opportunity to gain a body and progress in godliness.

entered "a state of innocence, having no joy, for they knew no misery; doing no good, for they knew no sin" (2 Nephi 2:23). But God's plan of salvation did not conclude with human beings as naive children—it continued with them becoming "free forever, knowing good from evil; to act for themselves and not to be acted upon" (2 Nephi 2:26). For us to achieve this level of awareness, Adam and Eve needed to pass through a second doorway we call the Fall.

The Fall represents a significant change where we became mortal for a period of time, cast out of God's presence, entering into a probationary state where we might repent and improve our condition (see Genesis 2:17; Moses 4:25, 31; 2 Nephi 2:21–22). In our mortal, fallen state, we are subject to the "natural man" (Mosiah 3:19), our flesh or genetics. We can also be subject to social and environmental influences that can limit our abilities by clouding our understanding (see Doctrine and Covenants 123:12). And we are subject to Lucifer who can tempt and try us. God allowed these conditions to influence us so we could know the "bitter" and learn to prize the "sweet" (see Doctrine and Covenants 29:39).

This test—overcoming our fallen condition—is very real, with each of us learning to calm the storm of emotions and worldly desires and the subsequent flood of temptations that come with them. This experience is essential for our progression to godhood. God's objective during this period of development seems to be for us not to eliminate our passions but to "bridle" them (see Alma 38:12)—to become disciplined enough to choose our response to them rather than allowing our passions to rule over us (see Alma 38:12). Thus, our development requires self-mastery and discipline.

Continuing on with the progression of our souls, God provided yet another doorway where we are to accept His gospel by covenant at baptism (see Acts 22:16; Doctrine and Covenants 39:10). Our baptismal covenant allows us access to the heavenly gift of the Holy Ghost. Through the power of the Atonement of Jesus Christ, the Holy Ghost helps sanctify (or purify) our souls.[129] He functions through Christ's Atonement to give us strength to overcome our sinful desires and become godlier still.

While there are additional covenants we need to make, I will not discuss those here.[130] Our focus in this book is to realize the value of accepting baptism and receiving the gift of the Holy Ghost. In so doing, we place our feet on the covenant path of discipleship. This path gives us fuller access to the divine grace of Jesus Christ and His redeeming power.[131] And as we progress along the covenant path, we come to the penultimate doorway: the gateway we call the temple.[132]

---

129. See 3 Nephi 27:20. Elder D. Todd Christofferson taught that repentance comes a combination of our act of changing, Jesus's Atonement through His grace, and the administration of the power of the Holy Ghost. He said, "This is help that can come only through divine grace, administered by the Holy Ghost" (D. Todd Christofferson, "Why the Covenant Path," *Liahona*, May 2021, 118).
130. While there are other doorways for men, specifically receiving the Aaronic and Melchizedek Priesthoods, I will leave the conversation of this doorway for another time. If you desire to know more, you could study the topic of the oath and covenant of the priesthood. See also chapter 6 of this book.
131. In his seminal book *The Mediation and Atonement of Jesus Christ*, President John Taylor explained the Savior's power to assist us in bringing about this change. This book is worth studying to better understand Jesus Christ's redeeming power.
132. One could argue there are more doorways than I outline in this chapter. For instance, death could be seen as the final doorway of this life, leading to our resurrection, which designates the kind of body we receive (see 1 Corinthians 15:40–42). And ultimately, our final judgment signifies the conclusion of our progression, where we are permitted access into the celestial kingdom. For simplicity, I am considering these events as conditional to the Savior reintroducing us into the presence of the Father. I am assuming each of these foregoing moments does not need to take place for us to be reintroduced into God's presence. I believe Joseph Smith had his calling and election made sure prior to these events. I see our calling and election as a formative moment in our progression, which leads to the kind of resurrection we receive and subsequently our inheriting eternal life (see Doctrine and Covenants 131:5; 2 Peter 1; Guide to the Scriptures, "Calling and Election," scriptures.ChurchofJesusChrist.org).

A Gateway to the Celestial Kingdom

Returning to the account of Adam and Eve, we recall from Abraham 3 that we left our heavenly home where we resided in the presence of God. The conditions Adam and Eve were born into were paradisiacal, a *terrestrial sphere* where they could live indefinitely and God could personally interact with them. At the time of the Fall, they were "cast out" of God's presence and, by extension, we with them. As a result of the Fall, we all entered a *telestial condition*, where suffering and fatigue affect us and hunger and thirst are constant. We no longer live in God's presence and are subject to temptation and sin. Eventually, we all will die physically, ending our mortal condition and this probationary period. Lehi said of this event, "Adam fell that men might be; and men are, that they might have joy" (2 Nephi 2:25). Thus, our step down in glory was also a step forward in progression toward eternal life. We gained bodies, allowing us to become more like our Heavenly Father, but in these bodies, we now face the "natural man" (or "natural woman" as the case may be). In response to the Fall, we needed power to overcome sin and death. Jesus Christ provided this power, which gives us the ability to rise from our fallen condition and return to the presence of God glorified and exalted.

In addition to the Savior's Atonement, the temple provides for us a gateway between the world we now live in and the world we desire acceptance into. Hugh Nibley explained this gateway relationship. He described how we currently live in a telestial state, and the temple and its ordinances provide the means for us to mediate between the telestial world and celestial world. Speaking of an early Christian text, Dr. Nibley wrote, "The purpose of such [temple] ordinances is to bridge the space between the world in which we now live, the telestial world, and that to which we aspire, the celestial world. Therefore, the events of the temple were thought [by these early Christians] to take place in the terrestrial sphere."[133] Nibley continued by noting that the word *telestial* implies someone who is an initiate into the sacred rites of the

133. Hugh Nibley, *Temple and Cosmos* (Salt Lake City: Deseret Book, 1992), 27.

temple, a beginner, or one who seeks to achieve his or her *telos* or "complete" or "perfect" self. He also explained that the mysteries of God refer to the sacred, holy rites of the temple. There in the temple the initiate would gain power to achieve the perfection he or she sought for—the celestial glory of God.

These thoughts align with what we know from the Doctrine and Covenants. The temple is governed by the Melchizedek Priesthood. The temple is the place where we can receive all of God's ordinances and covenants pertaining to the celestial world. Of these ordinances, we learn that "this greater [Melchizedek] priesthood administereth the gospel and holdeth the key of the *mysteries of the kingdom*, even the key of the knowledge of God" (Doctrine and Covenants 84:19; emphasis added). In the Greek New Testament, the word *mysterion* is commonly understood to mean the "secret rites" given only to those who are initiated into the Church.[134] These mysteries are the truths revealed by God to those who are prepared to receive them. In the restored gospel of Jesus Christ, we receive these mysteries, at least in part, through the ordinances of the temple, and without them the "power of godliness is not manifest unto men in the flesh" (Doctrine and Covenants 84:21).

We believe that worthiness to receive these mysteries comes through entering the covenant path of baptism and staying on the covenant path by keeping the promises we made. Then we must continue until we qualify for the blessings of the temple and become someone who is "recommended to the Lord"[135] as one worthy to enter His presence. Thus, through the process of making and keeping covenants, we enter the gateway between the telestial, fallen world and

134. *Theological Dictionary of the New Testament* (Grand Rapids, MI: Eerdmans Publishing, 1977), s. v. "mystērion." (Accessed via the e-Sword mobile application, see G3466.) See also Galen W. Wiley, "A Study of the Word 'Mystery' in the New Testament," *Grace Theological Journal*, 1985, 349–60; and Hugh Nibley's *Temple and Cosmos*.

135. Ronald A. Rasband, "Recommended to the Lord," *Ensign* or *Liahona*, Nov. 2020, 22.

the celestial, exalted one. The temple is our gateway between where we are and where we want to be.

Access to the Grace of Jesus Christ

The Savior enables us to receive a greater abundance of God's love so that we may overcome the "natural" or "fallen" element of our current condition. One way He helps us receive His grace is in the temple. President Russell M. Nelson explained, "Everything taught in the temple, through instruction and through the Spirit, increases our understanding of Jesus Christ. His essential ordinances bind us to Him through sacred priesthood covenants. Then, as we keep our covenants, He endows us with His healing, strengthening power."[136] As we qualify for His help and strength through our righteous desires and actions, the Savior is bound to us through covenants, and then His power can bless us in many ways. The following examples illustrate some of these blessings.

Marriage is a potent source of potential happiness. At the same time, it holds an equal possibility for misery. Think of all the damaged lives people experience because of broken marital vows. It's no wonder I once heard a man say to his friends, "Trust me, I've been married. No one in his right mind would want to do that. It was awful!" Many factors can lead to a miserable marriage. Selfishness, health challenges, incompatibility of interests, differing life choices, and a host of other factors can contribute.

When my wife and I first met and started dating, one evening we were talking about activities we might do together. I've always loved being outdoors in nature, but my wife-to-be didn't know that yet. Freely sharing her thoughts, she said, "In my family, we have the F-word, 'fishing,' along with the H-word, 'hiking,' and the C-word, 'camping'!" Immediately I realized that, for her, all my favorite activities were swear words! What went through my mind was, "I could

---

136. Russell M. Nelson, "The Temple and Your Spiritual Foundation," *Liahona*, Nov. 2021, 93–94.

never marry this girl!" Well, I was wrong. We've now celebrated 27 years of marriage together, but not without difficulty.

We've had many disagreements. Our interests and likes are very different. And sometimes those disagreements have been intense. When we've faced significant challenges together, we've always overcome them through love and patience. We have learned to set aside our differences. The greatest strength we have that binds us together is our temple covenant. When we got married, we promised each other and God that we would stay together, not for time only but for all eternity. We have had to say to each other more than once, "So, what are we going to do about this problem?" And each time, we have prayerfully continued to work through our differences.

Throughout these experiences, we've both become less judgmental and have removed many biases. We are more capable of understanding and certainly more compassionate toward each other. For us, none of these qualities have come easily. We have to qualify for them so the Savior can refine us, for it is *He* who has changed our hearts. As a result, we are new people, healed by the supernal power of Christ's grace extended to us through His Atonement and sealed upon us through temple covenants. To me, this portion of our conversion is most satisfying because I truly love my wife and want to be with her for eternity. The fulfillment of this desire can only come through repentance and change, enabled by the Savior's power to refine us and seal us together forever.

In one of my favorite Old Testament passages, the Savior said to a lost and scattered house of Israel, "A new heart also will I give you, and a new spirit will I put within you: and I will take away the stony heart out of your flesh, and I will give you an heart of flesh. And I will put my spirit within you, and cause you to walk in my statutes, and ye shall keep my judgments, and do them" (Ezekiel 36:26–27). This change—a true conversion from the old, natural self to the new, spiritual person—has come into our lives through remaining connected to the grace of Christ. Our temple covenants have solidified our determination to remain on the covenant path so the Savior can bring about this change.

The example of our change together is not the only one I have witnessed. For example, when I was serving in a priesthood calling, I counseled with a woman who had learned of an adulterous affair her husband had entered into. He lost his Church membership but eventually repented. Miraculously, I saw this woman forgive her wayward husband, taking him back into her life with full love and trust. Her compassionate act transcended her human capabilities, reaching into the divine realm of eternal love. Through her faith in Christ, she honored her temple covenants and remained with the man she was sealed to. Like the Savior who did not condemn the adulterous woman, this wife and mother did not condemn her sinful but repentant husband. Rarely have I witnessed such Christlike tenderness as she exhibited toward him.

I am not saying that the choice to divorce an adulterous spouse is never warranted, or that every situation should be met with this kind of acceptance. What I am saying is that the potential for healing that's available from the Savior—through His covenants and His grace—can overcome the deepest divides if people can accept Him into their hearts. Faith in temple blessings can bring motivation to accept the Savior's healing even in extremely difficult circumstances.

This kind of happiness, as President Russell M. Nelson taught, has "little to do with the circumstances of our lives and everything to do with the focus of our lives."[137] This sweet couple was able to taste this happiness. In addition, my sweet wife and I have also moved through our challenges to feel the redeeming power Jesus Christ offers to each of us. While your challenges may be different, there is no limit to the infinite power of the Savior's Atonement to heal broken hearts if we remain faithful to His covenant path.

---

137. Russell M. Nelson, "Joy and Spiritual Survival," *Ensign* or *Liahona*, Nov. 2016, 82.

A Vision of Eternity

In addition to helping us through the doorways back to our Heavenly Father's presence, there are essential teachings that can help us progress. While we may not openly discuss what we learn and experience inside the temple, we can comment on temple-related scriptures. These passages help us understand God's holy house. As we examine some of these scriptures together, we can find in them visions of eternity—a heavenly perspective. This perspective allows us to better understand how to prepare to return to the presence of God. We can learn from these passages who we are, why we are here, and what is to come when we return to God.

What we need are criteria to help us find temple scriptures. One such criterion is to examine the sacred experiences of prophets who went to "the mountain of the Lord" (Isaiah 2:2). The temple in Jerusalem was built on "the temple mount," a place of elevation. In scripture, prophets often went to a solitary, high, or hilly place to have sacred experiences. For instance, Jacob went to Bethel where he covenanted with God and saw angels descending from heaven to earth. *Bethel* in Hebrew literally means "house of God." The place commonly identified as modern-day Bethel is a hilly place, where Jacob could retreat from civilization to be alone in the presence of God.

One important temple-mountain scripture is Psalm 24:3-4. Some clarifying language from a Hebrew and English Lexicon helps us see the temple in these verses. The scripture reads, "Who shall ascend into the hill of the Lord?" The Hebrew word *har* translated as "hill" can also be read as "mountain."[138] Thus, "Who shall ascend into the *mountain* of the Lord?" Or, in other words, who can enter God's temple? A careful student of the scriptures could look for such temple scriptures and learn significant truths from them.

Another clear example is found in Moses 1 in the Pearl of Great Price. There, Moses "was caught up into an exceedingly high

---

138. *The Brown-Driver-Briggs Hebrew and English Lexicon* (Peabody, MA: Hendrickson Academic, 1994), s. v. "har." Accessed via the e-Sword mobile application (see H2022).

mountain" (verse 1) where he experienced the transcendent glory of God. What followed was a pattern based on Moses's experience that can help us understand our temples today.

First, Moses came to know God personally. There on the mountain, he "saw God face to face, and he talked with him, and the glory of God was upon [him]. . . . And the presence of God [after he had experienced it] withdrew from Moses . . . and [he] was left unto himself" (Moses 1:2, 9). Recognizing the difference of being in God's presence and then stepping out of it allowed Moses later to recognize Satan as he came to attack him.

In addition, Moses learned the reality of God and His true nature or character: "I am the Lord God Almighty, and Endless is my name" (Moses 1:3). In connection with this truth, he learned more about himself when God said, "Thou art my son" (Moses 1:4). This interaction portrays a powerful example of how each of us might increase our faith in God by knowing His nature. We must know God is real and what He is like if we are to exercise faith in Him. The *Lectures on Faith* elaborate on these two requirements, stating we cannot have sufficient faith unto salvation unless we obtain knowledge "that [God] actually exists" and obtain "a correct idea of his character, perfections, and attributes."[139] When we enter the House of the Lord, there in His presence we can come to know Him personally through the ordinances and covenants, the teachings we receive, and the personal revelation God gives us. This knowledge allows us to increase our faith in our Father in Heaven and Jesus Christ. Though we do not see God physically in the temple, we can still experience His spiritual presence there, which can be extremely powerful.

My experiences in the temple of coming to know God's character, perfections, and attributes have been instrumental in my spiritual development. Recently, I endured a trial of intense magnitude, possibly the most difficult experience of my life to date. Fortunately, it occurred when I was able to go to the temple frequently. While I was there, I took the opportunity to prayerfully study the scriptures.

---

139. *Lectures on Faith* (1985), 38.

When I go to the temple, I often ask the Lord, "What should I read while I'm here?" Often a scripture reference will come to mind, sometimes even one I'm not familiar with. I have never been disappointed when reading the scriptures in the temple, for I always find truths I need for the problems I am facing.

For me, the temple often acts like a spiritual windshield wiper, clearing away the filth of the world and leaving me with a clearer view of heavenly things. That was certainly the case during this particular visit. I felt directed to a chapter where the Savior was being wrongfully accused. As His accusers railed against Him, the scriptures say that He "answered nothing" (Matthew 27:12). As I pondered these words, I saw clearly the challenge before me, and the words in the scriptures were my answer. It was not easy for me when I finally approached the person I was to "answer nothing" to. Being wrongfully accused is a very difficult trial, and this situation was particularly painful. Yet in faith I tried to follow Jesus's example by saying nothing in my defense but simply listening to the person's concerns and feelings. To my tremendous relief, the person apologized without me offering any defense. I was praying earnestly that he might see the pain his words had caused me, and my prayer was answered. Placing my faith purely in the Savior's example stretched me to the very edge of my spiritual capacity, yet the Savior's way proved greater than my way.

In my experience, the temple is where I have come to know God's character, perfections, and attributes by reading scriptures there, going with a prayer in my heart, participating in the sacred ordinances offered therein, and observing the teachings I learn there. I believe the temple can offer each of us the relevant spiritual growth we need as we come to know God there.

Second, God revealed to Moses His plan of salvation. Moses was eyewitness to the creation (see Moses 1:4, 8). The scriptures state that he "beheld the earth . . . [and] also the inhabitants thereof . . . saying: Tell me . . . why these things are so, and by what thou madest them?" (verses 27–30). God then explained that He created the earth "by the word of my power . . . which is mine Only Begotten Son . . . and worlds without number have I created . . . by the Son. . . . And the first man of all men have I called Adam" (verses 32–34). He then explained His purpose in creating all these worlds, stating, "My work and my glory [is] to bring to pass the immortality and eternal life of man" (verse 39). Furthermore, He has created "worlds without number" and "as one earth shall pass away . . . so shall another come; and there is no end to my works" (verses 33, 38).

These verses suggest we too might learn something of the plan of salvation in our temple experience. Like Moses, we could behold the vastness of eternity there if we go looking for it. We too might see God's plan for us and find our place in the plan. President Gordon B. Hinckley taught that the temple "becomes a school of instruction in the sweet and sacred things of God. Here we have outlined the plan of a loving Father in behalf of His sons and daughters of all generations. Here we have sketched before us the odyssey of man's eternal journey from premortal existence through this life to the life beyond. Great fundamental and basic truths are taught with clarity and simplicity well within the understanding of all who hear."[140] Our temple experience can place our mortal lives into an eternal perspective, helping us see where we came from and why we are here on earth, and giving us hope for where we long to end up if we are faithful to our covenants.

For Moses, gaining this perspective led him to exclaim, "For this cause I know that man is nothing, which thing I never had supposed" (Moses 1:10). I don't read this verse as Moses being negative about himself. I see him as having his vision expanded to see God's greatness.

One of my daughters was married the end of December 2021. Shortly after the sealing ceremony, the temple sealer asked her and her new husband to stand between the two mirrors that face each other. He asked them to look behind them. "There," he said, "is a representation of all your ancestors who came before you. That's a lot, isn't it?" Then he asked them to look ahead. "There you can see a representation of your descendants. That's a lot too!" There was a laugh from all of us as we watched this exchange and saw the look of joy on the newlyweds' faces.

---

140. Gordon B. Hinckley, "The Salt Lake Temple," *Ensign*, Mar. 1993, 6.

What was happening for my daughter and her husband was that they were gaining an eternal perspective. The temple in many ways allows us to see the "welding link" the Prophet Joseph Smith described that binds us together in the eternities (see Doctrine and Covenants 128:18). Without Jesus Christ's Atonement, we could not qualify for these blessings. Without His Resurrection and our subsequent life after death, our sealing in the temple would be pointless. The Savior's power binds us together, and our experiences in understanding the plan of salvation in the temple help us find our place in the cosmos.

Third, gaining an eternal perspective can allow us, like Moses, to see our divine potential. Going back to the sacred vision found in Moses 1, God communicated to Moses his role in the plan, saying, "I have a work for thee, Moses, my son; thou art in the similitude of mine Only Begotten" (verse 6). Knowing of his divine nature must have been powerfully motivating for Moses. Likewise, each of us have within ourselves something of the divine. How we access that potential is an important realization each of us needs to achieve.

As human beings, we often think a lot about our similitude. We look at ourselves in the mirror. We compare ourselves to other people on social media. We look at someone else's house, car, clothes, or job and compare what we have, either to our joy or consternation. Yet God showed Moses a far more meaningful "mirror" to reflect upon: "I have a work for thee" and "thou are in the similitude of mine Only Begotten." Knowing God has something for us to do in this life can be a powerful motivator. For me, I have often gone to the temple prayerfully seeking to know more about my patriarchal blessing. I have felt deep and meaningful impressions there that help me see what God's "work" for me might mean. Each of us can go to the temple seeking this knowledge: "What is my work, Heavenly Father?"

Joy D. Jones shared in general conference the story of Renu Singh. Renu explained her experience growing up in India, saying, "I didn't really feel that I was very special." She continued, "My society and culture didn't really teach me that I had any value as an individual. When I learned . . . that I was a daughter of our Heavenly Father, it changed me. Suddenly I felt so special—God had actually created me and had created my soul and my life with value and purpose." She explained the transformation this knowledge had on her life. Before she learned the gospel, she found herself constantly having to prove to other people that she was "someone special." Once she knew who she was in God's eyes, she said, "I didn't have to prove anything to anyone. I knew I was special."[141]

We each need this kind of understanding to help us see our place in God's plan. How we come to know this truth is personal and can happen in many ways. Moses taught us that one of the powerful ways we can learn who we are is to go to God's temple. Regardless of where or how we discover it, we need to seek this "temple" knowledge, knowing who we are and that we have divine potential. It will change our perspective and deepen our self-worth.

Fourth, the endowment is a gift of power. The early Saints were instructed to gather to Ohio where the Lord promised, "There you shall be endowed with power from on high" (Doctrine and Covenants 38:32). Brigham Young taught, "Your endowment is, to receive all those ordinances in the house of the Lord, which are necessary for you, after you have departed this life, to enable you to walk back to the presence of the Father."[142] Thus, our principal gift of power is the ability to return to God and gain entrance into His presence. Yet there is so much more of the power of the temple we can receive if we seek it.

One way we can look at the endowment is as a gift of knowledge. Moses's experience was, in part, an endowment of knowledge. To explain this further, let me use an example related to my own home.

My wife and I have chosen to divide the labor at home along traditional lines. For example, she does most of the cooking. This decision was made primarily because she's an amazing chef and baker. It didn't take long for to me throw up my hands in defeat, thinking, "Why would I ever try to compete with what she can do in the kitchen?" But one of the unintended consequences of that decision is that I've

---

141. Joy D. Jones, "Value Beyond Measure," *Ensign* or *Liahona*, Nov. 2017, 13.

142. *Discourses of Brigham Young*, sel. John A. Widtsoe (1954), 416.

rarely worked at learning how to cook. Yet there are times when she needs me to take over things for her, and I'm seriously at a loss of what to do. It's not because I can't learn or because I don't care—I've just never taken the time to become familiar with what I might do in the kitchen. As a result, she's often frustrated when she gives me simple tasks and I don't know how to do them well. What is commonplace to her is foreign to me. Yet the reverse is also true. I've spent my time learning to work on cars and repair and remodel our home, and she wants nothing to do any of these greasy, dirty jobs. We've laughed at our equal differences between us. She would be completely lost under the hood of a car, wiring an outlet, or repairing drywall.

What we see from these examples is the power of knowledge and also experience using that knowledge. When someone knows nothing about the kitchen or auto mechanics, they are incapable of doing the most basic tasks. Likewise, when we know nothing of the knowledge of eternity, the plan of salvation, or God's power, we are limited in our understanding and abilities. If we fail to make and keep covenants associated with that knowledge, we cannot perform the godlike tasks we could otherwise engage in. Someone who has been invited into God's house to sit with Him and learn from Him can obtain infinitely greater power to overcome evil and perform godlike acts of righteousness. The temple endowment is a gift of power, and one of the ways that power comes to us is in the form of knowledge about who we are, why we are here on earth, and where we can end up if we remain on the covenant path. That knowledge is powerful.

Fifth, Moses's understanding of his role in the plan specifically gave him power over Satan. After seeing the heavenly vision of the Creation, Satan came to Moses. In response, "Moses looked upon Satan and said: Who art thou? For behold, I am a son of God, in the similitude of his Only Begotten; and where is thy glory, that I should worship thee?" (Moses 1:13). Some of God's glory remained with Moses after God left him. As a result, he could discern Satan's lack of heavenly light. Finally, Moses responded to Satan's belligerent attacks to worship him by "calling upon God." In doing so, "he received strength, and he commanded the devil, saying: Depart from me, Satan, for this one God only will I worship, which is the God of glory. . . . In the name of the Only Begotten, depart hence, Satan . . . and he departed hence" (Moses 1:20–22). From this temple-like experience, Moses learned the power of the Savior to overcome the adversary. Through prayer and in Christ's holy name, Moses rejected the devil and all his nefarious efforts.

Likewise, we increase our power over Satan as we attend the temple. This power can come from many sources, but the most influential is the increased understanding of Jesus Christ that we gain there. In addition to the specific teachings shared in the temple that emphasize the Savior, we can see His influence in many other ways. For example, we can see it through our personal worthiness to attend the temple. Without the Savior and His Atonement, we could not be worthy to attend. While our actions certainly influence our worthiness, His atoning sacrifice makes our worthiness efficacious. Also, the priesthood that functions in the temple is the Melchizedek Priesthood. We are told the ancient name of this priesthood is "the Holy Priesthood, after the Order of the Son of God" (Doctrine and Covenants 107:3). Thus, all things in the temple function through Jesus Christ. While one could argue this is true of everything in Christ's Church, it is especially relevant in the temple. Each person who enters the temple for him- or herself does so only one time. Every other time, which represents nearly all of our temple service, we perform work for someone who is dead. Without the sacrifice of Jesus Christ, He would not have vanquished death and performing this work would be pointless.

In Luke 16, we learn the parable of the rich man and Lazarus. In the parable, the rich man, after his death, found himself in the next life "tormented" in spirit prison as he experienced the effects of spiritual death. He called out to Lazarus, who rested in the "bosom" of Abraham in spirit paradise, to come and "dip the tip of his finger in water, and cool my tongue; for I am tormented in this flame" (verse 24). Abraham responded to the rich man, saying that his suffering was a just reward for his wicked behavior in life. "And beside all this, between us and you there is a great gulf fixed: so that they which would pass from hence to you cannot; neither can they pass to us, that would come from thence" (verse 26).

Referring to this parable, Joseph Fielding Smith explained, "Christ came and through his death bridged that gulf, proclaimed liberty to the captives, and the opening of this prison door to those who sat in darkness and captivity."[143] Jesus not only conquered death but crushed the gulf between the spirits in prison and those in paradise, making possible the work of salvation for the dead. As a result, the temple represents one of the great testimonies of the Savior and His power. Without Him, the work for the dead would be fruitless. Through Him, spiritual death "shall deliver up its dead . . . by the power of the resurrection" (2 Nephi 9:12). Then, by the power of His priesthood and through the vicarious work performed in the temple, the dead can become free from the grasp of sin that held them—free from spirit prison. The temple is one of the great symbols of Jesus Christ and His power.

One evening in temple, my wife and I were performing sealings and finishing a long list of names in the Mason family. There were many names, and we had stretched out this effort over a number of months. This was one of the last people to be sealed to her spouse. As we completed the sealing and were waiting for others to finish their names, I sat pondering. I did not hear a voice or see anything, but a feeling overwhelmed me, and I was positive the feelings reflected what this woman was experiencing. The thought came to my mind, "We are free!" And a feeling of total joy accompanied the thought. I pondered what could be happening in the spirit world at that time, and I had the idea that somehow this woman and her husband's ability to interact with each other had changed and that it meant they would be together.

While I do not know the details about living arrangements in the spirit world, the thought that was with me was, "What if they could not live as husband and wife until now, yet somehow these two

---

143. Joseph Fielding Smith, *Doctrines of Salvation*, comp. Bruce R. McConkie (1955), 2:158.

happily married people now could experience a relationship together they were not capable of experiencing beforehand?" While I have no way of knowing precisely what is happening in the spirit world, whatever that change was, they were free and filled with immense joy. I got to feel a portion of that joy with them. Each of us can experience the joy of bringing freedom to our ancestors as we engage in temple work. That feeling is akin to what the Savior must feel as He frees all of us from sin and death. We can participate with Him in bringing to pass the "immortality and eternal life" (Moses 1:39) of God's children.

Finally, we learn from Moses about an event with Adam and Eve that set in motion a way of life for us that is dedicated to making sacrifices in the name of God and His Son. The account states that after being driven from the Garden of Eden, Adam and Eve heard God speaking from the garden. He said they should worship Him by offering "the firstlings of their flocks, for an offering unto the Lord" (Moses 5:5). The account continues, "After many days an angel of the Lord appeared unto Adam, saying: Why dost thou offer sacrifices unto the Lord? And Adam said unto him: I know not, save the Lord commanded me" (verse 6). What Adam and Eve learned then transformed their understanding. The angel said, "This thing is a similitude of the sacrifice of the Only Begotten of the Father, which is full of grace and truth" (verse 7).

We can interpret this experience as Adam and Eve learning of the Savior and His eventual sacrifice for them. He overcame their transgression in the Garden of Eden, making it possible for them to return to the presence of God and overcome their sins in mortality. Yet there is something else they learned from this experience. The angel went on to say, "Wherefore, thou shalt do all that thou doest in the name of the Son, and thou shalt repent and call upon God in the name of the Son forevermore" (Moses 5:8).

Speaking of animal sacrifice, the Prophet Joseph Smith wrote, "Certainly, the shedding of the blood of a beast could be beneficial to no man, except it was done in imitation, or as a type, or explanation of what was to be offered through the gift of God Himself—and this performance done with an eye looking forward in faith on the power of that great Sacrifice for the remission of sins."[144] In other words, no animal sacrifice could save us. Yet Adam and Eve were expected to offer sacrifices to God, obviously commemorating the Savior's sacrifice. Was this offering just to teach them about what Jesus would do?

I suggest there is another meaning we could learn from. I believe offering the animal was not the real sacrifice. The angel asked Adam and Eve to combine with the offering an act of repentance, and I believe *this* act was the real sacrifice. Neal A. Maxwell also taught, "So it is that real, personal sacrifice never was placing an animal on the altar. Instead, it is a willingness to put the animal in us upon the altar and letting it be consumed!"[145] Thus, Moses's temple experience teaches us that we in Christlike ways can learn to sacrifice our sins to God. This is what it means to repent.

Each of us does things we know we should not do. We get angry with people, listen to things we know are bad, or watch things we know we should not. We certainly cannot say that doing them is "in the name of the Only Begotten." The sacrifice we can offer in the similitude of the Only Begotten is to remove these things from our lives. Likewise, there is a host of things we know we *should* be doing that we do not do. We could be better ministers, engage more in scripture study, or spend more time with our children. The list is long. Beginning to do one of these things is also a sacrifice of our will and our time in the name of the Only Begotten.

Originally, in the temples of old, such sacrifices of lambs and doves and such were brought to the temple, and people offered them there to remember what God had done for them in delivering them from Egypt. Thoughtful temple-goers realized the message from Adam that the real deliverance was from sin and death. But those who were even more thoughtful accepted that the animal was not the sacrifice, but rather it represented what they should give up or start doing in the name of Jesus Christ or in similitude to His sacrifice.

---

144. *Teachings of Presidents of the Church: Joseph Smith* (2007), 48.

145. Neal A. Maxwell, "Deny Yourselves of All Ungodliness," *Ensign*, May 1995, 68.

For us, we can make this kind of temple sacrifice as well. We know Jesus is the Lamb of God (see Revelation 12:11). We know that in Gethsemane, Jesus was offered as the Lamb for us, and that prior to the event, as He ate the Passover meal with His disciples, He introduced the ordinance of the sacrament (see Matthew 26:17–30). There, the bread and wine (or for us, water) became the emblems of His body and blood. We too can come to the sacrament and think of His death and Resurrection. We can offer to God our sacrifice of "a broken heart and a contrite spirit" (3 Nephi 9:20). But this offering is not the bread and water—it is our hearts changing and spirits uniting with God to sacrifice our sins.

As I have thought about this kind of sacrifice, I have realized how this kind of thinking might change me. It's clear that God wants me to give to Him. When I combine the Savior's efforts to offer Himself with the idea of me making my offerings "in similitude of the Only Begotten," I feel a different sense of power. I want to give like Jesus gave. I want to show my appreciation to Him for all that He did for me.

Speaking of this idea with a young man I know, I saw in his face a total change of countenance. I asked him what he was feeling because of this idea. He said, "I'm not afraid to serve a mission anymore." I asked him why. He said, "I love hockey. It's my life. I've been so afraid to serve a mission because I would have to give up playing hockey. I now understand that Jesus loves me, and if I'm supposed to play hockey after my mission, He'll bless me with that. I'm not afraid anymore to give up hockey to serve Him." I saw in this young man the power of sacrificing something in the similitude of the Only Begotten. Each of us can learn to make sacrifices in His name. This concept, according to scripture, is a temple concept. Engaging in sacrifice helps us think more about the Savior and encourages us to strive to be more like Him. This is the essence of the temple.

The temple is central to understanding Jesus Christ and coming to know Him personally. We can experience this kind of relationship as we worship in the temple. There, we can learn to know God personally, we can accept the ordinances and covenants of the priesthood, and we can learn to become more like the Son of God. As we pass through the sacred doors of the temple, we are reminded of the journey we are taking from God's presence to earth and back again. Like Adam and Eve, we too left God's home and now live in a fallen world. What we gain in the temple will help us overcome sin and death and return worthily to God's presence. There we strengthen our testimony of Jesus Christ and learn to become more like the Only Begotten.

10

THE ATONEMENT OF JESUS CHRIST

MDM

"Therefore I would that ye should be perfect even as I, or your Father who is in heaven is perfect."

—3 Nephi 12:48

In 1988, I found myself in Bishop George Matthews' office. I needed his help. I told him what I was doing in my life and that I knew I needed to change, and then I held my breath. I fully expected Bishop Matthews to tell me how awful I was. Instead, this loving man looked me in the eyes and said, "Do you know what you need? You need to come to know Jesus Christ. I want you to read the Book of Mormon every day until you find Him."

I remember thinking, "That's it? I can do that." I began reading immediately that evening. I don't remember many details about my experience at first. I recall gradually feeling better about myself. Little changes started happening, like who I associated with, what I listened to, how I spoke, and what I did. The transformation was gradual, but it was powerful just the same. As I continued reading, my experiences became more meaningful, until one day something significant happened.

Sitting in the City College of San Francisco Library, I was reading 3 Nephi 17. This day was different than the previous days of study. I felt like I was there with Jesus when He asked the people to bring forward all who were sick and afflicted and then healed them. When He knelt on the ground and prayed words that were not lawful to be written, I longed to hear those words. Then, when He gathered the little children around Him and blessed them and prayed for them, I felt like I was one of those little children. When the Savior wept for them, something happened inside me. I felt He was weeping for me. I felt His love. I knew He loved me. I felt set free.

As I was growing up, every time I did something wrong, I thought God was out to punish me. I thought he was the Reckoner of Justice. I expected to be punished by Him for every sin, and I feared Him. That moment in the library, I began to realize who He really was. Jesus became for me someone who weeps when I sin—not out of disappointment but because of the pain sin causes me and how hard my life becomes as a result. Writing these words, I feel again His great love, not just for me but for everyone who needs Him. Jesus loves us despite our weaknesses and sins. He wants to forgive us so we can become free.

With these thoughts in mind, His words ring out, "Come unto me, all ye that labour and are heavy laden, and I will give you rest" (Matthew 11:28). Rest from what? In one sense, from our sins of course. Carrying our sins is heavy work, and coming to Christ and letting go of our sins will lighten our load as we set down the heavy burden. Yet the prophet Moroni added, "Come unto Christ, and *be perfected in him*, and deny yourselves of all ungodliness . . . that by his grace ye may be perfect in Christ" (Moroni 10:32; emphasis added). The Savior also commanded, "Therefore I would that *ye should be perfect* even as I, or your Father who is in heaven is perfect" (3 Nephi 12:48; emphasis added). Becoming perfect is the ultimate rest that the Savior can offer us.

That said, with all our sin and weakness, how will we become perfect? This gap between where we are where we want to be can feel daunting. It feels so far off, and there are so many challenging aspects ahead. Like someone walking and pausing in the woods, we too might think there are "miles to go before I sleep."[146] How will we get there? What strength will be required to take us from our mortal state to becoming like God? As we'll see, this can only be accomplished through the Atonement of Jesus Christ.

Christ's Power to Heal and the Virtue and Efficacy of His Covenant Path

As we make and keep covenants through God's priesthood power, we gain powerful access to the Atonement of Jesus Christ. This access becomes full when we receive God's grace to deliver us from this world of sin and make us sanctified and holy people, the Saints of God or the sons and daughters of Light.[147] Jesus Christ possesses power to change all lives and overcome all problems if we permit Him.

As I recently read Elder Jeffrey R. Holland's book, *Christ and the New Covenant*, I realized the scope of the Savior's power. Elder Holland quoted Isaiah 49 to show the many ways Jesus Christ delivers us. He raised up the scattered tribes of Israel and restored them through Moses, and He will do so again in the latter days. He is a "light to the Gentiles" (verse 6) through the Restoration of the gospel to redeem them from the Apostasy. Those who have served kings and princes will be free to worship Him. Those who have been isolated on the isles of the sea will know Him; that is, no one will be left out,

146. Robert Frost, "Stopping by Woods on a Snowy Evening," *The Poetry of Robert Frost*, ed. Edward Connery Lathem (Ballwin, MO: Holt Rinehart & Winston, 1969).

147. See Hugh Nibley, *Temple and Cosmos*, 309–310. Dr. Nibley referenced many apocryphal writings where those who have received the ordinances of the temple anciently became the Sons of Light. Obviously, in our day we would add "Daughters of Light" to describe women who have received temple ordinances. "They are those upon the right hand of the Father, for it is by their faithfulness in these things that they show they are worthy to return and inherit the Kingdom." As we participate in temple ordinances, God blesses us more fully with the grace of Jesus Christ. See also chapter 9 of this book, specifically the section "Access to the Grace of Jesus Christ."

even those in the remotest of places. Those of the "desolate heritages" (verse 8) who live in lands destroyed by war or famine will come to know Him and feel His power and peace. Those who "are in [the] darkness" (verse 9) of ignorance, oppression, or sin will be set free by Jesus. "They shall feed in the ways, and their pastures shall be in all high places" (verse 9). Truly, the day will come when Christ returns and both physical and spiritual hunger will end.

Jesus and His covenant path are the answer to all of us becoming perfect. There is no one who will be left out because the Savior forgot them. He seeks to save all. John has written that Jesus "will wipe away all tears from their eyes; and there shall be no more death, neither sorrow, nor crying, neither shall there be any more pain: for the former things are passed away" (Revelation 21:4).

I picture the day when Christ returns to earth and takes us in His magnificent arms, one by one, and dries our tears and whispers in our ears the consoling words: "It is finished. Through me, you have overcome the world." The power of Christ to heal is infinite. If we come unto Him, we can experience His love, for He is "mighty to save" (2 Nephi 31:19). Whether we experience His return in our lifetime, or we die and return to His presence, we each have the opportunity to experience this magnificent reunion and moment of healing embrace.

While we know the Savior possesses power to heal everyone, I have noticed that sometimes we doubt that healing power will come to us. We may have various reasons for our doubt, but the result is the same. Our faith in Christ is weakened, not because of His lack of power or devotion to us but because of our weakness to remain true to Him.

I began to understand the Savior and His Atonement more completely when I understood better what it meant that I had made a covenant with Him. The way I understand the Savior's covenant promise is that if I will accept Christ though faith in His name—repenting of my sins and being baptized and confirmed by proper priesthood authority—then He offers to me the power to continually overcome my sins and eventually become like Him. This process—a lifetime of repenting and trying again—allows the Savior to refine me. However, there is another obstacle I had to overcome: I had to believe Christ would accept me.

I came to know He loved me, as I mentioned, while reading 3 Nephi 17. Now, I had to reconcile the distance between Him and me as I was finding myself on a very long path to becoming His disciple. As I am not yet completely like Him, I learned that I am on probation. He is watching to see what I will do. Alma described this period as a time to repent, "a time to prepare to meet God; a time to prepare for that endless state" (Alma 12:24) that is coming. I began to realize what a blessing life can be if I use the opportunities of this life to my advantage. Will I strive to progress? Or will I take the easy road and just expect Him to change me? Will I return to my former ways and forsake the One who rescued me? These are the kinds of questions that have entered my heart as I have learned to consider my ways.

As I have now journeyed a long way since that day in the City College Library, I have discovered that I have many weaknesses. If I am to become perfect, I need to overcome them all to be more Christlike, but I cannot do so in a day, week, month, or even year. This predicament has caused me a lot of stress because even though I love Jesus intensely and want to follow Him, I do so imperfectly. What happens to me while I am learning, growing, and changing but all the while imperfect in my discipleship? Am I guilty every minute I cannot live a perfect life?

For a long time, I felt a constant guilt because of my imperfections, and I was very unhappy. I felt stress because of my repeated need to repent, sometimes of things I thought I had already mastered. I could not reconcile my faith in Christ with my imperfections and constant need for Him. I kept wondering, "Why am I always feeling down about the fact I am not capable of following Him completely, despite knowing I can repent and that He loves me?" I kept wondering, "What am I missing?"

Over many years of striving to change, and of prayerfully studying the scriptures, I began to mature and thought, "I believe in Christ. I trust in Christ. I have faith in Christ. He has atoned for my sins. How can He atone for me and yet I continue to struggle, sin, and fall short?" Over time, I concluded that because of my covenant, Jesus has accepted me as His. He owns me. He purchased me. I belong to Him. This includes my sins. He paid the price for all of them—past, present, and future. As long as I am under His covenant and striving to the best of my ability to keep it, I am under His protection. He is my Master; I am His servant. My sins are His as I am His. He has accepted me in my sinful and imperfect state if I will continue to accept His covenant and strive to progress as best I can, continually repenting as I sin and fall short. His grace will be mine. His power to change my life will continue to function as He helps me. What I concluded was that I must always believe Christ, believe He is my Savior, and trust in His power to redeem me. I cannot save myself through my own obedience. I am incapable of going even one day without sin. But if I am connected to Him through my covenant, I am covered in Christ.

In the Old Testament, the Hebrew word *kawfar* is often translated into English as "atonement."[148] Some meanings of this word are "to cover," "to cover over," or "to be covered over." I do not take this word to mean God looks the other way when we sin. Instead, I think it means that when we make a covenant with God, He accepts us as one of His lambs and He becomes our Shepherd. He protects us from Satan, the wolf, and from sin and the natural man in us—destructive forces that seek to devour our lives if we give in to them.

Jesus stands as our protector. He is the One who has defeated the wolf and our fallen nature. He not only knows how to win against Satan and sin, but He has also carried all our specific sins. His love, power, and strength all become a covering for our sins while we work to overcome them through faith in Him, obedience to His commandments, and honoring our covenants. Then, as we receive the Holy Ghost, we can experience the process of sanctification. Conditional to our repentance and forgiveness, God requires that we endure to the end. We can never quit in this process. As long as we continue

---

148. *The Brown-Driver-Briggs Hebrew and English Lexicon* (Peabody, MA: Hendrickson Academic, 1994), s. v. "kawfar." Accessed via the e-Sword mobile application (see H3722). See also Russell M. Nelson, "The Atonement," *Ensign*, Nov. 1996.

along the covenant path, the Savior continues to own us and to provide a covering for our sins. Through our faith in Him, we are free to progress.

This thought has freed me from the burden of feeling weak and incapable of doing all that is asked of me. With this understanding of Christ, Nephi's words make more sense to me: "And now, my beloved brethren, after ye have gotten into this strait and narrow path, I would ask if all is done? Behold, I say unto you, Nay; for ye have not come thus far [along the covenant path] save it were by the word of Christ with unshaken faith in him, *relying wholly upon the merits of him who is mighty to save*" (2 Nephi 31:19; emphasis added). This idea of relying wholly upon Christ and His merits, not *my* merits, gives me tremendous peace. I don't have to be able to do it all because He has already provided the way. He has provided the means for me to be saved. I have made the decision of a lifetime, the decision to rely on Christ and never return to the path the world offers. With this determination, I can follow Nephi's advice. However, no matter how far I may progress, my progression will always be the result of Christ's grace, for I have relied solely on His merit.

"Wherefore, ye must press forward with a steadfastness in Christ, having a perfect brightness of hope, and a love of God and of all men. Wherefore, if ye shall press forward, feasting upon the word of Christ, and endure to the end, behold, thus saith the Father: Ye shall have eternal life" (2 Nephi 31:20). The key now is to always press forward, relying on Christ. This idea of pressing forward, while we are considering our ways, is essential to "work[ing] out our own salvation with fear and trembling" (Philippians 2:12). Our salvation is going to require work—not just a weekend of work at church, but a lifetime of work. The "fear" and the "trembling" come from many sources. Fear of failure. Fear of facing our weaknesses and having them revealed. The trembling comes as I exert myself to my limits. It also comes as I realize the consequence of not continuing. All of it leads to question, "How far can I go on the path of discipleship?"

The Greatest of All Ultra Marathons

Recently, a colleague of mine named Jared helped me answer the question, "How far can I go?" At lunch we were talking about our upcoming weekend activities. During the usual chatter, Jared told me his weekend would involve a 30-mile training run. "What?!" I exclaimed. "Why?" He explained he was preparing for a 100-mile race in a few months. My mind reeled. Considering how people talk about marathons being excruciating, I thought, "What would *this* race be like?"

I have since learned that what Jared runs is called an ultramarathon. A marathon is a race of 26.2 miles. Ultramarathons are races of any distance longer than a traditional marathon. Some of them qualify as baby-ultras of 30, 40, and 50 miles. Others cover more extreme lengths and include challenging conditions, like 154 miles through the deserts of Morocco, or the Ultra-Trail du Mont Blanc that covers 103 miles through the Alps of France, Italy, and Switzerland, with over thirty thousand feet of positive altitude change. Many of these races are run in extreme heat or cold, over rocks, jungle, desert, and mountain terrain. After numerous conversations with Jared, and reading several running blogs, I realized that enduring to the end of the covenant path is the ultimate ultramarathon.

What we are pressing forward toward is a sense of oneness with God. In English, the words *atonement* and *atone* are compounds from *at-one-ment* and *at-one*. This idea of us becoming "at one" with God conveys many layers of meaning. One meaning I prefer is that we are uniting with God in His thoughts, feelings, attitudes, and behaviors. Obviously, as mortals we cannot fully be "at one" with God—we would have to be perfect right now—nor will we be fully be "at one" with Him by the end of our lives. God is perfect, and we have many challenges we will yet face throughout the spirit world and beyond to become perfect like Him. Further still, this change is not humanly possible. Such a change to our nature can only occur through the grace of Jesus Christ as He transforms us into "new creatures" (2 Corinthians 5:17), or literally a "fresh creation" of ourselves.[149]

I love this metaphor of God creating us again as new people. There is a sense of "death" that we must undergo, where "old things are passed away" (see 1 Corinthians 5:17). What dies might be our love for, thoughts of, and behaviors that embrace anything in opposition to God. We become new people, "born again" in Christ because we forsake our old ways for a new path and a new life on that path, which is the covenant path (see Mosiah 27:25). Further, just as with a child's birth, there is growth and development with this change of heart. Infants are not born as adults, neither are converts born into spiritual maturity.

As new creatures in Christ, we engage in a great adventure of self-discovery as we come to know what Jesus is like compared to what we are currently like. As we recognize the gap between God and ourselves, through repentance and covenant-keeping we gradually close the distance between us to become more like the Son of God. Thus, with each new iteration of ourselves, we grow and mature. This process of considering who we are currently, aligning our hearts with God, and then striving to repent and change our nature qualifies us for the Savior's gift of grace to make us into new creatures. Through this process, we become more and more "at one" with Jesus Christ as we become more like Him. As Mormon taught, when we develop Christlike attributes, then "when he shall appear we shall be like him, for we shall see him as he is; that we may have this hope; that we may be purified even as he is pure" (Moroni 7:48).

I witnessed this kind of change through a young man named Chris Taylor. With Chris's permission, I share his conversion experience:

> I was baptized when I was eleven years of age. Growing up in my neighborhood was a little rough. My brothers and I were excluded from playing with the majority of the neighborhood kids because

---

149. *Thayer's Greek-English Lexicon of the New Testament* (Peabody, MA: Hendrickson Academic, 1995), s. v. "kainos" and "ktisis." Accessed via the e-Sword mobile application (see G2537 and G2937).

> we were not members of The Church of Jesus Christ of Latter-day Saints. My mom thought if we became members of the Church, it would help with friends, school, and sports. This is why my mom, all but two of my siblings, and I were baptized. Except for me, they are now all inactive. My dad is still not a member. Even though I was baptized when I was eleven, I was converted my sophomore year in high school through the efforts of a close friend.

It was during Chris's junior year in high school that I met him. One day, he described an experience he had over the weekend. Chris comes from a football family, and he was playing high school football at the time. He explained that when he came downstairs on Sunday ready to attend church, he found a table filled with food and his family ready to watch the Sunday game. They called out to him, "Chris, stay with us! It's going to be so much fun." He told me, "It was so hard. I wanted to be with my family, but I left and went to church."

Recently, when Chris reflected on this experience, he told me, "My family was against the Church, especially my mom and dad. I love football. My whole family loves football too. But I was never really convinced to stay home from church to watch football." Because Chris had developed true faith in Jesus Christ, he felt the Savior's love personally and was able to overcome this difficult opposition. Like the Savior, when He faced temptation, Chris also resisted the adversary's call to forsake his covenants.

Chris finished his high school years remaining active and faithful to the gospel of Jesus Christ. After high school, he received a three-quarter scholarship to play football for a university in Iowa. Upon completing a successful freshman year, the Spirit began working on him, inviting him to serve a mission. Over time, he accepted the need to serve the Lord and to be true to his covenant.

Chris learned that the consequence of his choice meant the school would not hold his scholarship. He told me, "I realized if I obeyed the Spirit and served a mission, I would forfeit $16,000 in scholarship money. How was I supposed to tell my nonmember father, who already disliked the Church, 'I'm going to give up all of this money and possibly my college and future to serve a mission for a church you do not belong to, and worse, one that you don't like'?"

Despite the opposition, and after a great deal of contemplation and prayer, Chris turned down his scholarship and served an honorable mission. Knowing the truth and understanding the doctrines and principles of the gospel, Chris acted on his faith and became more "at one" with Jesus than ever before. He overcame tremendous opposition to remain faithful, even in his young age. Now, years later, married in the temple, Chris's faith is stronger than ever. He is running the ultramarathon of being a disciple of Jesus Christ. He is finding through the Savior's grace the power to change and become more like Him.

Accepting Christ's Love Is the Only Way to Eternal Change

Of course, the fact that the Savior offers us a covering for our sins and allows us a probationary time to correct those sins does not give us the excuse to remain in sin. The strait and narrow path we are called to walk as we follow Christ requires us to change. One problem we will all experience is when the Lord's commandments conflict with our inability to perform everything God expects of us. As God's expectations intersect with our lack of ability to obey, we face an important choice. Speaking of this choice, Elder D. Todd Christofferson explained: "We don't have to attempt the impossible in trying to rationalize our sins away. And on the other hand, we don't have to attempt the impossible in erasing the effects of sin by our own merit alone."[150]

These two opposing options present a challenge that each of us faces. When we sin, we can err by rationalizing the sins away, thinking, "That was just a small or insignificant matter. I won't do it again." Yet rationalizing our sins does not assuage our guilt, and it certainly does not qualify us for God's forgiveness. The Lord has stated, "No unclean thing can dwell with God" (1 Nephi 10:21). Clearly,

150. D. Todd Christofferson, "The Love of God," *Liahona*, Nov. 2021, 17.

rationalizing away our sins will not work on the Day of Judgment if we desire to live in God's presences. We must be clean of all our sins.

The opposite path is one where we try to keep the commandments perfectly, seeking to save ourselves from our sins through our obedience. This kind of perfectionism is also impossible. As Paul stated, "All have sinned, and come short of the glory of God" (Romans 3:23). Regardless of our best efforts, we will never receive celestial glory because of our obedience alone. So, perfectionism is off the table. We just can't manage that level of Christlike, perfect obedience in our lives.

The only viable solution for our predicament is the strait and narrow path. For us, walking this path begins with our baptismal covenant. Included in this covenant is a willingness to keep God's commandments, one of which is to repent of our sins. As we do so, Elder Christofferson said, "Ours is not a religion of rationalization nor a religion of perfectionism but a religion of redemption—redemption through Jesus Christ. If we are among the penitent, with His Atonement our sins are nailed to His cross, and 'with his stripes we are healed.'"[151] What I am suggesting is that through our covenant, all our sins are nailed to His cross, so we ought to rejoice in our hearts and embrace the gift He has given to us. He alone could provide such freedom to progress. Fall at His knees and accept His merciful love.

One of the great scriptures often quoted is John 3:16: "For God so loved the world, that he gave his only begotten Son, that whosoever believeth in him should not perish, but have everlasting life." Too often we fail to read on, leaving out the next verse: "For God sent not his Son into the world to condemn the world; but that the world through him might be saved" (verse 17). The Savior's love is not condemning—it is freeing. We condemn ourselves when we ignore our need to change, or when we constantly feel guilty because we cannot keep the commandments well enough.

The Savior wants to forgive us. A frequently quoted example comes from John 8 when the scribes and Pharisees cast a woman taken in

151. D. Todd Christofferson, "The Love of God," 17.

adultery at the Savior's feet. We all can appreciate the shame and guilt this poor woman must have felt—half naked, tearful, and afraid, dragged somewhere onto the temple grounds, and accused in front of those who were present. When asked if He would stone her for her sins, the Savior replied with words that stunned both her and all who heard them: "He that is without sin among you, let him first cast a stone at her" (John 8:7). Then, as her accusers each departed and she was left alone with the Son of God, He said to her, "Woman, where are those thine accusers? hath no man condemned thee? She said, No man, Lord. And Jesus said unto her, Neither do I condemn thee: go, and sin no more" (John 8:10–11).

The Savior's Atonement offered her a covering for her sins. Although she was naked physically, more seriously she was naked spiritually, her guilt and shame fully exposed. Her sins were significant, and her salvation was in jeopardy if she continued along the path of sin. But if she would repent and enter the covenant path, Jesus would take upon Him her sins, and she would no longer be exposed to the weight of justice that one day would come upon her in full force. As Elder Dale G. Renlund taught, "Surely, the Savior did not condone adultery. But He also did not condemn the woman. He encouraged her to reform her life."[152]

What happened to her as a result of the Savior's love was a miraculous transformation. Elder Renlund continued, "The Joseph Smith Translation of the Bible attests to her resultant discipleship: 'And the woman glorified God from that hour, and believed on his name.'"[153] The covering Jesus offered her was His cloak of forgiveness. Though we are spiritually naked and exposed to justice and its demands, Christ's Atonement covers all of our sins, past and present, if we will repent. And He will cover our sins as long as we persist in our repentance and continually return to the covenant path.

152. Dale G. Renlund, "Our Good Shepherd," *Ensign* or *Liahona*, May 2017, 30.
153. Dale G. Renlund, "Our Good Shepherd," 30.

Faith to Endure as We Continue Becoming More like Christ

My desire throughout this chapter has been to address what we as faithful followers can do about the gap between ourselves and Jesus. If God commands us to become perfect, how do we avoid falling into guilt when we know what is right, want to do it, but continually fall short of meeting all of God's expectations? This challenge, of course, extends beyond the sins of commission, the "thou shalt not" kinds of sins. It also extends into the sins of omission, the "thou shalt" expectations, of which there are so many. They can become endless when we consider not just doing something with them but also refining our abilities at them or giving priority to them when we already feel stressed about life.

Certainly, as stated already, when we become aware of sin, we can repent and return to the covenant path. Yet an additional personal struggle can develop: feeling overwhelmed. For instance, as we listen to the many talks in sacrament meeting where someone invites us to do more, we may already feel like we're giving a lot. For example, you might hear, "You need to be a better minister, like Jesus was," and start thinking, "Well, at least I'm trying to text them when I can." Or when you hear about people's amazing experiences with *Come, Follow Me* where it sounds like angels are singing and children are crying with joy, you might think, "Ha! You should sit through *our* study of *Come, Follow Me*. It's a fight to get the kids to even join in with us and stay off their phones."

But then there's more. "Make sure you give a generous fast offering. There are hungry people. And while you're at it, make sure you sign up for the welfare assignment. Oh, and don't forget to put the temple on your schedule. That's what Jesus would do." All the while you might be thinking, "I completely forgot today was fast Sunday and already ate breakfast. I didn't even know we had a cannery. And I haven't been to the temple in six months. Oh, geez! How will I ever get better when I'm struggling so hard just to keep up? I guess I'll never be perfect!"

Knowing that being perfect means "complete, finished, or fully developed" still might not be enough to fix this problem.[154] The doctrine of continually striving for perfection *can* bring relief when we feel optimistic and hopeful about our future, but if it doesn't—if the constant need to improve leads us to think, "I'm just plain finished, I'm a complete waste, and the only thing I'm going to develop is an ulcer trying to do all this"—then we need to reevaluate our perspective. For me, I needed to develop a particular focus so I could overcome the anxiety I felt trying to constantly improve when I was just barely keeping up with life's other challenges.

I believe the problem arises because we know Jesus does not condone our sins and that we cannot rationalize them away. Yet our repeated sinning can make us feel hopeless. Further, we know we cannot get to heaven through our efforts to keep the commandments perfectly, because we have failed so many times trying and we get discouraged with our lack of progress or the slowness of it. We know we can and get back on the path, but the gap between where we are and where we need to be begins to feel so long, and the path seems so steep, that we start questioning, "Even with repentance, will I ever make it?"

It's these moments when we realize this is the longest ultramarathon ever, and we feel so stressed and anxious, so worn out and overwhelmed, that we don't know if we can keep going. So, what do we do then? How do we stay on this long covenant path to the end of our lives without the guilt trips and feeling overwhelmed to the point of wanting to quit? How do we listen each general conference like we're drinking from a fire hydrant and not feel, "Who can do all of this? It's just too much!"

The peace Christ offers us at times like these can come from multiple perspectives. First, it comes from knowing who we are. The Psalmist taught, "All of you are children of the most High" (Psalm 82:6). This means that regardless of our current status, we have the infinite potential of one day being completely like our Savior, of

154. See Matthew 5:48, footnote *b* for the Greek definition of the word *perfect.*

finishing the long and arduous climb and fully developing into the mature, godlike person our Father knows we one day can become. To help us remember this truth, we can consider the following scenario. When a little child who is learning to walk stumbles and falls, how do good parents respond? Loving parents would not berate the child for being weak and small. They would not criticize them for failing while they were learning to walk. When the child finally takes those first steps, they wouldn't say, "But you're not running yet! Why are you still just walking?" Nor, once their child finally mastered running, would they condescendingly say, "Why aren't you keeping up with that Olympian over there who runs a four-minute mile?" Like loving earthly parents, our Heavenly Father sees our potential and invites us to continue to rise. If we can remember who we are and what we ultimately can become, it will increase our peace. We are God's children, and as children, we need time to grow and develop.

Second, we need to remember that each Sunday, and at every general conference, the Savior needs to inspire all of us, regardless of our current condition. Of course, we can always do more. That's what eternity is for. After all, we believe in eternal progression, which implies we have a long time to complete this journey. And I don't think we will be finished anytime soon. During this ultramarathon, God can inspire each of us, line upon line, to know what to do to move forward on the path toward perfection.

Third, we need to remember that the gospel metaphor for our progression is a strait and narrow path—the covenant path. Remembering the nature of a path can bring us peace. A path has a definite beginning and end. Between them there are miles and miles to travel.

One of my favorite hikes begins on the Mueller Park trailhead in Bountiful, Utah, and ends at a place the locals call "elephant rock"—I suppose because it's as big as an elephant. The hike is long, especially for young children, and increases significantly in elevation. I've carried many a child on my back while we as a family made our way toward elephant rock. Sometimes we've hurried. Sometimes we've gone very slowly, even stopping for food and water or just to see the sights. There have been times when one or more of my children said, "Dad,

I don't want to go any further. Let's just go home." It usually took encouragement and some snacks to keep them going. Once, my daughter fell and seriously injured her hands when she landed on the rocks. It was an ugly wound that made me question why I ever brought my family on that hike.

Despite all the adversity we sometimes face on this hike, in the back of my mind, I've always thought, "But I know where this hike leads, and I know the view. It's stunning! The kids are going to love it. They've just got to keep going." So, with repeated breaks and some songs, jokes, and stories, I've helped each one of my children to pick up his or her feet at one point and keep moving along the path. Eventually, we've all made it to elephant rock. The looks on their faces as they see that enormous rock and climb out onto it is precious. They look out on the valley below and all the effort finally seems worth it. "We made it," I think. "It's finished. We completed the journey."

Life on the covenant path has much in common with our family hike. We place one foot on the path and soon we've covered some ground. We get tired, though, and think, "This path is too long. I think I want to stop. Can't someone give me some 'spiritual' water and help me move forward again?" Then our Savior, with His infinite power of grace, reaches out with His Spirit to encourage us along. He might send a friend who shares His love and serves us. Or He lifts us with a scripture that reminds us why we got on the covenant path to begin with. Or we take time away from the drudgery of life to attend the temple, where we feel the refreshing power of the Savior's love and sense the majesty of the covenants we've made. After whatever brings the needed reprieve, we try again. We keep trying again and again to move a little farther down the path and get that much closer to our destination.

When we struggle along the way and feel like quitting, from His elevated view, our Heavenly Father looks down on us, His children, and says, "Oh, little ones. I cannot let you stay where you are. If you only knew what was coming. If you could see the view from where I am, you would not want to get off this path." So, He too "sings us a song," maybe revealing it through the beauty of the earth. Or perhaps

He shares some moment of blessed humor with our children that motivates us to keep trying, or tells us a story of faith through a wonderful friend in a sacrament talk. Whatever the source He may select, He sends His encouraging love to say, "You need to keep moving forward because the end of this long journey is a reward that's worth all the heartache and toil." Through it all, our job is to pluck up our courage and try to walk again. As long as we keep moving forward, the process is working.

An important lesson we learn from the metaphor of the "covenant path" is this: As people put their feet on the path to "elephant rock" and stay on that path, continuing however slowly they may go, eventually they will end up where the path leads. Likewise, if we enter the covenant path and remain on it throughout our lives, it will lead us to the celestial kingdom. This principle is powerful. If we stay on any path and do not get off, we will reach our destination. The comfort in this thought is that regardless of how slow our progress may be, eventually we will make it to the celestial kingdom.

With these thoughts in mind, we need not despair when we hear all that God expects of us that is yet ahead. Wherever we are right now on the path is a matter of fact. We cannot sprint to the finish line. This is an endurance trail. There are no shortcuts to our eternal progression. We need to accept where we are now, appreciate the ground we've covered, and faithfully anticipate our Lord's help to cover the remaining miles ahead. He's not going to leave us. He has said, "I will not leave you comfortless: I will come to you" (John 14:18). In the meantime, while we anxiously anticipate the journey's end, the answer is to keep our feet moving, no matter how slowly we progress. Just move another step forward and see if we can't cover a little more ground today.

I regularly need the message of constant, steady improvement. That's what I rely on when I am sitting in sacrament meeting or listening to general conference talks and start feeling overwhelmed. As I remember the path I'm on and where it leads, I can feel good about where I am currently. Nephi once said, "We know that it is by grace that we are saved, after all we can do" (2 Nephi 25:23), but we can't forget he too had a moment when he cried out, "O wretched man that I am!" (2 Nephi 4:17).

If I can visualize the distance I have come and, with faith in Christ, acknowledge I have many more miles to go, then I can keep moving forward. If I do, I will eventually arrive at my destination. This perspective allows me to accept the one task I can handle today. I'll work on it, whatever it is, and keep pressing forward until I can master that thing. Then, in the end, when I have accomplished it, I acknowledge, "I have only come this far by the grace of Christ." He has given me a covering for my past sins whenever I have repented. And because of my covenant, He has promised me that as long as I keep trying, He will continue to cover my sins, even my lack of being able to do all that is asked of me. He covers those sins too. He knows my capabilities, and He can help balance where I currently am with my potential to become greater. Thus, I put my trust in Him. The trick is to stay on the path and not give up. He will help me overcome not only my current weaknesses but my future ones that I am not yet even aware of.

Christ has made this promise to all who willingly come unto Him, make a covenant with Him, and then seek throughout their lives to keep it. He is firm and fixed to us. So fixed, in fact, that He has asked, "Can a woman forget her sucking child? . . . Yea, they may forget, yet will I not forget thee. . . . I have graven thee upon the palms of my hands" (1 Nephi 21:15–16). He will never forget us as we walk along the covenant path. As we strive to obey Him and repent of our sins, He covers us. His Atonement covers us—the past, present, and future versions of us—as long as we stay on the path. The answer to the dilemma is to never get off the path, no matter how long and difficult it may seem, and to keep going, regardless of how slowly we may be climbing, for ahead of us is eternal life.

Understanding the Savior's Love for Us

What is required for us to press forward in faith and successfully endure to the end is knowing with a surety that the Savior loves us.

While I have already referred to this love, I believe there is more for us to consider, allowing the full weight of Christ's love to sink deeply into our hearts.

In the Old Testament, Moses gave the children of Israel a law of performances, which included many sacrifices. The general pattern for these sacrifices included important steps.[155] First, the person presented the sacrifice to the priest at the door of the tabernacle. The animal needed to belong to the one making the offering. Then, the priest would place his hands on the animal's head and dedicate it to God. Through this process, he also stated that the animal now represented the person who offered the sacrifice. Next, the priest required the person offering the animal to kill it.

I can imagine the thoughts that would go through my mind as the priest would hand me the knife to cut the throat of a little innocent lamb. With blood on my hands, and guilty feelings in my heart, I might have asked, "Why did the Lamb have to die?" A sensitive person, who understood that the lamb represented Jesus Christ, the Messiah, would find this experience deeply personal. As the lamb bled to death, the priest would have captured its blood in a basin. He then would have been literally holding in his hands the life of the lamb, represented by that blood. Next, the priest prepared the animal and roasted it on the altar of sacrifice. Additionally, there were variations to the procedures of sacrifice, depending on its purpose. One of these variations included the Lord's command that the priest "shall pour out all the blood thereof at the bottom of the altar" (see Leviticus 4).

The experience of offering sacrifice to God for those who understood its meaning would have changed people's hearts and drawn them nearer to Jesus Christ.[156] As we look back on those events from the past, we, like Isaiah, might now make an important connection. Speaking of Christ and His sacrifice, Isaiah wrote, "Surely he hath

155. Bible Dictionary, "Sacrifices."

156. It is our belief as members of The Church of Jesus Christ of Latter-day Saints that from the days of Adam and continuing on through Moses, the act of worshipping God through sacrifice was always connected to Jesus Christ. See, for example, Moses 5:5–8.

borne our griefs, and carried our sorrows. . . . He was wounded for our transgressions, he was bruised for our iniquities: the chastisement of our peace was upon him; and with his stripes we are healed" (Isaiah 53:4–5). Through these potent words, the prophet communicated a sense of personal connection to Jesus Christ and His suffering for our sins, as seen in the animal sacrifice. Then, Isaiah further connected Christ's Atonement to the sacrificial offering when he wrote, "Yet it pleased to Lord to bruise him; he hath put him to grief: when thou shalt make his soul *an offering for sin* . . . he shall prolong his days" (Isaiah 53:10; emphasis added).

Now, had we been there when the animal was dead and its body roasting in the fire of purification, we could have known more perfectly that Jesus was the offering for our sin. I can imagine how it might have felt for those participants to eat the sacrificial lamb. I hope I would have been one to consider all that it cost for me to consume that meal. He truly would have been the sacred food that sustained my soul. Yet Isaiah went further still and drove the point home as he continued, "Therefore will I divide him a portion with the great, and shall divide the spoil with the strong; *because he hath poured out his soul unto death*" (Isaiah 53:12; emphasis added). These words allude to the moment the priest took the remaining blood in the basin and poured it out on the ground.

Who can read these words with understanding and not shudder? Picture in your mind the priest holding the basin of blood, the life of the lamb. Now consider that the High Priest is Jesus (see Hebrews 4:14–16), and that He was the one who handed us the knife. We slew Him through our sin, and He caught all His own blood and held it in His hands. Then, finally, He voluntarily poured out His precious soul unto death, spilling His blood on the ground for us.

Who would do this? Who would hold his own life in his hands and willingly pour it on the ground, where animals defecate and urinate and people walk all over? Only One with an infinite power to love and a complete capacity to see the potential and future greatness of each of God's beloved children. We, the ones with the knife in our hands, have slain Him—not out of malice but out of need. He had to die that we might live. This was decided during that powerful moment in heaven when Jesus, the future great High Priest, was blessed and anointed to come to earth and take upon Him our sins, while we looked on, knowing that without His death we could not return and live with our Father. Then He came to earth and fulfilled the Father's plan. Although He groaned, "Father, if thou be willing, remove this cup from me" (Luke 22:42), He did not "shrink" but drank all of the bitter cup (see Doctrine and Covenants 19:18).

Now, having partaken of His bitter cup, He turns to each of us every Sunday. Rather than handing us a knife to take the life of the Lamb, He has His priests bless and brake the bread, the symbol of His body, and prepare cups of water, representing His blood. And they pass these emblems of His sacrifice to us, modern-day Israel. As the priest in ancient times would have handed the faithful follower the knife that took the Savior's life, in our day the priests present to us the emblems of the life already given. Jesus drank all the cup He had to drink; we now hold in our hands the flesh and blood of the One who died, and we eat and drink. We take Him into us, accepting of His offering. Yet we cannot forget. What's in our minds and heart during this sacred act is a measure of our love and devotion to Him. Through our thoughts and feelings, we can reflect on Him. Our actions during this sacred time can become the image that fuels our desire to endure. Accepting His love can stoke the fire of our faith to burn away our impure thoughts and sinful deeds.

Elder Neal A. Maxwell has helped us in modern times to see beyond the sacrifice of animals and look to the sacrifice within us. As quoted in the previous chapter, He has said, "So it is that real, personal sacrifice never was placing an animal on the altar."[157] It was always a symbol pointing to Christ, but because the sacrifice was always personal and belonged to the one making the offering, it needed to become something more. Elder Maxwell continued, "Instead, it is a willingness to put the animal in us upon the altar and letting it be

157. Neal A. Maxwell, "Deny Yourselves of All Ungodliness," *Ensign*, May 1995, 68.

consumed! Such is the 'sacrifice unto the Lord . . . of a broken heart and a contrite spirit,' (Doctrine and Covenants 59:8), a prerequisite to taking up the cross, while giving 'away all [our] sins' in order to 'know God' (Alma 22:18) for the denial of self precedes the full acceptance of Him."[158]

Thus, we come full circle. We each must "consider our ways." We need to examine ourselves and see what offering we need to make. Then, with full faith in Jesus Christ, we can trust in His love and grace and find the power of His Atonement. To assist us, the Savior has given us many resources that will help us make it through life, this massive ultramarathon. As we make covenants and seek to keep them, we can find the power to endure to the very end of our lives, being faithful to our covenants "even until death" (Mosiah 18:9).

As we endure, a process of change takes place. We can become converted and changed into a new soul—a Christlike soul, one that thinks more like how God thinks, loves more of what God loves, and strives to do more of what God does. We are each changed so that we "receive his image in [our] countenances" (Alma 5:14). It has been our desire to help you along this journey. We sincerely hope that what we have written will help you come unto Christ and be healed, strengthened, and lifted to press forward in faith, taking hold of His word, and find peace and assurance through your faith in Him. We know that He lives and that He loves us. And we know that through the Savior's power, we each can return and live with God again.

---

158. Neal A. Maxwell, "Deny Yourselves of All Ungodliness," 68.

11

HAPPINESS—ARE WE THERE YET?

CRG

"Happiness is the object and design of our existence; and will be the end thereof, if we pursue the path leads to it; and this path is virtue, uprightness, faithfulness, holiness, and keeping all the commandments of God."

—Joseph Smith[159]

Many years ago, I was waiting at the bus stop to catch a ride to work. I had gotten off the train and was expecting a normal day. But the events that happened at the bus stop caused me some reflection and concern. The following experience stands out in my mind as a key day in my life.

The bus was running late for some reason. Most of us were very anxious to get on the bus. I had a professional development class I

159. Joseph Smith, in *History of the Church*, 5:134–35.

needed to get to at work (which incidentally I was facilitating), and it would start promptly at 7:00 a.m. The bus that day was about fifteen minutes late, and I am one who does not like to be late to anything. An older gentleman came up to me with some money in his hand and asked if I had change for a five so that he could take the bus (which only took exact change). I looked at him and said, "I'm sorry, but I don't." He started to walk away, but then he came back to me, looked me in the eye, and said, "You need to be happier and smile more often." I was a little shocked that a stranger would tell that to my face. I smiled back at him and told him that I *was* happy. He returned a smile and then walked away.

I found this exchange in my life very interesting, especially with regards to its timing. At that moment in my life, I was going through much tribulation, I was under a lot of stress, and I had many professional assignments I had started working on that needed completed. My church assignments also kept me very busy. To add to that, my daughter Casey had just been admitted into Brigham Young University, and I was worried how we could help her financially while supporting our son Collin out in the mission field.

I stood there at the bus stop pondering over what this gentleman had just said to me. For me, it was an eye-opening and life-changing experience to have a complete stranger tell me that I need to be happier and smile more. I am a very happy person, but the problem at the time was evidently a disconnect between what I was feeling on the inside and the expression I showed on my face. I wondered how I could tell my face the happiness I was feeling on the inside.

This reminded me of the happiness that we all feel when we live the commandments of our Father in Heaven. When we ponder this, or have this pointed out to us, and count our many blessings, it helps us to recognize just how happy we really are. King Benjamin from the Book of Mormon recognized this fact when he said, "And moreover, I would desire that ye should consider on the *blessed and happy state* of those that keep the commandments of God. For behold, they are blessed in all things, both temporal and spiritual; and if they hold out faithful to the end they are received into heaven, that thereby they may dwell with God in a state of never-ending happiness. O remember, remember that these things are true; for the Lord God hath spoken it" (Mosiah 2:41; emphasis added).

Heavenly Father desires that we find true and lasting happiness. One thing we all have in common as sons and daughters of God is our desire to be happy. We are told from the Book of Mormon that the people of Nephi "lived after the manner of happiness" (2 Nephi 5:27). This resulted from their pressing forward in their faith in Jesus Christ six hundred years before His mortal ministry. They understood and followed the prophets of their time and understood the plan of salvation and happiness. Likewise, the Jaredites understood that happiness came from their submissiveness to the Lord's will, and despite their difficulties, they were able to maintain a sense of gratitude for God's blessings and goodness. Humility and gratitude are twin characteristics of happiness. Despite the hardships we all face, we have been given many resources to help us along our path.

I love the analogy that scholar W. Jeffrey Marsh teaches that compares the travels of the Jaredites to our sojourn through life and its attendant difficulties and challenges. For example, note the following passages and commentary.[160]

"For it came to pass after the Lord had prepared the stones which the brother of Jared had carried [before Him] . . . behold, they did give light unto the vessels" (Ether 6:2).

The Lord expects us to do our part—to carry before Him all we are capable of doing ourselves—and to ask Him to "touch" our efforts.

"The Lord caused stones to shine in darkness, to give light unto men, women, and children, that they might not cross the great waters in darkness" (Ether 6:3).

We have been given many "stones" in our lives, including patriarchal blessings, answers to prayers, wise and inspired counsel from

160. See W. Jeffrey Marsh, *The Light Within* (Salt Lake City: Deseret Book, 2000), 43–46.

Church leaders and parents, promptings from the Holy Ghost, and so on.

"They . . . prepared all manner of food, that thereby they might subsist on the water" (Ether 6:4).

We come to earth having prepared ourselves (and having been prepared by others) since the foundations of the earth were set. We were taught many lessons and prepared by God to do these things on earth long before we were born (see Doctrine and Covenants 138:53–56).

"And it came to pass that when they had done all these things they got aboard of their vessels or barges, and set forth unto the sea, commending themselves unto the Lord their God" (Ether 6:4)

This is very similar to us beginning our mortal journey. Like the Jaredites, we are starting a journey in uncharted waters. We commend ourselves to His watchful care and tender mercy. Although there are others who have traveled the path successfully, and there are others ahead of us, we all venture into the unknown. We have to exercise our faith in God to get through life, trusting He will guide us back successfully.

"And it came to pass that the Lord God caused that there should be a furious wind blow upon the face of the waters, towards the promised land" (Ether 6:5).

Opposition and trials of faith, like fierce winds, blow against us all through mortality. These challenges help define us and make us better people. We grow from them. We are humans *becoming* something better, rather than just humans *being*. Becoming is better than just being.

"Thus they were tossed upon the waves of the sea before the wind. . . . They were many times buried in the depths of the sea, because of the mountain waves which broke upon them" (Ether 6:5–6).

Life's challenges seem, quite often, to be just as overwhelming as this verse describes. The heartaches and the crosses we are called to bear sometimes seem about to crush us. But the Lord has promised us strength. Remember Doctrine and Covenants 122:7, wherein the Lord tells us that "all these things shall give [us] experience, and shall be for [our] good." Also, I am reminded of scholar S. Michael Wilcox's book *The Fourth Watch*, built on the premise that our Savior is a "fourth-watch" individual and will come at the very moment we need him (see Mark 6:48, 50).

"Therefore when they were encompassed about by many waters they did cry unto the Lord, and he did bring them forth again upon the top of the waters" (Ether 6:7).

Prayer will unlock the door that leads to God's help. With God as our friend, we have no need to fear. We also need to remember to have faith in His timing as well. His help is given "in his own time, and in his own way, and according to his own will" (Doctrine and Covenants 88:68).

"And it came to pass that the wind did never cease to blow towards the promised land while they were upon the waters" (Ether 6:8).

Brother Marsh explains the restraints or limitations that trials place on our lives. The pain, mental anguish, or heartache that accompanies them can sometimes last throughout our entire lives. I am reminded that we need to "submit cheerfully and with patience to all the will of the Lord" (Mosiah 24:15).

"They did sing praises unto the Lord; yea, the brother of Jared did sing praises unto the Lord, and he did thank and praise the Lord all the day long, and when the night came, they did not cease to praise the Lord" (Ether 6:9).

Gratitude for God's blessings, even the smallest ones, often has a direct correlation to our humility and meekness. I am reminded of the ten lepers who were healed by our Savior in Luke 17:16–17. Nine of the ten who were healed forgot to express gratitude. When we express our gratitude, it shows God that we trust Him.

"Thus they were driven forth; and no monster of the sea could break them, neither whale that could mar them; and they did have light continually, whether it was above the water or under the water" (Ether 6:10).

If we put our trust in God, He will continue to provide that light or revelation for us to strengthen us and protect us.

"Thus they were driven forth, three hundred and forty-four days upon the water" (Ether 6:11).

That's a really long time when you think about it. It's almost an entire year. I was deployed to Southwest Asia for seven months during my time on active duty in the Army, and that separation from my family felt like an eternity! Yet when we put on our eternal lenses, mortality is very short.

"They did land upon the shore of the promised land. And when they had set their feet upon the shores of the promised land they bowed themselves down upon the face of the land, and did humble themselves before the Lord, and did shed tears of joy before the Lord, because of the multitude of his tender mercies over them" (Ether 6:12).

Can you imagine the joy we will feel when we return to God's presence? I feel that tears of joy will surely flow from each of us at that moment.

Our Father in Heaven and Savior Jesus Christ desire that we find true, lasting happiness in our own lives. President George Q. Cannon described God's blessing and rewards in these words:

> We may pass through the fiery furnace; we may pass through deep waters; but we shall not be consumed nor overwhelmed. We shall emerge from all these trials and difficulties the better and purer

for them, if we only trust in God and keep his commandments. Then He has a future for us. That bliss which we have a foretaste of here, we shall have a fullness of hereafter. You who have received the Holy Spirt; you who have felt its power; you whose hearts have been gladdened under its heavenly influence, you know how sweet it has been; you know that there is nothing on earth so sweet as the outpouring of the Spirit of God on a human being. No matter what experience you may have had in riches and in all that earth desires, there is nothing that compares with the heavenly sweetness and joy of the Spirit of God. This is a foretaste of that which is to come. We shall receive a fullness of that, if we are faithful. If we hold on without flinching, and without turning to the right hand or to the left, our God will lead us straight on until we are brought into His presence and crowned with glory, immortality and eternal life; which I pray may be the happy lot of every one of us.[161]

A Series of Questions to Help You "Consider Your Ways" to Become Happier

Since that experience I had at the bus stop, I have tried to ask in my personal prayers that my inward happiness may show outwardly. For me, this has changed everything. It changes the way I look at my professional work, the way I look at service, and even more importantly, the way I treat my family and others. This is much more difficult than it sounds, but if we ask our Father in Heaven for His help, we can radiate the happiness that we feel. This happiness can be physically expressed personally and spiritually. I learned this principle line upon line and know that it's true. This is the apex of enduring discipleship. The following principles help me to externally radiate my internal happiness.

Count your blessings daily and focus on all that is good in your life. Remember there are people who would give anything to have what you have. You get to decide in each moment what you will

161. George Q. Cannon, in *Collected Discourses Delivered by President Wilford Woodruff, His Two Counselors, the Twelve Apostles, and Others* (1988), 2:185.

focus on—the good or the bad. Focus on what's good and trust that the bad is there to serve you and shape you into a better person. This will help you to draw closer to your Father in Heaven. Are you doing this now? If not, consider your ways.

Never set conditions on happiness. Make a personal policy that you will never say, "I'll be happy when . . ." It never ceases to amaze me when I hear of people who think that their entire sphere of influence is contingent upon the size of their house, or the calling they have at the time, or the type of car they drive. Understand that happiness is a choice you make now, in this very moment. You have just as much power to choose happiness today as you will have in the future. You do not need a big house, a visible calling in the Church, or a large fancy car to be happy. For me, my happiest times are when I am around my family and they laugh at my silly "dad" jokes. Are you setting conditions on your happiness now? If so, consider your ways.

Decide that happiness is the essence of your character. You get to decide what kind of person you want to be. Don't let others dictate that to you. See yourself as a happy person. People naturally gravitate toward others who they perceive as happy, non-complaining, and fun to be around. Are you one of those? If not, consider your ways.

Have more fun and be more fun. Laugh more often, and collect appropriate jokes and funny stories to share with those around you. Make it fun to live with you or to be around you. Be spontaneous, adventurous, and positive. Write those funny experiences down in your journal so you can recall them years after the fact. Be flexible and easygoing. Find ways to make whatever you do fun. Turn boring, frustrating things into a game. I truly believe that we have more natural ability to play and express happiness than we realize. Are you creating fun in your life at the moment? If not, consider your ways.

Never gossip, criticize, or judge others. See everyone as a student in the classroom of life, with the same infinite value as you. Miserable people tend to focus on the bad in others, but happy people don't need to do that. Strive to see others with wisdom and compassion and you will like yourself much better, which will create more happiness and show in your countenance. Pray for charity in your life, then act like you already have it. As you exercise this gift of the Spirit, our Father in Heaven will make it more evident in your life, line upon line and precept upon precept. Do you have charity in your life now? If not, consider your ways.

Keep things in perspective. Remember what matters most and what does not. Understand that good and bad things may happen to you to help you learn and grow as a child of God. Are you taking things out of context or blowing things out of proportion in your life? If so, consider your ways.

Choose to respond to every situation with love and charity. Learn better communication skills, which will improve your relationships with your spouse, children, and friends. Building rich relationships starts with better communication. The Church has wonderful resources available to help so many people. These resources are available online or can be acquired through your local distribution center. Many motivational videos are also available to see on YouTube or on the Church's website. Oftentimes, watching these motivational and inspiring videos helps me improve how I treat others and see them through the lens of charity. Do you respond to your life situations with love and charity? If not, consider your ways.

Simplify tasks and take more breaks. You cannot create happiness if your life is too full of stressful obligations. (I learned this the hard way.) Find some quiet downtime to relax, unwind, and have fun. No one can give this to you. It must be a priority to make sure you get time for leisure activities. For me, finding time to be alone when the house is still and quiet (generally early in the morning) is a great way to get my bearings and learn some new revelatory perspective. It takes a little bit of discipline to get out of a nice warm bed, especially when you are tired, but the implications are eternal. Are you making things easier things in your life to find more balance? If not, consider your ways.

Set goals and keep growing, learning, and experiencing new things. People who are engaged in learning are always happier. Setting learning goals will influence your self-worth. If you are not doing this, consider your ways.

The little things are the big things. Remember that to be a faithful disciple and press forward on the covenant path of Jesus Christ, we need to nurture the faith that He has blessed us with. This includes daily scripture study, prayer, worthily partaking of the sacrament each week, temple attendance, and lifting where you stand while finding joy in the journey. Mark and I have tried to be as thorough as possible in our explanations to you about the importance of doing the little things. However, don't do it just because we've told you to—do it because it's the right thing to do and because you are a son or daughter of our Father in Heaven. If He can't trust you in the little things, He certainly won't trust you in the big things. We show our love, gratitude, and commitment to Him by doing all the little things we can, which ultimately add up to the big things. If you are not doing those little things, consider your ways.

Take care of your body, eat healthy food, exercise, and get plenty of rest. Most of these topics were covered in chapter 2. Remember that your body can't have a zest for life if you aren't taking care of it. Exercise is a great cure for depression, and losing some weight will give you more energy. (I'm still working on this!) If you are not doing this, consider your ways.

Remember that life is a journey, not a destination. You must enjoy the journey and choose to appreciate the little incremental wins, small blessings, and sunny days. Take the time to "smell the flowers."[162] When we realize that we are here on earth for a higher purpose, we are able to more fully prioritize that which matters most. Our emphasis in life becomes more about what we can do to lift others to a higher level. We serve others so that they can serve others and so on. If you are not doing this, consider your ways.

Perhaps you have additional ideas that can be added to this list. It is certainly not all-inclusive. As we consider our ways and press forward in Christ, He can impress upon our minds and influence our

---

162. Many of the suggestions in this list come from Kimberly Giles, founder and president of ClarityPoint Coaching (claritypointcoaching.com), with some significant modification by the authors.

behaviors so as to yield more happiness, contentment, and joy. This process of spiritual rebirth begins to unfold as we diligently press forward along the covenant path. Brother Brent L. Top helps to identify some of the fruits of spiritual rebirth and what happens to us individually when we consider our ways. We have:

- peace of conscience (see Enos 1:6; Mosiah 4:2);
- a feeling of joy and divine love (see Alma 36:20–21; Alma 19:29–30);
- no desire to do evil but to do good continually (see Mosiah 5:2; Alma 13:11–12);
- increased love for our fellowman (see Ezek. 36:26, Enos 1:9–13);
- increased spiritual understanding (see Alma 19:6; Mosiah 5:3); and
- the image of God engraved upon our countenances (see Alma 5:14).[163]

Hopefully, you can begin to see how we, as mortals, can overcome our natural tendency to "take the road more easily traveled" and put ourselves onto a path that is so much narrower yet eternally rewarding. The answer lies simply in how well we have become converted. We hope that now you can see the benefits of enduring discipleship. Elder David A. Bednar of the Quorum of the Twelve Apostles teaches us the following:

> Conversion is an enlarging, a deepening, and a broadening of the undergirding base of testimony. It is the result of revelation from God, accompanied by individual repentance, obedience, and diligence. Any honest seeker of truth can become converted by experiencing the mighty change of heart and being spiritually born of God (see Alma 5:12–14). As we honor the ordinances and covenants of salvation and exaltation (see Doctrine and Covenants 20:25), "press forward with a steadfastness in Christ" (2 Nephi 31:20), and endure in faith to the end (see Doctrine and Covenants

163. See Brent L. Top, "Spiritual Rebirth: Have Ye Been Born of God?" in *The Book of Mormon and the Message of the Four Gospels*, ed. Ray L. Huntington and Terry B. Ball (Provo, UT: Religious Studies Center, Brigham Young University, 2001), 201–17.

> 14:7), we become new creatures in Christ (see 2 Corinthians 5:17). Conversion is an offering of self, of love, and of loyalty we give to God in gratitude for the gift of testimony.[164]

The Lord has said to "prove me now herewith" and He will "open you the windows of heaven, and pour out a blessing that there shall not be room enough" (Malachi 3:10) to receive the promised blessings. Even though this scripture is used in the context of tithing, it is certainly a true principle that extends to all of God's commandments and promises. We can discover for ourselves the joy that comes from pressing forward in Christ and having those windows of heaven opened to us.

One sign that we are increasing in our spirituality and considering our ways is that we have a greater awareness of where we fall short in this life—a keener sensitivity to our weaknesses. Elder Bruce C. Hafen wisely pointed out that it "doesn't mean we are drifting away from Him. It may well mean that we are drawing closer. Like a good coach, a good tutor will always help his students see and correct their mistakes. When we understand that, correction is motivating, not discouraging. For because of the [Lord's] Atonement, we can learn from our mistakes without being condemned by them."[165]

Elder Joseph B. Wirthlin of the Quorum of the Twelve Apostles taught us this important principle, emphasizing the need to stay on the strait and narrow path laid out by the Lord:

> Satan will try, at every step of the way, to lead you off course. His objective is to make you unhappy and miserable like he is (see 2 Nephi 2:27). Vast sums of money are spent each year to package and disguise sin and evil to make them appear enticing, attractive, even harmless.
>
> However, regardless of appearances, "wickedness never was happiness" (Alma 41:10) and never will be. Never find yourselves in the position of the Nephites just a few years before the birth

---

164. Elder David A. Bednar, "Converted Unto the Lord," *Ensign* or *Liahona*, Nov. 2012, 107.

165. Bruce C. Hafen, *Spiritually Anchored in Unsettled Times* (Salt Lake City: Deseret Book, 2009), 29.

> of the Savior. They "sought . . . for that which [they] could not obtain, . . . for happiness in doing iniquity, which thing is contrary to the nature of that righteousness which is in our great and Eternal Head"(Helaman 13:38). You cannot find happiness in sin and iniquity.[166]

Adding to this point, happiness comes as a direct result of our obedience to our Father in Heaven and our corresponding courage to follow that path until the end of our days here upon the earth, despite the difficulties we may have. Lehi obviously had many trying circumstances when he warned the inhabitants of Jerusalem. They mocked and ridiculed him and sought to take away his life. (This seems to be the lot of all ancient prophets.) Yet Nephi said, "I . . . will show unto you that the tender mercies of the Lord are all over those whom he hath chosen, because of their faith, to make them mighty even unto the power of deliverance" (1 Nephi 1:20).

The Book of Mormon details an inspiring account of the condition of the people shortly after the visit of the Savior on the American continent. One of the key takeaways is that the people "had all things in common among them" (4 Nephi 1:3). Here was a people entirely committed and dedicated to living the principles they had been taught and additionally had the love of God in their hearts so that there was absolutely "no contention in the land" (4 Nephi 1:15). The account says that "surely there could not be a happier people among all the people who had been created by the hand of God" (4 Nephi 1:15–16). They were living in a community of commonality, dedicated to living the principles of the gospel, and having the love of God in their hearts. This is what Nephi meant when he said his people established a society founded on gospel truths, stating that they "lived after the manner of happiness" (2 Nephi 5:27).

During one of our stake councils recently, our stake president, Ryan Robinson, asked what "theme" or ideas may be good to share with the wards during ward councils in 2022. That was a loaded question, and I needed time to ponder it. However, it was wonderful to

---

166. Joseph B. Wirthlin, "Running Your Marathon," *Ensign*, Nov. 1989, 75.

hear the comments and suggestions from other participants in the council. For me, it's such a magnificent experience to hear the words of others who all have the same objective as I do and who are working each day to become better people. Sometimes I write down what they say to include in my journals because it resonates with me and makes me a better person. In my opinion, this is truly revelation in action. Most of the comments touched on the need to teach and remind others who they are, or teach them more about charity, service, or feeling the Spirit. All of these are true and wonderful lessons in and of themselves, but the thought that came to me during my personal pondering was that we need to be reminded to have "the end in mind" while we live.

As mentioned in the first chapter of this book, one of Stephen R. Covey's principles to be an effective leader is to "always begin with the end in mind."[167] We need to think about how we would like to turn out before we get started on our ambition or quest. When I had that thought during my personal pondering time, I likened it to our pre-earth life. In that sphere, we saw our Father and Heaven. Clearly, we wanted to be like Him. We worked with Him, and we knew Him. We saw Him with our eyes, heard Him with our ears, and perhaps more importantly, we could feel His spirit. As a result, we wanted to be like Him, despite the hardships and difficulties that mortal life would present. We saw our potential through our association with Him. Hence, through seeing Him as He was—an immortal being who had gone through and passed all His tests—we became more motivated with the "end in mind" concerning our purpose and potential.

I think that during that ward council meeting, I understood more than I could describe or write. As indicated in the introductory quote of this chapter, Joseph Smith once said, "Happiness is the object and design of our existence; and will be the end thereof, if we pursue the path leads to it; and this path is virtue, uprightness, faithfulness,

---

167. Stephen R. Covey, *The 7 Habits of Highly Effective People* (New York: Simon and Schuster, 1989), 172.

holiness, and keeping all the commandments of God."[168] I wonder if sometimes we forget that by doing all that our Father in Heaven asks us to do, it will ultimately lead to our own happiness. We get so caught up placing emphasis on one thing over another that we forget what the "end in mind" looks like.

Experiencing happiness while in mortality is not an unreachable goal. It will require us to dedicate ourselves to the Savior Jesus Christ, live His teachings, love as He did, and adopt those righteous characteristics that He manifests. We will then see and understand that part of our purpose in considering our ways will be to lead joyful, meaningful lives that our Father in Heaven wants for us, ultimately living "after the manner of happiness" (2 Nephi 5:27).

168. Joseph Smith, in *History of the Church*, 5:134–35.

CONCLUSION

Therefore, What?

CRG

"'Consider your ways' (Hagg. 1:7). If that witness has not been given to you, isn't now the time to seek it? Come and join with us, and let us continue to build the kingdom of God here and now."

—Elder L. Tom Perry[169]

Down through the ages, and even today, the one constant that prophets and apostles have taught us—the one common denominator—is the metaphor of the two gates and the path each one leads to. As with the people of King Benjamin in Mosiah 5, the beginning of the strait and narrow path starts with the recognition of Jesus Christ and the need for His help and grace. Second comes faith in Jesus Christ and in His power to redeem. Third, we must act, which includes repenting of our sins, entering the waters of baptism, and receiving the Holy

169. Elder L. Tom Perry, "Consider Your Ways," *Ensign*, May 1973, 21.

Ghost. And additionally, other saving ordinances must be done, like receiving temple ordinances and, for men, receiving the priesthood.

Through all of these things, we gain access to heaven, to its powers, and to the love and mercy of our Savior Jesus Christ. He is the one who gives us the strength to endure and become more like our Father in Heaven. There will be challenges, bumps, and bruises along the covenant path, but with His help, it *can* be done. He did it, and He has enabled us to follow His lead as well. Additionally, we have so many other examples to learn this from who successfully navigated that narrow path. We will learn important lessons and gain valuable experience. And the Savior will always help us, be with us, take us by the hand, and lead us. As it says in the Book of Mormon:

> Wherefore, my beloved brethren, I know that if ye shall follow the Son, with full purpose of heart, acting no hypocrisy and no deception before God, but with real intent, repenting of your sins, witnessing unto the Father that ye are willing to take upon you the name of Christ, by baptism—yea, by following your Lord and your Savior down into the water, according to his word, behold, then shall ye receive the Holy Ghost; yea, then cometh the baptism of fire and of the Holy Ghost; and then can ye speak with the tongue of angels, and shout praises unto the Holy One of Israel.
>
> Wherefore, *do the things which I have told you I have seen that your Lord and your Redeemer should do*; for, for this cause have they been shown unto me, that ye might know the gate by which ye should enter. For the gate by which ye should enter is repentance and baptism by water; and then cometh a remission of your sins by fire and by the Holy Ghost. (2 Nephi 31:13, 17; emphasis added)

We need to develop our own capacities, working as a partner with our Savior. Many great people have said that success in life doesn't mean never falling but rather rising every time you fall. Life is full of problem-solving, and in solving our problems, we grow and mature and develop into Christlike beings. We also need to have a willingness to serve. The attitude that the Lord has revealed to all of us in the restored gospel of Jesus Christ is the forgetting of self—willingly giving what we have to others.

Here I'm reminded again of my friend's dream that I shared in chapter 7—the one about following the current of inspiration and allowing yourself to become "immersed" in the water through total submissiveness and faithfulness. By fully and completely trusting in our Savior, we allow Him to mold, shape, and refine us into better people. It takes great faith to be able to say (and really mean), "Thy will be done," when the world is becoming increasingly more difficult and caught up on titles, power, money, appearance, and material possessions. If you've ever tried walking in water at various depths, you know how difficult it can be in places, especially when it gets over your knees. Even though we all may be going the same direction, moving toward the same goal, it becomes much easier when we go "all in" and allow the Savior to "carry us" through the currents of life to our destinations.

Thus, as the prophets have said, the ultimate test of mortality is to see whether or not we will believe in Jesus Christ, exercise faith in Him, trust in Him, and obey the laws and ordinances of the His gospel. We need to acknowledge that inviting the Savior into our life is the first and most important aspect of the plan of happiness. I love the counsel that President Henry B. Eyring has given: "The greatest test of life is to see whether we will hearken to and obey God's command in the midst of the storms of life. It is not to endure storms, but to choose the right while they rage. And the tragedy of life is to fail in that test and so fail to qualify to return in glory to our heavenly home"[170]

A second way of moving along the covenant path and pressing forward in Christ is understanding that our time on earth is a time of testing or probation. What we do during this time has eternal ramifications. The power of this idea is expressed in the third article of faith: "We believe that through the atonement of Jesus Christ, all mankind *may* be saved, by obedience to the laws and ordinances of the Gospel" (Articles of Faith 1:3; emphasis added).

---

170. Henry B. Eyring, "Spiritual Preparedness: Start Early and Be Steady," *Ensign* or *Liahona*, May 2015, 38.

As I indicated earlier, there are many barriers to eternal life and therefore many dimensions of salvation. Each is essential, but each conveys only a part of all that must occur for us to achieve eternal life. Some dimensions come to us unconditionally as a free gift from the Savior. For example, all of us will overcome death through the Resurrection, and none of us will be punished because of the Fall of Adam and Eve. All of us will return to God to be judged of our own works. However, some dimensions of salvation depend on *what we do*. This is true of salvation from sin, from hell, from spiritual separation from God, from ignorance, from the natural man, and from our weaknesses and mistakes. The word *may* in the third article of faith is important here. For while it is eternally true that we cannot overcome any of these barriers by ourselves, and thus must depend on the grace of Jesus Christ in all of them, it is just as eternally true that our salvation ultimately depends on what we do.

Tying It All Together to Help Us Press Forward in Christ

Finally, let's tie this all together and see how these chapters we have discussed[171] help us to press forward in Christ despite the hardships life may give us. The principles in these chapters, in combination with Jesus Christ's Atonement, will enable us to draw closer to Him. We will see mighty changes in our life, including the following.[172]

1. There begins to develop within our hearts a desire to do more to further the work of the Lord and to become better people than we are currently.
2. We begin to view the Church as a place where we go to share, to give, and to contribute.

171. There are many other subjects we could have written about that are not included in this book. For example, we become better people through service, prayer, acting instead of just being acted upon, trifling not with sacred things (see Doctrine and Covenants 6:12), and in many other ways.

172. This list combines Brent L. Tops's suggestions with Robert L. Millet's ideas found in his book *The Holy Spirit*, with some significant modifications from the authors.

3. We gradually begin to view commandments, laws, and Church directives differently, no longer seeing them as guardrails, barricades, or hindrances to life's enjoyments but rather considering them as helps, guides, and kind gestures of a benevolent Father in Heaven.
4. As we earnestly search the scriptures, we begin to see patterns, connections, parallels, and principles closely related to our own experiences.
5. We begin to be more secure and settled in our faith and less troubled by unanswered questions.
6. We begin to face trials, challenges and the vicissitudes of life with less defensiveness and anger.
7. We begin to feel a deeper sense of love for and loyalty toward the apostles and prophets, those charged to guide the destiny of the kingdom of God.
8. We come to accept the humbling fact that we are unable to fully identify and correct our weaknesses on our own. We ask regularly, "Lord, what lack I yet?" (see Matthew 19:20)

It is our hope that we—you and I—will stay true to the word and endure to the end. It is our prayer that we remain faithful to our covenants and, by doing so, are able to receive *all* of His promised blessings and not just some of them. If you feel you are only receiving some of His blessings, then perhaps now is a good time for you to consider your ways. This is the path and the gate that lead to eternal life. As we wrote in the introduction, the path is strait and narrow, but it is sure and true. If we follow that path, we follow our Savior. It is His path. He is the Way. It is essential to enter the gate. As Nephi said, "We must press forward with a steadfastness in Christ" (2 Nephi 31:20) with hope and faith and endure to the end.

Additionally, take time to ponder and reflect over Appendix A on the next page. You will find that as you consider your ways and press forward in Christ despite the hardships of mortality, you will come to love the Lord more assuredly. You will obey his commandments more fully. You will have a greater desire to repent of all your sins because you will want to become more like Him. A mighty change of heart will begin to take place in you because your motives and desires will more closely align with His. You will begin to experience the Holy Ghost more in your life, and you will become more pure and shaped by Him because of this change.

It is our prayer that we will become more devoted disciples of Jesus Christ by pressing forward in Christ, which will enable us to become more Christlike. "Learn of me, and listen to my words; walk in the meekness of my Spirit, and you shall have peace in me" (Doctrine and Covenants 19:23).

APPENDIX A

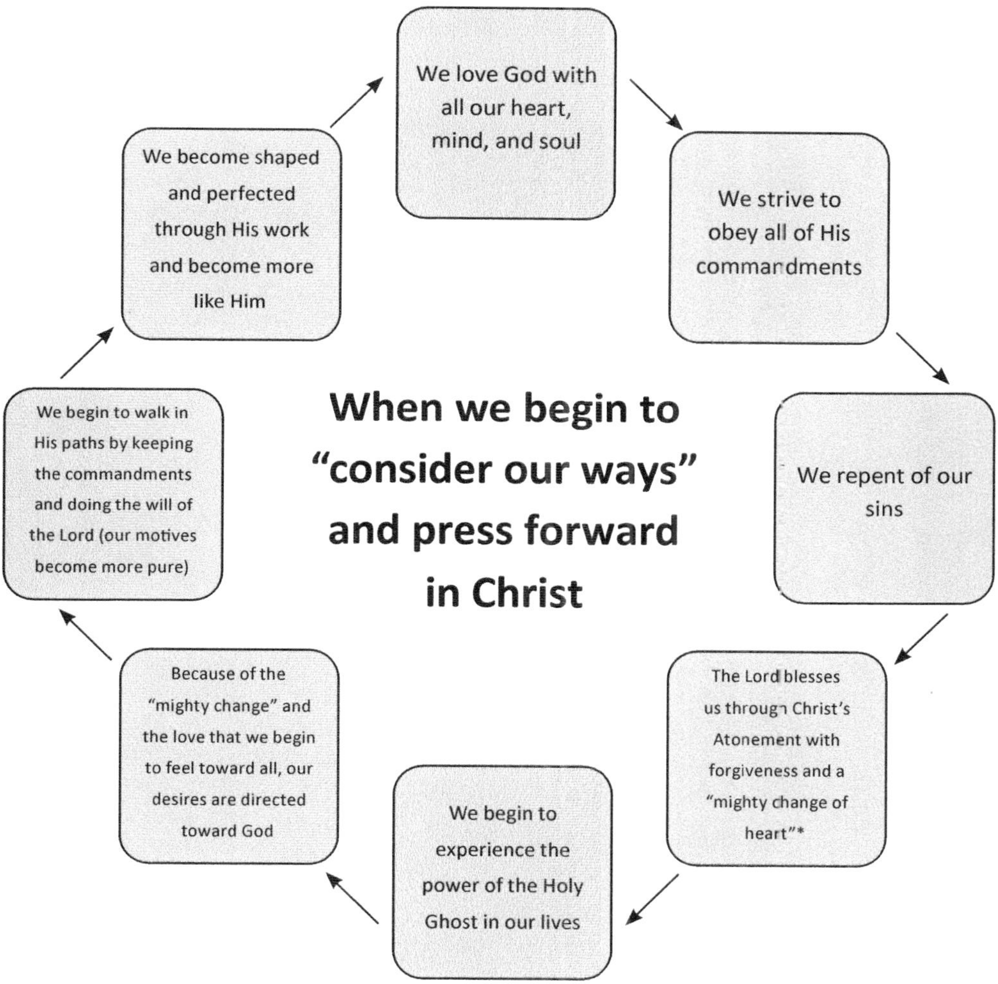

* All along the way, the Atonement of Jesus Christ gives our life's attempts meaning, purpose, and power.

ABOUT THE AUTHORS

Christopher R. Greenwood

Christopher R. Greenwood is the noted author of two prior works, *A Mighty Change: The Process of Going from Good to Better* and *Spiritual Atrophy*. He has also written several Church-related articles.

Chris served a mission in Brisbane, Australia. He is a graduate of California State University, Sacramento, and the U.S. Army Logistics Management College in Virginia. He has appeared in several Latter-day Saint productions, most notably portraying the part of Martin Harris in the Martin Harris Pageant. Additionally, he was the writer, director, and narrator for the Latter-day Saint Church Printing Center documentary film *So Let It Be Written*.

Chris currently works for the Department of Defense. He and his wife, Tami, have five children and are currently living in Indiana.

Scan to visit

www.pressforwardinchrist.com

Mark D. Mason

Mark D. Mason is a first-time author with the completion of *Press Forward in Christ*. He decided to write a religious book because he has seen the power the Savior has in his personal life and wants to share that influence with everyone. He gained his love for understanding and teaching the gospel as a missionary in the great Ohio Columbus Mission.

Mark graduated from BYU–Provo with a degree in philosophy and a master's and PhD from Utah State University in instructional technology and learning science. He is a teacher and an administrator by profession and has also written curriculum.

Mark was born in California and raised in Utah. Most recently, he and his family moved to the Tampa Bay, Florida, area. He and his wife, Tricia, are the parents of seven children and soon-to-be grandparents twice over. Their family enjoys the outdoors, board games, music and singing, college football, and reading.

Scan to visit

www.pressforwardinchrist.com

NOTES

NOTES

NOTES

NOTES